WHAT SERVICE PROVIDERS SAY ABOUT *MARKETING YOUR SERVICES*:

Accounting
Even though I have an MBA with a marketing focus, this is just what I need as marketing director. It has a real-world flavor you don't get in text-books. Crandall manages to transform a mysterious, intimidating, often unpleasant function into a series of doable, interesting, and even fun activities. Read it, and use it to make your marketing better.

Linda Carlton, CPA, MBA

Advertising
Crandall's unique method requires nothing more than a modicum of common sense and a lot of enthusiasm. You're going to love this book. I wish I'd had it thirty years ago. Even though he's a little tough on media advertising, his down-to-earth advice on how to sell your services is right on target.

Alan Cundall
Executive Vice President and Creative Director
Hayes Orlie Cundall, Inc.

Architecture
This helped me understand my weaknesses. My successes were due to using Crandall's points without realizing it. Now I can go to the next level.

Rick Bertolina, AIA

Banking
A great user-friendly marketing tool for the financial services industry.

Don Cvietusa
Senior Vice President
Silicon Valley Bank

Business Consulting
Very practical. A fast and easy read.

Jim Halm
Excellence Seminars

I've learned more from your *Marketing Your Services* book than from all the business materials I've read combined.

Linda Naphilz, Ph.D.
Solutions Focused Consulting

This book is one of the best I have ever read and used for my business. Many of the topics are rarely if ever covered in MBA school, nor does an MBA program provide you with the kind of thorough step-by-step help offered here. Each chapter provides ideas and recommendations that you can try out *now* without spending a lot of time or money.

Bridget E. Robinson, MBA
Strategy Consultant

Career Consulting

Here's a no-nonsense book packed with actionable information. Usually this subject puts me to sleep, but this one woke me up.

Edward Coletti
California Career Consultants

Construction

I don't read anything I don't have to. But I'm reading this book cover to cover. The ideas I've checked already will add $30,000 to my next year's gross."

Adam Ellis
Licensed Contractor

Finance

A pointed overview of how consultative selling builds good relationships, with just the right relevance and insightful humor to make the point.

Bill Row
IDS Financial Services, Inc.

Insurance

The genius of this book is that it plows through the most complex marketing ideas quickly and gets down to what you can do today to strengthen your marketing."

Fred Kissling
Editor/Publisher
Life & Health Insurance Sales magazine

Legal

Crandall's book is terrific. Instead of vague and abstract advice, he recommends definite and specific actions which, in my experience, are very effective. I try to use at least one of his ideas every day.

Stuart A. Bronstein
Attorney-at-Law

Law schools teach law, not marketing, so lawyers have to learn to sell on their own, or not at all. This book can take years of fits and starts off a lawyer's marketing education.

Douglas L. Hammer
Shartsis, Friese & Ginsburg

Mechanics

The book is easy to read and interesting. I wish I could write like that! As a mechanic running a service business, I didn't think I would find much of interest. But I found a lot of valuable information that I could actually use.

Al Weisman
Mechanic

Nonprofit Groups

I've used Dr. Crandall for years as a marketing consultant in many areas. He's a genius. What the book says is right on for nonprofits. Relationships, honest value, long-term thinking: This is how you build support for a group, or any other cause or business.

Simon Ellis
Administrator, Moose Lodge 550

Psychology

It helped me overcome my inhibitions about marketing. Easy to read and full of concrete suggestions.

Richard Allen, Ph.D.
Director of Counseling and Psychological Services
UC Santa Cruz

Public Relations

It's pathetic how many marketing books sit on my shelf collecting dust like empty tombs. This one sits on my desk next to my Rolodex and calendar. It's filled with Post-it Notes, paper clips, and highlighting. To say it's user friendly is an understatement. From the first day, it was a tool of everyday necessity.

Peter Beardsley
Public Relations Consultant

Real Estate

The summaries are great for the busy professional. After reading the chapters and getting ideas I wanted to use, the summaries were there to remind me of the main points so I didn't have to take notes. That was really a time saver.

Nancy Marquez
Realtor

Sales Management

Dr. Crandall has hit the nail on the head! Building and nurturing relationships is the key to growing a business. This clear and informative book should be a must-read for all entrepreneurs/business owners.

Jack Sweeney, CRMC
Radio Sales Manager

Software

Don't be deceived by the easy reading. This book is packed with usable ideas even for the experienced marketer.

Marc Fine
Software Executive

Surveying

For the professional in private practice, [this book] is just what you need to increase the quantity and the quality of your clients.

William Schroeder
Land Surveyors

Window Washing

[The] emphasis on building relationships versus trying to make a quick sale reflects my own style, and is a welcome confirmation. Rick Crandall lives out what he preaches—he has successfully provided thousands of local businesspeople, including myself, with opportunities to network with one another.

Richard Fabry
Owner, window washing company
Publisher, *American Window Cleaner*

WHAT EXPERTS SAY ABOUT *MARKETING YOUR SERVICES*:

I haven't said anything good about a marketing book in a long time. But this one I liked. When you combine solid business experience with insight, you get Crandall's practical guide to marketing. A must read for any service provider.

Michael Phillips
Marketing Without Advertising

Crandall's book is a practical start-up manual for those who want their marketing to do more than just put an ad together. I like it.

Don Peppers
The One to One Future

I'm one of those people who hates the idea of selling. But, I know it's important. This book brilliantly injects creative new ideas, along with some novocaine for those like me who think of marketing as disgusting and sleazy.

Robert Townsend
Up The Organization

Entertaining, well-organized, and loaded with practical strategies.

Dr. Ronald Goldsmith
Department of Marketing
Florida State University

I believe this book has strong sales potential to small-practice law firms, architects, optometrists, travel agents, gardeners, consultants, accountants, etc....

James Carman
Professor of Services Marketing
UC Berkeley

You'd have to bend over backwards not to make money with the information in this book—it's that powerful. Crandall is especially good when he talks about referrals.

David Garfinkel
Referral Magic

[It] flowed so well, I couldn't put it down. I liked the various definitions, the different perspectives and angles on marketing. It's great how [Crandall] ties them all together and then gives you mini-marketing plans.

Randy Sloan, Publisher
Santa Rosa Business Journal

Strangely enough, I've been in marketing for over 45 years and yet, I've always been one of those 'people who hate to sell.' Crandall really hit my hot button with this one. [This] book is a real businessman's (and woman's) bible!!!

Jerry Buchanan, Editor/Publisher
Info Marketing Report

If you're looking for a book that you won't want to put down—a book that is crammed with ideas you can put to use right away—you'll want to read this. . . . The writing is absolutely tremendous.

Don Bagin, Publisher
Communications Briefings

Rick Crandall is one of the most savvy marketers I know. His systematic approach to marketing takes the guesswork out of success.

Bob Nelson
1001 Ways to Reward Your Employees

If you want to jump-start your own business, leverage your career, or sell your services, read this book.

Louis Patler, P.h.D.
If It Ain't Broke, BREAK IT!

Learn how to turn on your own powerhouse marketing machine with Crandall's new book. Crandall provides BIG solutions to everyday marketing problems. He's not just a writer. He's been there and it shows.

Bruce David, Editor/Publisher
Starting Smart
Author, *Mercenary Marketing*

Fast-paced and everything you can do right now to get new business on a budget.

Marv Q. Modell, Editor/Publisher
The Salesman's Insider

Marketing
Your
SERVICES

Marketing
Your
SERVICES
For People
Who HATE
to Sell

EXPANDED & UPDATED EDITION

RICK CRANDALL, Ph.D.

McGraw·Hill

New York   Chicago   San Francisco   Lisbon   London   Madrid   Mexico City
Milan   New Delhi   San Juan   Seoul   Singapore   Sydney   Toronto

The *McGraw·Hill* Companies

Library of Congress Cataloging-in-Publication Data

Crandall, Rick.
    Marketing your services: for people who hate to sell / Rick Crandall.—Updated and expanded ed.
        p.   cm.
    Previously published: Chicago: Contemporary Books, 1996.
    Includes bibliographical references and index.
    ISBN 0-07-139871-6 (alk. paper)
    1. Service industries—Marketing.   I. Title.

    HD9980.5 C73   2002
    658.8—dc21   2002070986

Interior illustrations: Oliver Chen and Carolynn Crandall

3 4 5 6 7 8 9 0   QPD/QPD   1 0 9 8 7 6 5 4

ISBN 0-07-139871-6

McGraw-Hill books are available at special quantity discounts to use as premiums and sales promotions, or for use in corporate training programs. For more information, please write to the Director of Special Sales, Professional Publishing, McGraw-Hill, Two Penn Plaza, New York, NY 10121-2298. Or contact your local bookstore.

This book is printed on acid-free paper.

CONTENTS

PREFACE

I feel quite humble about the success of this book in the earlier editions. It has been called the best marketing book ever—not because I'm a great writer, but because the book has great information.

This book also has several advantages:

- It is designed for service providers, not products.
- It has sidebars and other quick points on every page.
- It provides lots of real examples for large and small service providers.
- It uses a conversational, easy-to-read style.

As an editor, I look at hundreds of books a year. Many are uninviting to read and look boring. My goal is to give you the best marketing information you can use now, with lots of examples to borrow or adapt.

If the first four pages don't convince you that this book can help you—and be an enjoyable read—I haven't done my job. I'm so sure this book will benefit you that I offer my personal money-back guarantee in the introductory pages.

I also want to thank my thousands of seminar students and other readers of my books. (Most recently, Ed Challberg, Linda Napholz, and Tamara Sanner made detailed comments.) They told me what worked for them and gave me a pool of examples that helped me write this book. (If you'll send me your success stories, failures, and marketing materials, I'll send you more, or answer your questions.)

Finally, remember that no matter what I say, what counts is what you do. Please use this book to take action on your marketing today!

RICK CRANDALL
rickcrandall.com
forpeoplewhohatetosell.com

CHAPTER ONE

MARKETING FOR REAL PEOPLE

If You're Proud of What You Do, You Can Market Easily and Effectively

I f you're like most service providers you not only hate the idea of selling, but are suspicious of marketing. Time after time service providers in all fields have told me that they don't want to be like the stereotypical "used-car salesman." I have good news for you. If you follow the guidelines in this book, you will market your business in ways that are:

- professional,
- enjoyable, and
- get results!

This book will not only show you *how* to successfully make marketing an automatic part of your work; it will show you *why* marketing can be comfortable for you.

Marketing will help you obtain more *and* better business—whether you're an accountant or a chiropractor, an attorney or a landscaper, in the United States or Europe, in Brazil or Russia. If you'll try some of the hundreds of ideas in this book, you have my personal *money-back guarantee* that you will see results! (See Chapter Fifteen for details.)

This book is more practical and more complete than any other book of its kind. It explains all the key types of marketing with lots of examples. It is all you need to successfully market, whether you are a new service or an established one, a giant law firm or a one-person contractor. Reading this book is an investment: If you'll spend just one hour per chapter to read it, and then take action, it will pay you dividends your entire career.

While marketing *is* work, effective marketing sets up systems that result in *less* work for you as they become simple and routine to apply. Other people can even do much of your marketing for you.

A QUICK OVERVIEW OF THE BOOK

In this book, you will learn how to:

- build lifetime relationships with clients,
- create simple and effective marketing plans, and
- use hundreds of time-proven examples successfully.

This chapter is a bit more complex than most of the later ones. It defines *marketing* in a number of ways. It explains a philosophy of marketing based on relationship building. It shows you why marketing and selling are not "sleazy" or unprofessional when done right. It also starts you on the road to planning your marketing, with an emphasis on customer service.

Chapter Two provides short examples of practical marketing that you can do immediately. Chapter Three covers the "technicalities" of marketing concepts.

The chapters from Four on are much more concrete. Each covers clearly the "how-to's" that you need to apply the marketing method highlighted. They start with the most common marketing methods and move to those that are more effective—and usually less expensive—for service providers.

IF YOU DISLIKE "SELLING"

Selling Sounds Sleazy

I understand your attitude about selling. In my Ph.D. program in psychology, they looked down on people who promoted themselves or weren't "pure" academics. However, marketing doesn't have to be unprofessional. By the time you've finished this chapter, I'll show you how you can market successfully in a dignified, comfortable way that fits your personal style.

I've taught thousands of people how to market their services in ways they actually enjoy. Few had any background in marketing. They went into business—or to school—to be a Realtor, an architect, a banker, an accountant, an engineer, an insurance agent, or something else. They did not want to "go into sales."

A BAD IMAGE FOR MARKETING

Most people define marketing as either personal selling or advertising. You probably think of selling as pushy, imposing yourself on others and trying to get them to purchase something they don't want. After you read this book, you should think of advertising as expensive, impersonal, and often ineffective. These are the two best known areas of marketing. Hardly a recommendation to like it!

So, why did I write this book? Because there's another way to approach marketing. You can serve others in an honest, socially responsible manner. You can improve your marketing without being pushy or using "hard-sell" tactics—and you can even enjoy doing it!

DON'T APOLOGIZE ABOUT YOUR SERVICES

If you provide a valuable service, you should be proud of it. *Marketing isn't sleazy if you're not!* You're helping people by letting them know about your services. Why be apologetic when you can be a passionate evangelist who crusades for better dental hygiene, lower legal costs, or healthier lawns?

MARKETING = RELATIONSHIPS

My approach to marketing your services focuses on building relationships and friendships—on helping other people. You show yourself at your best while minimizing rejection and imposition on others.

Long-term business is more about relationships than about what you offer. For instance, Michel Landel of the French food service giant

The economic revolution of the American economy since 1900 has in large part been a marketing revolution caused by the assumption of responsibility for creative, aggressive, pioneering marketing by American management.

Peter Drucker
The Science of Management

Creative Relationships

Why should people pay attention to you from among the many alternatives they have? If you use creativity, both you and your prospects will have more fun. For instance, Bill Blades has his own postage "stamps" that he puts on letters to get attention. He uses other devices to be humorous and get attention because it fits his personality. You need to be creative when approaching people or you will look just like your competitors.

Sodexho says, "You have to touch [customers'] hearts, because it's a very emotional business."

If you orient your entire business to serving customers, you will be more successful. This means you don't sell *your* services. Rather, you use your skills to help customers meet *their* needs.

To improve your relationships with customers, you develop new skills to meet their ongoing requirements. This better serves customers *and* gives you an edge, since it's been estimated that it is five to ten times more profitable to sell an existing customer a new service than to sell a new customer your first service.

The relationship-oriented service provider is:

- the Realtor who educates first-time home buyers.
- the banker who encourages you to refinance, even when it cuts the bank's fees.
- the travel agent who acts as a consultant, not an order taker.
- the insurance agent who contacts you more than just once a year when your policy is due.
- the stockbroker who encourages you to invest for the long term, even though it means lower commissions.

Your best marketing is a personal approach. It's an honest approach that reflects your personality, whether you're talking one-on-one with people or writing articles that help them understand your field. It is the opposite of mass media commercials hammering at people who don't want to respond. It's building relationships.

Do Clients Like *You*?

If relationships are the key, it means that, as long as you're good at what you do, *who you know and their relationships with you*, not what you know, is most important to your business success.

This may not seem fair. But most of your clients probably aren't knowledgeable enough to really judge your competence. So they make decisions based on your *relationship* with them, how you treat them, and how comfortable they feel with you—decisions such as whether to stay with you, and if they will refer you to their colleagues and friends!

For instance, take the case described by Tom Peters of Dr. Tattersall, an M.D. from Australia. Dr. Tattersall randomly created two groups of patients. After visits by patients in one group, he sent a pleasant follow-up letter. Patients in the other group received nothing. Later, both groups were asked to rate their satisfaction with their medical visit. Three times more patients in the group who received a letter rated themselves completely satisfied. Peters concludes, "A doctor's consultation plus a letter is an entirely different service from a consultation without a letter."

> [Your business success] is proportional to
>
> 1. the thickness of your Rolodex,
> 2. the rate of Rolodex expansion,
> 3. the time devoted to Rolodex maintenance.
>
> Tom Peters

WHO ARE YOU?

One overlooked aspect of marketing is that if you're going to build business relationships with others, you must be clear about who you are and what your services represent. In order to be uniquely attractive to others, and capture their trust, you need to project very precisely with whom they are entering a relationship. This involves positioning and other factors (explained in Chapter Three). A simple way to start thinking about who you are is to ask how you differ from your competition. If competitors could use the same Web site, brochure, newsletter, and so forth that you do (just by inserting their names), then you're not telling your prospects and customers who you really are.

Be clear about your uniqueness. As discussed later, it could come from your personality, your technical skills, the exact types of clients you serve, or many other factors. The underpinning of this book is to show you how to use marketing to build relationships. To do this, you should continuously think about who you are in those relationships and how to communicate this more distinctly to others.

HOW THIS BOOK WILL MAKE IT EASY FOR YOU

This book is different from other business books. It is designed to be an easy-to-use guide and "cookbook." It allows you to read a little, and then actually produce something that can help you immediately.

I promise that if you'll read for twenty minutes (often less), you will always discover several suggested marketing activities for both big and small firms. If you'll pick one of them and carry it out, you'll boost your marketing.

I can't guarantee that you'll get an immediate response from everything you do. But I can guarantee that you'll be far more aware and effective than you've been in the past!

If you already have a marketing plan, or need to find quick help in a particular area—such as publicity or sales—you can skip to individual chapters at any time.

MARKETING SERVICES IS DIFFERENT

Most marketing books are product oriented. Marketing your personal services is different from marketing cars, appliances, or retail goods. With products, people generally know what they are buying. Services are more intangible; with services, people are buying *you*—it's a much more personal transaction. This is why you feel rejected when people don't buy your services.

A FIRST DEFINITION OF MARKETING

Marketing is an umbrella concept. Under it are all of the different specific techniques that can create business for you.

The term *marketing* is greatly misused. Too many people use the term *advertising* to mean marketing. Other people use the word *marketing* to mean only one part of the overall process.

The correct usage is that *"Marketing is anything you do to get or keep a customer."* This definition, from Harvard professor Michael Porter, is simple but complete. It includes reaching out to new prospects *and* getting more work from your existing clients (more about this later).

Marketing is an ongoing experiment to find methods you are comfortable with that appeal to your audiences. As you find techniques that succeed, marketing can become a simple routine that takes less of your attention. So the goal of great marketing is for it to become easier and easier while you have more and more fun interacting with people you enjoy (clients and prospects).

WHAT MARKETING DOES

Marketing brings you into contact with people. And then, depending on the impression you make and the strength of their needs, some of these people will use your services or refer you to others.

To improve your marketing, you need to increase the reach and effectiveness of your contacts. My guess, based on my research and teaching, is that when you look at how you found your last five clients, you'll find that most of them came through some sort of personal contact, directly or indirectly. They heard about you from someone else or met you because you participated in the same activity. (As discussed later, certain services, such as plumbing, are exceptions.)

I guarantee that the more effort you make to keep in touch with existing clients and intelligently reach out to possible customers, the more business you'll get. But no one can predict which methods will be most effective for you. Much of that depends on your personality, your interests, and the kinds of people you know and meet.

THE FIRST THING TO DO

This chapter will give you an overview of marketing to help you make more intelligent decisions about the specifics. If you'll do a little bit of work first, it can help you now—and later.

One activity that will be very useful to you has already been suggested. List your last five clients, and where they came from. By writing these names down and noting their sources, you've taken the first step to effective marketing: keeping track of what works for you.

Where did your last five clients come from?

Client #1 _____

How obtained? _____

Client #2 _____

How obtained? _____

Client #3 _____

How obtained? _____

Client #4 _____

How obtained? _____

Client #5 _____

How obtained? _____

Keep Track of What's Happening

When one of my seminar students wrote down the source of her clients, it was the first time she'd realized that more than a third of her work was due to a single person.

She'd known this person had referred people to her firm, but she hadn't realized how important the referrals were. You can bet that once she realized this, she paid much more attention to her relationship with this person!

Referrals are worth their weight in gold. Be sure to thank anyone who refers a prospect to you. Perhaps, like me, you've given people referrals and never received a thank-you call or note. (Whether or not it produced business, you certainly should acknowledge others for sending someone to you. Your referral sources will notice the absence of a "thanks," whether they mention it or not!)

Here's a more concrete example of keeping track of what's happening. I've owned a lot of different businesses—from services such as consulting to retail. We advertised one of our service businesses in two different newspapers in two different counties.

One newspaper was twice as expensive as the other, so when times got tough, we cut back the advertising in the more expensive newspaper. When we finally started keeping a little tally—just asking callers where they saw the ad—we found out that the newspaper that was costing twice as much was producing four times as much business! So, it was actually half the price of the "less expensive" newspaper. Such a mistake can make a big difference in your advertising decisions!

Where Else Do Your Clients Come From?

Look at the list of where your last five clients came from. Do they represent the sources of all your clients? If not, add other sources here.

Where other clients come from
(for example, referrals, met at a group, and so on):

_____

_____

_____

_____

_____

Now, write down a few things you are willing to do to get more clients from all of your sources (for example, go to more group meetings, thank people for referrals).

	Source	*How I can get more work from that source*
1.	_____	_____
2.	_____	_____
3.	_____	_____
4.	_____	_____
5.	_____	_____

Many things you can do to obtain clients are almost free. Consider adding these to your list: talking to more people when at meetings; calling people; and writing letters, articles, and press releases (more about these later).

WHAT METHODS WORK FOR YOU?

All methods will differ in effectiveness, depending on your marketplace and how good you are with each strategy.

Big Versus Small Firm

Throughout this book, there will be some ideas that only work for big firms and some that only would be used by one-person firms. Surprisingly, though, the basic principle of building relationships works for both. Every client needs to have a relationship with a service provider that makes them feel well taken care of and loyal.

For instance, two different bookkeepers each contacted new business listings in their area (these so-called DBAs or fictitious name filings are published when businesses register a company name in their county).

One bookkeeper wrote the new businesses a letter. For every one hundred letters she sent, she received essentially no responses. The other bookkeeper sent new businesses a letter and consistently got one to three responses per one hundred who became clients. The second letter worked while the first didn't. Why? The second letter was simply better written.

The first bookkeeper followed up with telephone calls. She would get several clients per one hundred through these calls; she was better on the phone.

In general, the phone is a more expensive *and* more effective method. But the first bookkeeper, in particular, was better on the phone than she was at writing letters. The bookkeeper who was better at writing letters never used the phone.

No one can say what will be most effective for you. It depends on your prospects and your personal skills and comfort with a method. What can be said is that *something will work for you*. And the harder you work at marketing, the more clients you'll get, whether they come directly from what you do, or indirectly through word of mouth.

If you have staff, everyone should be involved in marketing. As discussed later, clients' interactions with your staff may determine how good your customer service is. All employees can contribute to marketing by improving relationships with existing clients, and employee referrals can be some of your best.

OTHER DEFINITIONS OF MARKETING

Now let's look at some other definitions of marketing to give you a sense of the different dimensions that can be important.

An Exchange That Satisfies Needs

One American Marketing Association definition of marketing includes something along the lines of "an exchange that satisfies the needs of both parties." That's at least descriptive of what's going on. And it reminds you that you have to meet people's needs—or they won't part with their money, which presumably meets *your* needs!

Most service providers actually would like more than money in the exchange. They'd like appreciation. They'd like an interesting client to work with. But the notion of *exchange* is valid in either case.

Marketing as Research

What you're really trying to do with your marketing is find people who have a need or desire for what you offer and the means to pay for it.

This is also a good definition of sales prospecting. If you have enough good prospects—people with strong needs and means—it's relatively easy to sell your services. When you find strong prospects, there should be little need for sales pressure. The key is to find people at the time when they realize they have a need for your services.

Marketing as Education

There are many more people who have a need than who have both the awareness of their need and the readiness to act. This is why some people look at marketing as an educational process. You help people analyze and understand their needs. You show them how your services can help them in ways they hadn't thought of.

This is all true. But the danger of looking at marketing as education is that you can spend forever educating people and never do any business with them! You're best off trying to find people who already have an awareness of a need or a problem. There will be plenty of educational work to do with them.

Test Marketing Methods for Yourself

Picking marketing methods to use is an art, a preference, and a science. It's an art to guess which methods might work best for your audience, but your personal preferences often determine how effective a method will be. Go with methods with which you're comfortable. Once you pick some methods to try, it's a science to measure precisely how effective each one is. For instance, Ford Saeks tried many methods from direct mail to advertising for a product he developed. It wasn't until he went to a trade show that he had great success by getting the right message in front of the right people, using the right marketing method.

A Transfer of Enthusiasm (and Faith)

An old friend of mine used to define marketing as the process of transferring your enthusiasm for your services to your prospects and clients. This is also why it's good advice to love what you do.

This is not a definition of marketing, but the notion of passion and emotion is very important. Selling your services is a personal interaction. When you are enthusiastic, you come across as sincere and credible. If prospects accept your enthusiasm, they will trust you and want to work with you.

Of course, some services are not as personal. If you're a plumber, people tend to hire you from Yellow Pages ads only when they need you.

If you think you have a hard time building relationships, think how hard it is for the plumber to maintain a relationship when he or she only sees people once every five or ten years when they have a clogged toilet!

OPERATIONAL DEFINITIONS

Now, let's define marketing in operational terms. The seven areas shown in Figure 1.1 are the major types of marketing.

Advertising, sales, and publicity are the "big three" of outreach marketing.

1. Advertising

Advertising is paid, mass-media, impersonal marketing. You can reach a lot of people through Yellow Pages, radio, online, and so on, but there's no chance for personal interaction. This is called a shotgun approach and is quite impersonal. However, advertising methods such as infomercials with 800 numbers are beginning to provide some interactivity to traditional advertising.

2. Sales

Sales, on the other hand, is personal, the opposite of mass media. You have a chance to receive feedback and change what you say, depending on

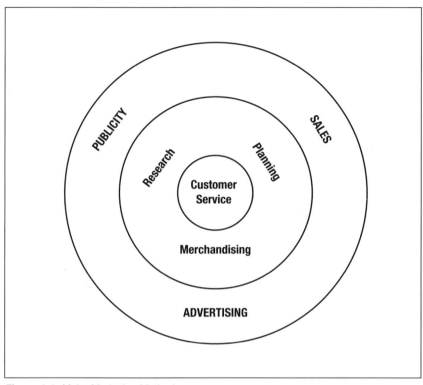

Figure 1.1 Major Marketing Methods

people's reactions. Most selling is one-to-one, usually face-to-face. However, it can be done in groups or on the phone in some cases. The infomercials mentioned above could also be looked at as combining selling with advertising.

3. Publicity

The other big outreach area of marketing, especially for services, is *publicity*. Publicity is traditionally mass-media exposure where you don't have to pay. Publicity is only part of the public relations area, but obtaining free publicity is a good definition.

In my work with print media, I've found publicity to be at least five times as effective as an ad of the same size in the same media. So getting someone to mention you in a story, or writing a guest column, is much more productive for you—and much less expensive.

4. Customer Service

The most important part of marketing (that people often don't think of as marketing) is *customer service*. (That's why it is in the center of Figure 1.1.) This is what you do to *keep* customers and get repeat business and referrals. If you're established, the majority of your work should be repeat business, so customer service should receive the majority of your marketing attention!

I'm assuming that you're good at what you do. If you're not, or you don't work well with clients, good marketing will make you fail faster! (More people will try you and pass the word that you're incompetent.)

Marketing Is Customer Service

People who say they don't like marketing are not thinking of the whole package. I believe that the state of customer service in the world is terrible. If you are trying to provide superior ser-vice to your customers, so that they really love working with you, you need to cast a very critical eye on how you're really treating people.

Research has now shown that customer *satisfaction* isn't enough. To have loyal, repeat clients, you need to go for customer delight, raving fans, or other similar results.

You should start thinking now about whether there is—or could be—anything about your service that thrills customers, that makes them want to work with you or makes them want to brag about you to other people.

Customer Service for Fanatics

You can probably think of a case of mediocre customer service you've received much faster than a case of great service. To deliver great service, you must have a fanatical commitment to customers. Speed is one way to do that. For example, Northwestern National Insurance cut quote time from days to zero by putting data on laptops; MadeToOrder.com cut order time for customized merchandise from weeks to fifteen minutes; Doyle Wilson won a Baldrige Award for quality, while still being the fastest home builder in Texas (which also makes it more profits by having its money turn over faster); Farnell Components answers more than 90 percent of customer calls *before* customers hear the ring. Speed may not work for you, but if you want to stand out from the pack, you need to find something that will.

My guess is that we all have lots of room for improvement. For instance, when clients or potential customers leave a message, do you return the message and then figure it's their turn again? Better service is to try several times for every one call of theirs. Be sure to leave specific times when you can be reached. This may be something you can do right now if you have a pile of messages on your desk!

All first-rank professional service firms . . . are organized in small groups around the customer . . . [The question is] how to best achieve symbiosis with the customer.

Tom Peters

5. Research

Two more subtle areas of marketing that people overlook are *research* and *planning*. Ironically, these two areas provide the foundation that will make your other efforts successful.

All marketing is a kind of research. You gather information about your market. You try something and test its effectiveness. You're trying to find the specific people who need your services. You're trying to find out exactly what they want. You're trying to find out how to appeal to them.

These are all research questions. The more answers you have, the better able you are to find new customers and serve your existing customers.

6. Planning

You really can't do anything in life unless you have some sort of plan. Throughout this book, I'll show you how to do simple, mini–marketing plans that get you focused and moving on one or more aspects of your marketing.

7. Merchandising

The last major area of marketing that I distinguish is called *merchandising*. It refers to such things as stores using displays with cardboard cutouts and putting merchandise at the end of the aisle or at a certain level on the shelf where it will be seen more easily by customers. This seems totally inappropriate for services. You're not a product. You're not in the supermarket.

How Merchandising Applies to You

Merchandising is not usually discussed for people who market services. But you have to remember that you are "merchandising" yourself. Every time you meet people, they are judging your "package."

People are buying *you* as much as they are buying the promise of solutions for their problems. Therefore, you have to look the part, and treat people the way they expect. If you're a plumber or a contractor, you should have a truck and the appropriate tools. If you're a lawyer or an accountant, you should dress well and look a little on the conservative side. (Few people want an accountant who's a "wild and crazy guy." He might take their money and run to Mexico!)

Merchandising also relates to your image, which will be discussed elsewhere. For instance, two people I know who run an interior design firm are exceptionally well groomed. Their office is always neat. Their careful "packaging" of themselves suggests that they will take equal care of your interior.

INTEGRATED MARKETING

I've just broken marketing down into specific types so you can think about them separately. However, your marketing is part of a *whole*. There are hundreds of specific marketing actions you can take within the seven areas I covered, but they need to be integrated within one "marketing personality." Think about building relationships with friends. It would confuse others if you were very outgoing one day and withdrawn the next day. Both personalities could make good friends, but people prefer you to show some consistency.

The Internet is a good example of integrated marketing because it can involve all the marketing methods mentioned. These all need to project the same message to your clients and prospects so they won't get confused about who you are as a service provider. A simple example is a woman I met with recently. She hired different people to do her Web site, brochure, and sales letter without an *integrated* view of what her firm really stood for. This can confuse your marketing message. When your Web site uses different colors than your letterhead or brochure, and emphasizes different strengths, the subtle disharmony can upset your audience so they are not as comfortable with you.

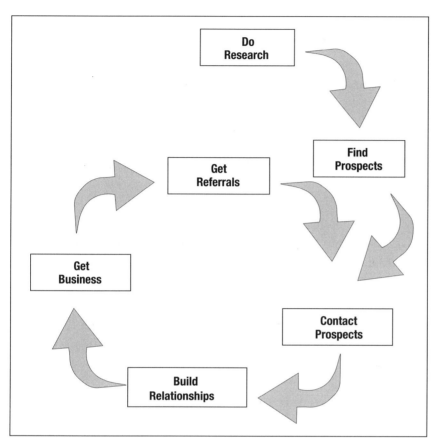

Figure 1.2 The Marketing Cycle

THE MARKETING CYCLE

Another way to look at marketing is as a cycle (Figure 1.2). You do research at the beginning to find possible prospects. Then you try to build relationships with them. Some of these relationships come to fruition and produce business. You also get referrals and repeat business to repeat the cycle with each group.

PRODUCING TANGIBLE SERVICE "PACKAGES"

Because services are so intangible in many cases, it helps to "product-ize" your services so that people can buy a package that will lower their taxes, improve their marketing, cut their electric bill, whiten their teeth, improve communication in their company, or other benefits.

Rather than buying your time, *people want to buy solutions to their problems*. Focusing on the benefits you deliver to them supports this idea in their minds.

TAKE ACTION TODAY (OR SOONER!)

Even if you're on the right track, you'll get run over if you just sit there.

Will Rogers

"

This chapter is introductory more than action oriented, but I hope you'll also act now to improve your marketing.

Once you agree to start marketing, a brief plan tells you what to do, when to do it, and how to do it. It sets goals and tells you when you've achieved them.

Every action in life requires these steps. Most of us plan in our heads without thinking about it. For instance, our "plan" for the day includes getting up, brushing our teeth, going to work, and so on. When we're performing services, planning is often forgotten because we've used a certain approach for so long.

So do a little specific planning now, even if it's not your normal style, but be sure to link it to action.

A MINI–MARKETING PLAN

Let's create some brief planning sheets for you.

Your Budget: Time, Money, and Attention

Your first step is to create a budget for marketing. Three things are going to be required of you: time, money, and attention.

Time and money can be traded off. You've purchased this book; it will teach you things that will save you money. If you have no time, you can buy help from other people to perform various aspects of your marketing (see the Appendix on hiring help). But, at some level, you must be personally involved in your marketing.

To make your marketing work, you must give it some attention and focus. It's going to take at least that much of your time until you establish effective systems that anyone can run for you.

Current Activities

The first thing to do that will support your later plans is to make notes about what you're already doing for marketing and what it's costing you in time and money.

Current Activities	*Cost* Time	*Money*
_____	_____	_____
_____	_____	_____
_____	_____	_____
_____	_____	_____
_____	_____	_____
_____	_____	_____
_____	_____	_____

Your Schedule

When you get going on your marketing, it will be woven throughout your entire day. It will become something that you do naturally and comfortably and think of as *an integral part of being a service provider*. But for the time being, let's budget a little time on a regular basis for you to read this book, think about marketing, and begin to take action. What kind of schedule works best for you?

- Do you want to do all of your marketing thinking and planning on the weekends?
- Do you want to do it one hour a day?
- Half an hour a day?

- Do you want to do it three hours a week?
- After five o'clock, so it doesn't interfere with direct service to clients?

In the space below, list the times of day and week that you will read this book or otherwise work on your marketing.

			Day of Week			
Time of Day	Mon	Tue	Wed	Thu	Fri	Sat/Sun
8 A.M.	____	____	____	____	____	____
Morning	____	____	____	____	____	____
Lunch	____	____	____	____	____	____
Afternoon	____	____	____	____	____	____
After dinner	____	____	____	____	____	____

Your First Mini-Plan

As a final step, make a list of the things you already think you'd like to add to your marketing. If you have a few ideas, jot them down to remind yourself. Come back and jot others down as you read Chapter Two. To the right, estimate how much time and money they'll take.

		Cost
What I'm Willing to Try Now	*Time*	*Money*
_____	_____	_____
_____	_____	_____
_____	_____	_____
_____	_____	_____
_____	_____	_____
_____	_____	_____
_____	_____	_____

_____   _____   _____
_____   _____   _____
_____   _____   _____
_____   _____   _____
_____   _____   _____

In each of the later chapters, I'll help you come up with more ideas. And I'll show you how to save money and time in carrying out any aspect of your marketing.

Now, there's one more element that I think you should add to your mini-plan.

RESEARCH

Research is the other thing you can do that's valuable to start your marketing efforts and move them in the right direction. It's ironic; as you've read, two things that most people don't think of as marketing—research and planning—often provide you the foundation that makes all of the other things you do successful.

What kind of research can you do now that will help you with your marketing later? If you're in business, your single best step is to send current and past clients a brief questionnaire. (If you're starting a business, you can use a similar questionnaire with your contacts who might become clients.)

It's a little difficult for people to tell you in person what they like or dislike about you or your services. A questionnaire is nonthreatening for both you and them. It will be easier for them to be frank in writing than when talking directly to you; it's quick; and, if you do it right, most clients will respond.

A Sample Client Questionnaire

On the next page is a sample letter for you to send out to all of your clients. It consists of only three questions. (If you have large clients, you should contact them more personally.)

Sample Letter to Clients

Dear _____:

I'm interested in your suggestions as to how I could improve my service to you and to others. Please take one minute to answer the three questions below:

   1) What did/do you like about working with me?

   2) What did/do you dislike about it?

   3) Is there anything else you can tell me that would help me provide better service?

Please feel free to include your name or not, but I'd love to talk further with you if you're interested.
Thank you very much for your time.

Sincerely,

Modify it to suit yourself, but keep it simple. Put it on your stationery. If at all possible, personalize each one with a brief handwritten letter or a Post-it Note. Explain to people that you're very eager for their input and would appreciate their response.

If your client list is not too large, send the questionnaire with a self-addressed, stamped envelope so that people can just take a minute or two, fill it out, and send it back.

This is very elementary research, but it results in a couple of interesting things. It gets people "talking." Even if they don't respond, it reminds them that you're there. And it gives you a reason to renew contact with them by following up with thanks or a summary of results.

There's a big bonus to this research. By asking people what they like about working with you, you get potential testimonials that can be used on your Web site or in a brochure.

Most important, you may get a few criticisms. These are the hardest to get and the most valuable, but by asking people to say something good and something bad, they are more likely to give you both testimonials and valuable criticism.

Gaining by Talking to People

Talking to your current or past clients will help you. One of my acquaintances sells landscaping services. Whenever business is slow, he calls past clients. And, usually, he gets a number of jobs.

Landscaping may be a little easier than some other services because people often need a tree trimmed, or something new put in the yard, but this can work the same way for more abstract services. I dragged a lawyer friend of mine to a Chamber of Commerce meeting once. Stu talked to seven people, and three of them had some sort of business for him. It was just advice on a lease, checking on a contract, or writing a letter, but it was quick business, and it led to more later.

Keeping in touch with past customers is extremely valuable. We'll talk about that more in Chapter Fourteen on referrals, and Chapter Nine on ways to stay in your clients' minds.

ACCEPTING CRITICISM

The number one customer complaint about service businesses such as banking, accounting, or insurance is poor communication. For instance, about half of the clients of lawyers said that the lawyers did not do a good job of keeping them informed about the progress of their cases. Yet when the service providers were quizzed, they underestimated the importance of both their ability to communicate and their personal styles.

Many of the criticisms that people make might seem trivial. For instance, they'll claim it was hard to reach you by phone when, in fact, they reached you every time but one. More likely, they won't remember any problems. If

Handling Complaints

When the customer picked up a load of dry cleaning, one shirt was ruined. The counterperson asked what would make the customer happy, then made the whole order free (far more than the customer asked for), thus building customer loyalty.

Unhappy Customers

A consumers' research center study showed that consumers felt a "pervasive discontent" about the services they received, including those from doctors, dentists, and lawyers.

!

people say that there's a problem, no matter how trivial, it is usually the tip of the iceberg that can help you make big improvements in your services.

How to Use a "Stupid" Criticism

Let's pretend a client says she had trouble understanding your bill. Your bill was itemized out in fifteen-minute blocks, and everything was specifically labeled. How could she not understand that?

In fact, what clients may really be saying is that they didn't like the fact that you itemized every little transaction because it made it look like you were nickel-and-diming them to death. (This is often a problem with attorneys and accountants; for instance, billing phone calls in six-minute increments.) Or, clients looked at the cluttered list of itemizations and didn't really want to cope with it so they didn't. Therefore, they didn't understand the details, not because the details weren't clear, but because, graphically and visually, or emotionally, they were repelled by the bill.

This may suggest something as simple as changing the format of your bill to cluster items under no more than three or four headings such as "Time on the Phone," "Writing Documents," or similar changes. This can eliminate the look of charging them for every little thing, while still providing them with enough information. Or, it may suggest a summary of the bill above the details, so that the cover sheet is clear and simple, and then the details follow for those who want them.

Try to Second-Guess Customers

It's your job to "second-guess" customers. They will often only give you hints of dissatisfaction. Most dissatisfied customers simply won't use you again, and they won't take the time to tell you why. If someone complains about something, the first thing you should do is say, "Thank you for taking the time to bring this problem to my attention." Then you have to make sure not to be defensive as you work to understand what caused the person to raise the hint of a problem.

But I'm jumping ahead to customer service. First, let's cover some more specifics to convince you that you *can* market better—without pain. That's what the next chapter will do.

AGENDA

*Things may come to those who wait, but only those things
that are left behind by those who hustle.*
ABRAHAM LINCOLN

There are hundreds of specific marketing suggestions in this book. The odds are that you won't be able to use some and you won't like others. Fortunately, it only takes a few good ideas to move your marketing ahead. Pick those that fit your and your clients' styles that you can carry out easily, then get started. Here are some possibilities suggested by this chapter.

Planning

► Document where your clients are coming from now. This may suggest actions to take such as thanking people for past referrals, visiting certain groups, or changing where you advertise.
► Create your first preliminary marketing plan. Include your budget and a schedule.

Reaching Out

► Can you organize some of your services into "packages" that can be sold for a flat price based on what they do for clients?
► Does it make sense for you to contact new businesses? (DBAs or fictitious name filings are listed in the paper and with your county clerk.)

Customer Service

▶ Institute a new rule: When you play telephone tag with clients, don't just leave one message and figure it's their turn. Try several times. And leave better messages: Ask what they need and tell them when you can be reached.

▶ Send out a one-page questionnaire to past clients to gather testimonials and feedback, and to renew contact.

▶ Look at your billing format to see if it could be presented better.

CHAPTER TWO

WHAT YOU CAN DO TODAY

"One-Minute Marketing"
for the Impatient

*Forget everything except what you're
going to do now, and do it.*
WILL DURANT

I've designed this book for those of you who want results fast. This chapter has a few ideas from later chapters that you can use right now. If you'll try three, you'll see results.

I'll also discuss why you shouldn't use some of the methods until you have a broader perspective and have analyzed your situation. One of the biggest problems with marketing is that many of the things that are most concrete and easy to do, such as advertising, are often expensive and not particularly effective.

Ideas are a dime a dozen,
but the person who
puts them into practice
is priceless.

Norman Vincent Peale

MARKETING STEPS TO TAKE TODAY

Let's look at the seven operational areas from the last chapter and see what you could do today in each one to get started on your marketing.

Advertising: Skip It for Now

Advertising is easy because people sell it to you. You only have to say "yes." But it's not particularly good for services marketing. It can be expensive to try to do something quickly in this area. So let's move ahead to other areas. (Advertising is covered in Chapter Four.)

Sales

The best thing you can do in sales is to build relationships. If you have clients, call a few to touch base. Set up a breakfast or lunch with one to get better acquainted. Getting to know them better when you're not "selling" often leads to business you didn't expect.

If you are new, or want additional clients, ask people you know for referral suggestions—people or companies you might contact. Go online to a search engine such as Google.com and search terms in your field. I always find Web sites of companies I might want to contact. When they're small, I often drop them an e-mail right then. If I send messages to ten companies I often get a few quick responses the same day.

Cashing In on Free Publicity

Publicity can get your name in front of people at no cost to you. Let's preview some things you can do right now.

Write a Letter

The simplest form of publicity is overlooked by most service providers. It is writing a letter to the editor! That letter might be to your local paper, your clients' trade magazine, or a professional newsletter. Your odds of getting published are high.

Letters Provide Visibility

Letters remind people who already know you of your existence. It wouldn't be unusual to receive a couple of calls saying that they'd seen your letter to the editor. It also provides the first "drop" of familiarity for people who don't know you. If they see your name three or four times, by the time they see something substantial from you, they are more likely to respond than if they hadn't seen your name earlier.

You Can Write About Anything

The interesting thing about letters to the editor is that they don't have to relate to stories that have been printed. You can say anything you want about any topic. The media uses letters to air public concerns.

No Limit on the Number of Letters to the Editor

Our local paper once published something like 562 letters from the same person. I know because this fact was mentioned in his obituary. So, papers don't stop you after one letter. In fact, if your letters are good, carefully reasoned, and clearly written, they are more open to publishing you later.

If there is anything on your mind this week, write it down. Perhaps you read about it in the newspaper this morning, or maybe it's been festering in you for a while. A letter with a little passion comes across as more sincere, but remember that the object of this letter is not to spout off. It's to build your image in a subtle way; it's to get your name out there one more time.

Keep Writing

Don't stop! Today you can write one letter, but it's only the beginning of a campaign. The same idea can be written about in different forms for different newspapers, trade magazines, newsletters, or other outlets. I've had the same basic note published in many online newsletters and discussion forums. For sample letters to the editor that may give you ideas, see the Appendix for Chapter Seven. Like all the Appendix material, you can borrow anything useful for your efforts.

Ask About a Column

The second thing you can do today is call editors and ask if they are interested in a guest column by you, covering your area of expertise. Your odds of immediate success here are not high, but all it costs is a phone call to try.

The easiest way to start is with professional trade newsletters or the weekly paper in your hometown. They are much more open to people helping them fill editorial space. The leading dailies and big trade magazines in any area are often deluged with material and are much less open until you've built up a relationship with them. (Building relationships with the media is discussed in detail in Chapter Seven.)

Customer Service by Phone

Now let's look at customer service. This is an area that all service providers know is very important.

Six Tips for Snappier Writing

1. **Don't Inhibit Yourself.** First get out as many words as you can in whatever fashion suits you. Only later, go back and edit for clarity and consistency.
2. **Write In the Active Voice.** The passive voice is impersonal and dull.
3. **Keep Sentences Short.** Avoid colons and semi-colons with multiple ideas.
4. **Use Short Words.** Don't try to impress people with your vocabulary. Use simple, short words whenever possible.
5. **Don't Waste Words.** For instance, "at some future date" can become "later."
6. **Keep It Simple.** Don't complicate your writing with asides that, however clever, are a distraction from the main point.

If you are established in business, it should be your main marketing effort.

Repeat business and referrals from customers are the least expensive form of marketing, and the most effective. There are entire chapters on customer service and building referrals later in the book (Chapters Thirteen and Fourteen). But what can you do about customer service today?

What Message Does Your Phone Give?

What can you change in your office to improve customer service now? Let's consider the message on your answering machine. (You must have some form of answering service if you're in business.)

The tone of voice on your message—or live answer—should be very friendly and sincere. A friend of mine in communications has an answering machine message that says, "We *really* want to get your message," with a tone of voice that makes it sound very insincere. I think he means to be humorous, but it doesn't come across that way.

Listen to your message now and see if you can warm it up or be more helpful to callers. Perhaps you get a lot of calls after hours with a particular question. Maybe you can put the answer to that question on the machine; for example, "For those of you who are calling about our upcoming seminar, it's at such and such a place, such and such a time; if you leave your name and phone number, we'll call you back, answer questions, and register you."

Answering the Phone

Now, take a look at how you or your employees answer the phone. "Smith and Associates; may I help you?" is considered a standard, professional greeting. I call it coldly professional the way most people do it. You sound different when you recognize the other person as a friend. You should tell your employees you'd like them to sound particularly friendly and enthusiastic on the phone today. A simple change in tone of voice could improve the image of your company considerably over time.

Look at the greeting, "Smith and Associates; may I help you?" If you look at it literally, it's stupid. They called for a reason, so of course you can help them! What if you changed your greeting to "Smith and Associates; *how* may I help you?" Now, you've already acknowledged they want help, and you've moved the conversation one step closer to them saying what they want.

If you don't know what your employees *are* saying when they answer the phone, that's something you can fix right now. Call your office and listen to the greeting with a critical ear. Decide the best way to answer the phone and implement a consistent program now.

Messages

Let's look at another customer service problem. Lots of people call a company and ask for a particular person. If that person isn't there, they say, "Fine, I'll call back," or they leave a message.

The message usually states, "George called at 4:00 P.M.; please call back." That doesn't allow you to be prepared when you call George back. It would be much better for George, and you, if you knew what it was about so you could pull appropriate files or do a little bit of thinking. When you call back, you'll be prepared to do a better job.

Don't Subject Callers to Phone Runarounds

Receptionists, secretaries, and others who answer the phone often know a lot about a company and sometimes are very helpful. When you encounter these people on the phone, try to remember to compliment them on their knowledge and how well they handled the call. They seem to appreciate it, so they must not get enough recognition at work. Remember that for your employees.

What about the runaround? When people call some numbers (if your company is big), are they told they have to call another number? Customers hate this. Often they don't get referred to the right place. Such referrals are set up for your convenience, not the customers'.

If at all possible, have the person who answers the phone deal with it, call the other person, transfer the call, and so forth. If the first person can't do this, he or she should give the caller a choice, saying, "Mr. So-and-So's at a different office. I can reach him and have him call you, or would you prefer to call his number directly?" Since you can't guarantee that Mr.

Help Your Customers and Prospects Leave Better Messages

I get lots of calls from authors who want to ask a question about their papers that we are publishing. Most of the people in our office could answer it. But the authors think only the editor can. So, when I'm not there, they waste their time, and mine, by not saying what they want.

One reason that customers and prospects don't like to leave messages is because many people on the other end of the phone act impersonal or uninterested. We're not used to helpful people on the line.

Instruct your staff to do what they can to pleasantly pull a little more information from people. One excuse my employees sometimes use is, "Dr. Crandall likes to be prepared when he calls back. He has files in several different offices. Can you tell me what this call is about?" If the caller won't say, or gets rude, she is usually selling something and you don't want to talk with her anyway.

So-and-So will be available to take the call, it becomes a little awkward. But if you try to do the work for the customer, it will be appreciated.

When a person answers the phone and transfers it to another, the first person should tell the other person who it is, and that person should pick up the phone and say, "Hello, Mr. Smith," not just, "Hello." That way, the person calling gets right into the system and is being dealt with as a human being.

An 800 Number?

Another idea you could implement today for customer service is to install an 800 number. It costs only a few dollars a month service charge, plus the tolls. In a regional area, it's not expensive.

The 800 number doesn't involve setting up a new line; it simply rings to your existing line(s). If the calls come in on your regular line, you won't even know that you're paying the charges. But your customers and prospects know that you've made it easier and less expensive for them to reach you. It's surprising how little things like that will make a big difference to people calling and asking a "dumb" question that allows you to enhance your relationship with them.

Call Clients

If you're a principal in your company, customers are a bit flattered to have the president or partner call. They know your time is valuable and that you are serious about the call. Say something about how you just called to see if there's anything you could do for them, to check on how their job is going, and so on. You could even try something like this: You can tell them that every day you try to call a couple of customers, and see if there is anything you can do for them. You like keeping in touch with customers because you don't get to see as many people as you'd like. This sounds friendly and natural, and people often will respond to it.

What you want to ask customers, of course, is, "How can we do a better job for you? How can we make you like us more so you'll come back and give us more referrals?" You can't ask this directly so make it more of a social call.

Don't say it's a survey. People are tired of that. Surveys are for *your* good. Make your call for *their* good. Just check in to find out how they're doing, then bring the conversation around to something related to your service.

Research

You can do research to help your marketing in each of the areas we've covered. You can do research on publicity or advertising possibilities. Build a file of the names and addresses of various publications, columnists, online advertising outlets, and so on. Is there a printed directory you should buy? There are directories of magazines, newsletters, associations, and even other directories.

You could scout out the local libraries and see what resources you can use. You can go online and begin to compile a list of e-zines, or even sources of sales prospects.

You can find the Web sites of prospects and competitors. You may even be surprised at what's on your clients' Web sites! Your clients will be impressed if you give them feedback on their Web sites. They may even be open to giving you an online link and testimonial. If you consider the different operational definitions of marketing talked about previously, here is some research you could do today.

- Talking to your customers has already been mentioned as sales and customer service. Of course, it often also involves research in finding out about their interests.
- You can do research on publicity possibilities. What's the address and phone number of the local newspaper editor or the trade magazine? What's the phone number of the business editor, the features editor, the editorial page editor, or the calendar editor?
- Go online and find key Web sites and online newsletters that you can sign up for in your and your clients' areas.
- Is there a CD-ROM that you could buy that would have lots of information relevant to your clients' industries?

Nowadays, there are many computerized databases of magazine articles, companies, research reports, and other material. It's not hard to be more informed than your clients or your competitors in most areas because few of them do much ongoing research. Try a few online searches in your field to see what you find.

I have faith that the time will eventually come when employees and employers . . . will realize that they serve themselves best when they serve others most.

B. C. Forbes,
founder of *Forbes*
"the capitalist tool"

Planning

To start your planning, fill in the brief form on the facing page. I'm not a fan of elaborate plans, but to get something done you do have to pick a goal and commit to doing it. You'll find that simple marketing planning will repay your efforts.

Merchandising

What can you do to "merchandise" yourself better today?

First, you can look at your clothing. Does it fit the image of your service? If you're a plumber, you should have bib overalls; if you're a lawyer or banker, you should have a nice suit. But how long since your suit's been cleaned? Is it getting a little frayed around the edges? Is there a button missing? Are your shoes shined properly? People often make judgments from subtle cues. Do you need a haircut? This is something you could do for your merchandising right now.

There's more to your appearance than clothes. How does your briefcase look? Does it fit your image? Do you have the proper tools, forms, pens, calculator, or other devices you need when you make a visit?

Brighten the Corner Where You Work

What does your office look like? Are there items on the wall that are attractive or show people how competent you are—testimonials, awards, articles you've written? Is your waiting room neat? Are there magazines or other material that show off your capabilities—portfolios, a binder with letters from grateful clients? These are the kinds of things people might browse while they are waiting and be quite impressed.

If you have receptionists, are they well groomed and friendly? They shouldn't be chewing gum or eating; they shouldn't be grooming themselves. If they don't have enough to do while waiting in front, they should be sorting, filing, or hand-addressing notes to past clients.

Your personal office should look clean and neat, even if there are piles of projects spread around carefully on tables and desks.

What Can You Plan Today?

Your plan could be to pick one idea and do it today. Is there something we've already talked about that appeals to you, such as changing the way your phones are answered? Perhaps calling a past client? Or maybe the chapter titles give you ideas, or you've been meaning to try something else.

So your plan today could be:

1. Decide to do something now . . . I *will* do something today.

2. Pick what you can do. _____

3. Think for a few minutes about how you can do it. _____

_____

4. Pick a time when you're going to do it. _____

5. Do it!

This is a minimal plan, but it helps get you focused. There's also something beneficial about writing things down, so write your own mini-plan on a sheet of paper.

Start an Online Community

One way to support customers and make your Web site a destination is to support discussion groups on your Web site. For instance, Royal Dutch/Shell (shell.com) supports many conversations about social issues, including criticisms of the company. Shell doesn't censor, and both it and its customers learn from the exchanges.

What About Your Location?

What about signage for your office? What do people see when they walk in the front door? Is there garbage in the parking lot? Is a plant looking dead? Walk out your door, come in the office, and look at it as a total stranger would. You'll often be surprised at what you've allowed to run down without noticing it.

Is your office building easy to find? In our building, people used to go by the entrance and miss it. They were annoyed, so they'd arrive at our office defensive or upset. It wasn't until a new tenant came in, who was in the graphics business, that something got done. The tenant said to the landlord, "Do you mind if I put up a better number on the street?" Now there's a much bigger number that's a great deal easier to see.

This is merchandising in a general sense, like a retail store. But if people visit you, it can be important for services too.

Here's another tip if your office is hard to find: Create a map. Take a regular map, scan it into the computer or trace it, then blow it up and exaggerate the details. You then have a map you can e-mail or fax to people with directions. It's simple, unusual, and better than online directions.

OTHER THINGS TO CONSIDER

What else can you do today?

You could write someone a note to build the relationship. A personal letter, personally addressed, is always read. Is there someone you've been meaning to check in with? This would be a time to call them or drop them that note.

Is your business card up to date? Your business card is your smallest possible "brochure." Are all your phone numbers current? Is your fax number on it? Your Web site and e-mail? Don't wait until you get the perfect designer card. You can go to some of the large office stores and get five hundred or a thousand business cards for $15 now, so there's no excuse not to throw out your old cards and get temporary up-to-date ones immediately.

If you are a good speaker, giving talks is a way of marketing your services. Perhaps today you can call the local community college, or Rotary or Lions groups, and find out how one becomes a speaker (more on that in Chapter Eleven).

SUMMARY

This chapter was designed to get you moving if you're in a hurry. It was also designed to convince you that there are things you can do right now, at low cost, with little effort, that can improve your marketing. It's important to get momentum on your side. Instead of always feeling that you're not doing enough marketing, make a commitment to do *something* on a regular basis. Some of the examples here are easy ways to get started.

The next chapter will cover some marketing technicalities; then each chapter will cover the details of one specific technique you can use. Each will have specific steps you can take and how you can move forward if you use that approach to marketing.

AGENDA

So much to do, so little done.
CECIL RHODES

Here are a few ideas from this chapter you could put to use today to improve your marketing and customer service.

Reaching Out

► Write a letter to the editor.
► Ask about a column in a trade newsletter or magazine.
► Visit a new business group, such as a chamber of commerce or a Rotary Club.

Customer Service

► Improve your answering machine or voice mail message.
► Decide how you want your phone answered and make it uniform, and more friendly.
► Take better messages. When forwarding a call to someone else, be sure he or she answers using the caller's name.
► Call three customers today and ask how they're doing.
► Install an 800 number.

Merchandising

► Clean up your office, car, wardrobe, and so on.
► Update your business card.

▶ Update your stationery with your fax number, Web site, and your e-mail.

▶ Develop a map to your office you can fax to first-time visitors.

Research

▶ Do some library research on your markets, a possible newsletter, or other information.

▶ Find out about giving a free local talk.

Most of all, commit to doing *something*!

CHAPTER THREE

YOUR "MINI–MBA" IN MARKETING

Don't Be Bothered by Technicalities

> jar'•gon, *noun.* The specialized vocabulary that those
> in the same line of work use to show how much more
> they know than their clients.

In this chapter we'll step back from concrete examples of marketing for a few minutes. I want you to feel comfortable with marketing concepts so you won't avoid thinking about marketing, and so marketing consultants can't "snow" you with technicalities.

I call this material the "mini–MBA" because if you understand the general ideas behind these terms, you'll know more than you'll need to know about the technicalities of marketing.

You won't know as much as an MBA after reading this chapter, but after reading this book, I guarantee you'll know more than most MBAs about how to really market services.

ALL YOU NEED TO KNOW

If you know about a dozen terms and what they mean, you'll know all the theory you'll need about marketing. The most important aspects of your marketing can be learned practically, by trying things and keeping track of the results.

All the technical terms boil down to two or three important concepts. They were developed by different people or from different perspectives, but they make many of the same points. When you learn these, you'll know the basics.

KEY TECHNICAL TERMS USED IN THIS CHAPTER

Features Versus Benefits	USP
Demographics	Branding
Psychographics	Market Segments
Rifle versus Shotgun	Niche Marketing
Target	One-to-One (CRM)
Positioning	Permission Marketing

FEATURES VERSUS BENEFITS

Perhaps the most basic distinction in marketing is between features and benefits.

Features are the aspects of the product or service. For instance, a law firm may offer litigation services for the construction industry. *Benefits* are what people get from using your service. For instance, people hiring an accountant might want to be able to not worry about their taxes.

Most people have routine features, such as their specialties, their pricing, their location, and so forth. These routine features are similar to those of many retailers.

More valuable benefits come from the particular results that you deliver. They're often not the obvious part of your service. Lawyers deliver wills that will encourage harmony among the heirs, beauticians deliver higher self-esteem, contractors build homes that make people feel comfortable, and so forth.

Your features don't always tell people the benefits they'll receive from you. People can't see your understanding of problems. They can't see your background. They can't see your ability to combine information from different sources, to provide solutions for them. This is why, when people are making a decision to buy a service, *they usually make it on how much they like you or trust you.*

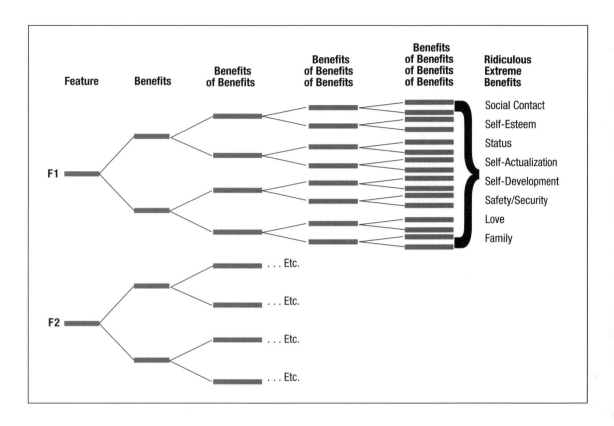

Feature	Benefits	Benefits of Benefits	Benefits of Benefits of Benefits	Benefits of Benefits of Benefits of Benefits	Ridiculous Extreme Benefits

Social Contact

Self-Esteem

Status

Self-Actualization

Self-Development

Safety/Security

Love

Family

Look for Benefits

In basic training for sales or telemarketing, instructors talk about features and benefits. They emphasize that you should be sure to communicate benefits to people, not features. They have you list your features and their benefits.

Knowing what benefits your services provide will both attract more clients and help you serve them better. I'm unaware of anyone else who structures the features/benefits link this way: Features lead to benefits, which lead to benefits of benefits, then benefits of benefits of benefits, down to "ridiculous extreme benefits."

I do it this way for three reasons. It forces you to list more total benefits from your work. It makes you think about the different classes of benefits that people might get from your services. And, most important, it reminds you that the immediate benefits of a feature may not be the benefits that people want.

For instance, let's take an accounting service: The benefits might be that it gives the customer more management information for making decisions, that it organizes records to make it easier for taxes, and so on.

But each of these things is not the customer's goal in life. They each provide other benefits. For instance, having management information better organized allows you to make better decisions. The benefits of this are saving you time, making you more money, doing a better job for clients, and other things.

The Ridiculous Extreme Benefits in Life

But what are the real benefits of having time and money? You can't eat money or sleep with it. You have to do something with your time. So, these are not the ultimate benefits. Ultimately, all benefits come down to what I call "ridiculous extremes." You use the money to purchase something that gives you pleasure. You use the time to be with your family, or to develop yourself. So, the ultimate benefits are always things such as social contact, self-esteem, status, self-actualization, and self-development.

To wake people up, I often tell them that if you can't tell others how your service will improve their sex lives, you haven't thought out your benefits properly! (When they have more time to spend with their spouses, or when they can take pressures off and go on a nice vacation, this will improve their sex lives!)

F-A-B ulous Benefits

Another way of summarizing the features versus benefits distinction is FAB, or fabulous. You want what you do to be fabulous. Your *features* provide *advantages* that provide *benefits* for your clients. Therefore, your service is *fabulous*.

Your Principal Benefit

Another thing that people often look for in determining their overall marketing strategy is their *principal benefit*. You can analyze fifty different possible benefits to come to a principal one. That's the one you'll focus on in your sales, advertising, marketing, and publicity.

To go back to our accountant example, most accountants think that their principal benefit is the services they provide. But if you talk to their customers, the real reason people use accountants and bookkeepers probably is *freedom from fear*. They want to get peace of mind from not having to worry about something they don't like, to have someone hold their hand if the IRS comes after them, and to avoid getting in trouble because of bookkeeping, taxes, bank reconciliations, and so forth. So, really, accountants should provide peace of mind.

RESEARCH TERMS: WHO YOUR CUSTOMERS ARE

It's awkward to organize the technical terminology of marketing because of the overlaps, but the words in this group all involve research in some way. The idea of most of these concepts is that the more you know about your prospects and customers, the more easily you can market something to them, or the better you know people, the better you can meet their needs.

The first two terms go together—demographics and psychographics. They tell you who people are and what might motivate them to hire you.

Demographics

Demographics is the measurement of differences among people (or companies), based on observable characteristics such as age, race, gender, income, neighborhood, and so on.

Why would we care about demographic differences among people? Because some products are purchased only by men or women. Some are purchased only by the young. For instance, most music CDs are sold to the young.

Life Stages

For selling investments, Kemper Funds defined five "life stages." Many companies sell different investments to different age groups, but, to meet needs better, Kemper used a new focus on why people in *each* stage buy.

You can look at businesses the same way if you're selling to them. Their size, industry, experience with services like yours, and other characteristics will influence how receptive they are to you.

In today's world, the differences among demographic groups are much less than the similarities. So, knowing that someone is a certain age, race, gender, and so forth doesn't tell you too much about him or her: If demographics are what's outside your head, psychographics are what's inside.

Psychographics

If demographics are things outside the head, psychographics are inside. *Psychographics* are differences among people (and companies) based on psychological factors. The main reason that demographic (or observable) factors might predict differences among people is that these differences are tied to psychological differences.

With psychographics, you go straight after motives and needs. For instance, some people look for the lowest price, independent of quality. Some people want the best service or best quality, independent of price. Some people are value oriented.

In a more psychological sense, some people like to buy safe services that are well established. Others like to be innovators. They often do a lot of research, and are opinion leaders to whom others look for decisions about new purchases.

Psychographics Should Indicate Needs

From an even more psychological perspective, you can look at how needs differ. Some people or companies want to fit in with others and identify with a group, so they look for service providers who are safe. For instance, there used to be a saying that nobody ever got fired for buying IBM equipment. Or perhaps a purchase gives them status ("the plastic surgeon to the stars"). Some people with low self-esteem may look for products that can make them feel better about themselves—such as a flashy car.

Many decisions to buy are made on a very emotional basis. By understanding the psychology of the buyer, psychographics can help marketers attract more people and meet their needs better.

For a few hundred thousand dollars, some companies will do a specific study of your market, and tell you what kinds of buyers are out there for your services. Without spending any money, you can analyze the types of buyers you work with best, along the lines already discussed.

Focus Groups

Focus groups are small groups of people—say, eight or ten—whom you think are similar to your customers. Typically, you either ask them questions about different services in your category or show them different ads to see which ones appeal to them. You get them talking. You have a moderator. You videotape the sessions. Often, executives watch through a one-way mirror.

Formal focus groups generally cost several thousand dollars to run. You are unlikely to need a formal focus group. However, you should develop an informal "kitchen cabinet," a customer panel, or a sounding-board group. Participants can look at your approach and give you honest feedback about what your customers might think. Focus groups are good for finding ideas for more accurate research, or for getting a general sense of how people will respond. They can be done online also.

Informal Focus Groups

At one time, the Bank of America used an interesting variation on focus groups. It enlisted five or six people who represented a specific market segment (such as corporate clients). These included happy customers, ex-customers, dissatisfied customers, and even prospects. Also included was an audience of appropriate managers who could also ask questions. Hearing actual customers discuss real experiences gave these sessions a lot of emotional impact on bank staff.

After the session, the group members had lunch together so managers could ask further questions. In the afternoon, action teams met immediately and dealt with issues brought up by the customers. They were empowered to suggest new general procedures, not just deal with one customer's issues.

"NRA" MARKETING

This group of technical marketing terms involve strategy. These are ways to find customers, ways to make a better impression on them, or ways to exclude competitors.

I've labeled the first three strategy terms the "NRA" aspects of marketing because they all sound gun related!

Targeting, rifling, and *shotgun* illustrate much of the overlap of different terms. When you hit a target and get a bull's-eye, you have more successful marketing.

Shotgun Marketing Has a Place

Sometimes shotgun marketing can pay—but the results are usually longer term and difficult to measure. Consider the following example.

A Butler, Pennsylvania, architectural firm ran radio spots on Pittsburgh's all-news station. (The company surveyed members of its target audience about their radio-listening habits to determine the station on which the ads should run.) The sixty-second spots, called "Design Considerations," ran twice a day. In them, one of the firm's partners talked about architectural-related matters. Topics included the importance of energy-efficient buildings, the best way to lay out an office, and the architecture of various local bridges (even though the company had never built a bridge).

What did the company get out of it? The company felt it did a public service by explaining a field it was proud of. Its name recognition went up tremendously, and its employees set themselves up as experts. The company figured the radio spots cost half of what it would cost for a direct mailing campaign to ten thousand people. The radio spots also differentiated the company from its competition.

This radio campaign generated a few calls. But its major value was in raising the company's name visibility so when employees called on prospects they got through the door.

Rifle Versus Shotgun

There are two ways to hit a target: with a *shotgun* or a *rifle*. A shotgun sprays a lot of pellets in a broad pattern. The pellets don't hit the target very hard; people may not notice. But for shooting a general area, shotguns are very effective. A rifle shoots a single slug long distances, and hits the target very hard, but it must be aimed well.

Target or *rifle marketing* means you have a clear idea where you're aiming with your marketing message. You're *targeting* a particular type of company or people, often determined on the basis of demographics, psychographics, or benefits that they're looking for. You're aiming your message at them.

Shotgun marketing means that you're just advertising in broad ways, such as the mass media. You're spraying your message far and wide, hoping some of it will hit. If your audience is hard to find, you use this general approach. It worked for AOL, who did "carpet bombing" mailings and other mass distribution of its disks to everyone, repeatedly. It was very wasteful, but achieved for them the leading position for Internet access.

The Advantage of Targeting with a "Rifle"

If you're an attorney and you claim to be able to take care of any legal need, that doesn't make much of an impression. You look a lot stronger when you focus in on a specific need.

For instance, there are a number of lawyers who advertise specific services. Listeners assume that if you specialize tightly, you're better at what you do. The "motorcycle lawyer" helps motorcycle riders who get into accidents, and has a phone number that spells out 1-800-CYCLE. In fact, at least two in our area have phone numbers that spell out something like that. Other personal injury attorneys are looking for people who have been injured on the job. Some attorneys advertise divorce "for men only." They specialize in a particular problem or a particular kind of customer. They are using a *rifle approach* in *targeting* their market closely.

POSITIONING

Positioning is a concept developed in a brilliant book (*Positioning: The Battle for Your Mind*) by Jack Trout and Al Ries. Positioning means who you are, compared to alternatives, in the minds of your customers and prospects. Historically, positioning has dealt mostly with retail products. For instance, certain cars over the years have been positioned by price and style; doctors bought Buicks, and so forth.

One of the classic positioning examples was Avis car rental: "We're Number Two. We Try Harder." It was a number two that was far behind then number one Hertz. It took its weakness and turned it into a strength.

When you say that you're number two, most people think it's probably because you're not as good as number one, and you're getting your brains beaten out in the marketplace! Avis turned this around, and said it was number two and trying harder. Americans like the underdog, especially the

> In a highly competitive context, you must be perceived as unique, or close to it, in areas of importance. [Such] narrowness has costs. Nonetheless, in crowded marketplaces like today's, "all things to all people" competitors are usually doomed.
>
> Tom Peters

scrappy underdog who's trying. We could believe that because Avis was number two, it was willing to try harder, willing to do more to satisfy our needs.

We happen to have an accidental experiment that suggests very strongly that this positioning statement was very effective. The campaign increased Avis's market share. Then the company was sold, the campaign was dropped, and market share decreased. The company was sold again, the campaign was reinstated, and sales increased again.

Marketing as Art and *Science*

The Avis campaign is also an interesting example of the difference between the art and science of marketing. By measuring responses to large, systematic marketing efforts, we can scientifically know what works best. However, deciding *what* to test is an art. Robert Townsend, who was president of Avis at the time, told me that no one really liked the new Avis slogan. Townsend had promised the ad agency a free hand. It felt that all rental companies were very similar (see the following section on USP). It picked the "try harder" position, but weren't thrilled with it. The rest is history, since after it worked so well everyone was happy.

How This Applies to You

Positioning is always *against* alternatives. You would seldom advertise your services as a computer consultant competing against IBM, or as a single lawyer competing against the biggest law firm in the country. But every time you're talking to prospects—people who are considering hiring you—they are comparing you to other alternatives. They may be comparing you to a big, expensive provider. They may be comparing you to other people like yourself. They may be comparing you to college student interns who can do part of the job.

Like all "art" in marketing, the best way to position yourself is a guess. However, most service providers never think about how they are different from others. If you don't have a passionate position about what you do and the way you do it, prospects who meet you won't be attracted to you. You need to spend some time deciding what you stand for and how to communicate it proudly. Be a spokesperson for a cause rather than just a vendor of a service and it will set you apart.

You Versus Nothing

It's also important to remember, and not always noted in discussions of positioning, that prospects are also comparing you to using no one at all.

In many cases, people won't move ahead in meeting their needs because they don't have a strong enough drive—a problem hasn't hit them in the face. I saw a statistic once that for every one person who goes to the dentist, seven people need to do so. Many, many decisions about using services can be put off. Your yard can grow more weeds, your taxes can get an extension, you can ignore a back pain. Inertia may be your biggest competitor. What it often takes to motivate people is an urgent problem—or your great marketing!

USP

USP is used in sales a lot and is a rather old-fashioned term. It stands for *unique selling proposition*.

After the term *positioning* came into use, USP has sometimes been misstated as "unique sales position." It's related to positioning, but it's also related to principal benefits from your research. Picking a USP is the art of marketing again. Based on what you know about your prospects and what you can provide, you try to develop a unique selling proposition to communicate the one benefit that you think will stimulate people to hire you.

This proposition becomes a benefits statement for clients and a positioning statement for you. For instance, a temporary personnel agency might choose as its USP the fact that it has a pool of prescreened candidates. Or it might focus on its ability to provide benefits for temporary workers. For many services, the most unique thing that

Successful USPs

The USP must do three things to be complete and powerful:

1. It must say to the consumer, "Buy this and you will get this specific benefit."
2. The proposition must be one that the competition either cannot, or does not, offer.
3. It must be so strong that it pulls new customers to you.

Rosser Reeves
Reality in Advertising

competitors can't match may be *your personality*. It's still about your relationships with others.

BRANDING

Branding is a concept that has gotten a lot of attention. Many firms have created brands that are well known, from Coca-Cola to IBM.

Investing money in "branding" often means increasing your visibility with techniques such as image advertising. It can build a general relationship with prospects. In many ways, *branding* is just a new word to give consultants something new to sell. It covers much the same territory as positioning and USP, with a lot of client awareness thrown in.

As already mentioned, when "new" terms like this come up, you'll be able to fit them into the framework of the concepts covered in this chapter. If a new concept appeals to you, use it, but make sure it is consistent with who you are and that it helps you build relationships with clients and prospects.

MARKET SEGMENTS

Another research-related term is *segment*. Like *target*, it can be a noun or verb. You can segment your market. That means you're breaking it up into

---

Worksheet for Pursuing a New Segment or Target Market

1. Can you identify your market clearly?   Yes_____ No_____

2. Is it large enough to support what you want to accomplish? Yes_____ No_____

3. Can you cost-effectively reach this market?   Yes_____ No_____

4. Is this market ready for your services?   Yes_____ No_____

5. Does your service have a competitive advantage?   Yes_____ No_____

6. Are you stronger than your competition in some way?   Yes_____ No_____

7. Do you have referrals into this market?   Yes_____ No_____

---

logical subgroups (often based on demographics or other factors) to provide better service or a more specific marketing message to them. As a noun, a segment is a particular target you're aiming for: men of a certain age, companies of a certain type, and so forth. For instance, if you pick a pop radio station, you'll get a listener segment of young adults aged thirteen to twenty-two.

Again, the purpose of breaking the marketplace into segments is to better serve those segments, or to better convince them to use your services. You can see how the "motorcycle lawyers" fit here. They've taken a small *segment* and made it their *target*. Before you pursue a new segment, see the worksheet on the facing page to estimate how effective it will be for you.

NICHE MARKETING

Niche was saved for last because it is the culmination of the research and strategy terms. In particular, you use your research and develop your strategy to create a *niche* for yourself. The actual term is similar in meaning to segment, target, or position. It simply comes from a more ecological perspective.

Your Home Field Advantage

A niche is a place in the ecology in which a species has an advantage over competitors. You can see why this can summarize the results of your strategy and research. When done right, research and strategy result in you having a protected niche where you will flourish.

In evolutionary terms, animals in a niche often adapt in ways that allow them to eat a certain food that others can't eat. You might develop a specialty that others don't have. A niche is a protected environment for you in which, you hope, you're totally dominant and can triumph over any competition. You want an "unfair" advantage!

Specialization

One lawyer specializes in representing cities that sue manufacturers of plastic pipe used in city water systems. Another has a "turnkey" system for distributors to sue a tool company. If you were a city (or tool distributor), wouldn't you want to be represented by "the expert"? Also, other lawyers make referrals because they can't know the specialty as well.

!

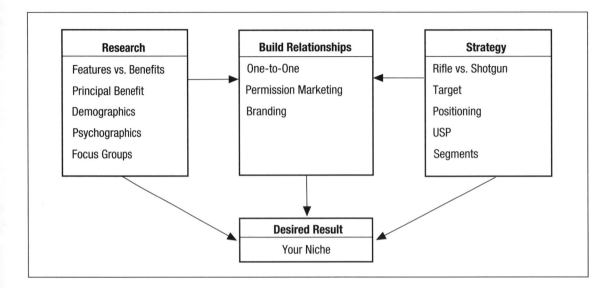

Research	Build Relationships	Strategy
Features vs. Benefits	One-to-One	Rifle vs. Shotgun
Principal Benefit	Permission Marketing	Target
Demographics	Branding	Positioning
Psychographics		USP
Focus Groups		Segments

Desired Result

Your Niche

You need a rich enough ecological niche to ensure that there's enough "food" for you to flourish. If it's very rich, the dangers are that you either outgrow your niche, or you encourage competitors who move into your niche because the pickings are easy. If you're a one-person shop, this won't be a problem for you. If you're a bigger firm, you need strong positioning and continuing innovation to remain successful.

Take Advantage of Your Differences

Test Your Uniqueness

See if your marketing strategies set you apart. Substitute the name of your closest competitor in place of your company's name. If it still sounds fine, it's not a strong marketing effort. Emphasize those things that are unique for you.

Most of you in architecture, law, banking, insurance, and other areas are quite similar to many other people in your field. But through accidents of experience and temperament, you've developed certain unique differences. You will always be in a stronger position—both *against* your competitors and *with* your clients—when you specialize in some way. Work to develop at least one niche.

Developing Your Niche

Your niche can be based on:

- the type of customers with whom you work
- the people who trust you and want to work with you (your network)
- the type of services you provide
- the way in which you provide those services
- your image or style
- your understanding of certain types of problems

Niche marketing can mean much the same as target marketing when you're aiming at a particular group of people who occupy a particular place in the "ecology." Or it can be like positioning if you are using your ecological advantage to show customers why you are better.

A niche can even be based on geographic location. If you're the only provider of your particular services within a certain number of miles, you'll naturally get local business.

CUSTOMER RELATIONSHIPS

The reason we have strategies, try to understand people, and try to put ourselves in the minds of the customer or prospect is to build relationships. Many people have acknowledged the importance of relationships, but few have put the customers' interests first when they conflicted with short-term profits.

General terms such as *relationship marketing* have been around for years. Two specific terms that have had major impacts are *one-to-one marketing* and *permission marketing*.

One-to-One Marketing/CRM

One-to-one marketing is based on a series of important books by Don Peppers and Martha Rogers, starting with *The One-to-One Future*. A support industry on customer relationship management (CRM) has developed with a focus largely on the computer tools to track, segment, and contact customers. For instance, Swissair knew it couldn't compete on low fares, so it built a data "warehouse" where all customer information is acces-

Customer "Radio"

Your customers and prospects are tuned into one frequency: WII-FM (What's in It for Me).

Target marketing and one-to-one marketing are not necessarily the same thing. Most target marketing programs segment your audience into groups. One-to-one marketing focuses on a segment of one.

Don Peppers and
Martha Rogers
The One-to-One Future

> Customers must usually buy a service to actually experience it. Thus, they must trust a service company to deliver on its promises and conduct itself honorably. The customers' trust is a service company's most precious asset.
>
> Leonard Berry and Kathleen Sanders,
> *Design Management Journal*

sible. Flight attendants now use it to track preferences of frequent customers and deliver enhanced service during the flight.

To oversimplify, one-to-one marketing says that the goal of a business should be to try to treat each customer personally. By setting up databases, keeping track of what customers do, and asking them what they want, you can learn more about your customers and treat them differently than others.

By making it worth the customer's time to educate you about his or her needs, you gain a competitive advantage. Once you've customized your services, a competitor cannot offer the same service, and, if you treat customers well, it's not worth their time to educate competitors to compete with you.

As usual when ideas become very popular, most of the early efforts at one-to-one or CRM probably failed; and many have argued that you can't customize for *every* customer. One-to-one is the logical extension of segmentation. Ideally, you develop segments of one customer. Even if you never reach that ideal, one-to-one is an important goal. Professional service firms have always tried to treat big clients this way, with the lead partner establishing close relationships.

Permission Marketing

The title of the book *Permission Marketing* by Seth Godin says what it is about. He developed it from work online where spam (junk e-mail) is a big problem. Godin generally offered prospects a specific benefit (bribe) to give permission to receive a marketing message. Just as in any relationship building, positive exchanges lead to further, deeper relationships. You have to build trust.

While developed from online work, permission marketing is a good way to think about relationship building in general. You:

- invite prospects to "raise their hands" for you to contact them
- keep track of permissions to contact people at different levels
- develop a series of steps to deepen the level of communication and build trust
- work to deepen permission and relationships with customers

The One-to-One Marketing Revolution

Tom Peters

In *The One-to-One Future: Building Relationships One Customer at a Time,* Don Peppers and Martha Rogers brilliantly reconceive the basis for marketing. They urge companies to "turn even the simplest products and services . . . into collaborative ventures with individual customers to create lasting, impregnable relationships." New technologies, they claim, make it "possible for . . . even the mass marketer . . . to assume the role of small proprietor, doing business again with individuals, one at a time."

The core mechanism is straightforward: Gather as much information as you can about customers, then tailor the entire enterprise to customers' very personalized needs. Customer segmentation (rather than product segmentation) already exists; e.g., American Airlines' variety of frequent flier programs, American Express's assortment of credit cards. But there's a much longer road to travel.

Though the authors acknowledge that the product or service remains important, they say the focus should change "from high-quality service to high-quality relationship"—with an emphasis on "share of customer" rather than share of market.

This shift entails fundamentally altering organization structure. To hold "marketing managers in your company responsible for concentrating on share of customer," Peppers and Rogers say, "you must first turn your marketing department into a 'customer management' organization" designed around portfolios of customers arrayed according to expected lifetime purchasing value. Even new product-development activities become secondary to the customer-management structure.

Those who effectively get their hooks into customers this way will likely have the basis for relationships that can, even in these fickle days, stand the test of time. While brand loyalty is atrophying at an astonishing rate, customer loyalty may be there for the taking—if firms are nervy enough to swallow the entire Peppers and Rogers prescription.

!

YOU PROFIT FROM REPEAT BUSINESS—IT'S STILL RELATIONSHIPS

It's very hard to make a profit from your initial marketing. Some people say that it costs five times more to get a client the first time than to keep a client. It may be fifty times more!

The point is, your real object should be to form relationships with customers so they will do repeat business with you. They call on you because they want to work with you, not because you're the low bidder.

Consultants Build More Than Satisfaction

Chapter Six on personal selling will cover Consultative Selling™. All of you are consultants in a way. When you are offering your services, you should get away from your own bias (that you want people's business no matter what). You should try to give "objective" advice as a consultant would.

This is what happens in relationships. When you care about the other person's needs in the long term, you don't manipulate. As a superior service provider, you work at building rapport with people and giving them advice in their best interests, not yours. With the right clients, your superior service then works in your best, long-term interests as well.

Relationships Vary, but They're Still Relationships

You don't have to be "buddies" with all your clients. Relationships can vary.

If you're the landscape gardener who trims people's roses every season, you may have a superficial relationship with clients. You may call them or send a postcard, and they may respond, "Sure, come by and trim my roses. Is it still $10 per rose?" They don't even see you trim them. You leave a few flowers, with a ribbon and note on their doorstep, haul away all the dirty clippings, and they feel they have a good relationship with you. But it's really quite minor. They see only the flowers and none of the thorns!

In cases such as those of attorneys or accountants and their clients, a close, trusting relationship is important. You may be working with clients' money or on their divorces.

Clients Judge You by How You Treat Them

There's another key reason why relationships are important. Clients are often not in a good position to judge your actual competence. They need to feel that you like them and won't take advantage of them. Ultimately, the best marketing does not just sell—it builds trust and relationships.

If you're good at what you do and enjoy it, then you have to enjoy the people with whom you work. Good clients are not a pain. (Fire clients who don't meet your standards. It will help your business.) Clients are people with whom you can socialize. They give you referrals and keep your interests in mind. This is another reason marketing is not something to fear or dislike.

Marketing means making friends and doing something you enjoy. You help others and get paid for it!

OLD MARKETING "INITIALS"

There is some old-fashioned jargon in marketing that continues to be used in the textbooks. There are three sets of famous letters in marketing. Two were designed to summarize broad aspects of marketing, and one is strategy oriented.

The Four Ps of Marketing

If you read a marketing textbook or take a marketing class, you'll hear about the "four Ps" of marketing:

- Product,
- Place,
- Price, and
- Promotion.

Product, in your case, would be your services—having services that are useful; providing the right services for the marketplace.

Place refers to location. Your actual physical location should not be particularly important, compared to that of a retailer. You may even go to clients' offices rather than have them come to yours. Sometimes

---

The 4 Cs

I actually prefer the lesser-known 4 Cs of marketing to the 4 Ps.

1. Instead of *Product*, you have *Customer Value;*
2. for *Price*, *Cost;*
3. for *Place*, *Convenience;*
4. and for *Promotion*, *Communication.*

The Cs make a lot more sense, especially for services. They are much more customer oriented—and you need to think like your clients to do the best marketing.

being in a status office building is an advantage for your image. But it can also make people think you will be too expensive.

Price is a factor when people don't have other differentiating information. They can't see your expertise. They can't see your insight. They can't see how your past experience will help you provide solutions for them. They *can* see price.

Sometimes if you are higher priced, people think that you must be better. But often, high fees will scare prospects away. (I cover different ways to price your services in the Appendix.)

When people are making a decision to buy a service, they will make it based on how much they like you or trust you in addition to price. Actually, the price isn't important if they're sure they're getting benefits worth more to them than the cost. For instance, if you charged $10,000, but saved them $20,000, they'd readily give you the $10,000. Price would be no object. This is value pricing. Prove your high value and price is secondary.

Promotion, in this "four Ps" summary, refers to all the marketing methods you use. Promotion actually has a more limited meaning in marketing, referring to things such as coupons, in-store games, and other techniques to push sales. But if the people who invented the "four Ps" used it the correct way, then the "Ps" wouldn't cover marketing well enough!

AIDA

The second set of famous letters in marketing is "AIDA." These letters stand for:

A ttention
I nterest
D esire
A ction.

They're particularly used in advertising.

Your marketing has to get people's *attention*. If people don't know you exist, they can't do business with you. Then, they need to either already have an *interest* in what you do, or you have to raise their interest. Next, you have to create a *desire* for your services. This means they actually begin to believe that you could meet their needs, and they want to use you. Finally, they have to take *action*. If they never take action, you have no business.

Again, while these acronyms are catchy and have been around a long time, they really aren't too helpful. It's better to focus on what you are that is unique and on what your customers want. Then you'll be able to get their attention, and meet your and their needs.

SWOT

SWOT is much loved by MBA programs. When you are analyzing yourself in the "market," you look at your *Strengths* and *Weaknesses*, as well as *Opportunities* and *Threats*. Of course, these are all useful things to analyze as you determine strategy and positioning. However, like all the "initials," the use of SWOT is largely a reminder of common sense.

THE POWER OF MARKETING: GOOD AND BAD?

One reason you may not like the idea of selling or marketing is that you think of it as manipulative. Ideas such as psychographics can be thought of from a positive perspective as better understanding and meeting your customers' needs. Or they can be thought of as usable from a negative perspective to manipulate people.

There are those who have made a living over the years writing books about the power of advertising. Vance Packard (*The Hidden Persuaders*) was one of the first. There are more recent ones in which authors talk about the power of subliminal advertising. For instance, you might discover that if you enlarge the picture of an ice cube in a drink ad one hundred times, then turn it upside down and look at it in a mirror, it looks like a nude man or woman, or a couple!

I suspect that this says more about the author's mind than the minds of the advertisers! But it's quite possible that once in a while an advertising art director with a sense of humor does put some little hidden figure in an ad. So what?

Subliminal Baloney

All the fear about subliminal advertising came from one weak study many years ago. In a movie theater, researchers flashed one or two frames in the movie that said something like, "Drink Coca-Cola," "You're thirsty," "Buy popcorn." Supposedly, sales at the snack bar went up at intermission.

The idea of being manipulated without our knowledge was so shocking that laws were passed, and subliminal advertising has been illegal almost from the day it was invented. There is some research suggesting that we sometimes can be influenced a little by things we can't identify. If things flicker by too fast to see, some part of our brain still may recognize something about them or some part of the message. But the great fears about manipulation through advertising are much overstated.

The Power to "Mold Men's Minds"—NOT!

If it were true that advertising had the power to mold or control men's minds like the old radio character, The Shadow, the big advertisers would be far more successful than they are.

Instead, we see that advertising is becoming less and less effective. Each decade, it's facing more and more competition, and greater and greater clutter. The average person sees thousands of ads every day, and most of them are ignored. Marketing through advertising is not going to be that effective, whether subliminal or otherwise.

The issue of manipulation is also important to you. As mentioned in Chapter One, many people feel that "selling" is bad, that it's manipulative, that you're twisting people's arms and shoving things down their throats. Perhaps you can do this with some things for some people. But think about how you like to buy services. Manipulation is obviously not the way to sell services or to have a relationship, and *relationships are the key here.*

SUMMARY

Now you have enough technical background to earn your "mini–MBA"!

You Know What You Need to Know About Technicalities

If you generally understand these aspects of marketing and ways of looking at things, you know as much as most MBAs about practical marketing as it applies to your case. You shouldn't be intimidated by consultants, books, or new terms that come along; they'll all fit within this framework.

If you studied for your MBA, you'd also deal with things such as formal projections, information systems, and corporate-level opportunity analysis. You might even hear about fancy statistical techniques such as "cluster analysis," "regression," or "connotical correlations." They're just tools. If you ever need them, you can follow Henry Ford's axiom, "When I need an engineer, I'll hire one." What's needed more for your marketing success is *your* commitment and direction.

Marketing is not based on technical terms. You don't have to remember the meaning of all the words in this chapter. You have more than the average MBA: You have a philosophy that transcends the technicalities. And you now understand why marketing equals relationships.

Your Niche

You understand the general ideas behind marketing in terms of research, strategy, and relationships, and then finding a niche or position for yourself in the marketplace.

This framework will help you develop a niche in which people appreciate what you do, where you're able to work with people you enjoy, make money, and make others happy. That's what marketing—and life—is all about.

Niche Research

Find out the trade publications of your customers in *Standard Rate and Data* at the library. Even easier, ask customers for old copies of magazines they get—many publications have coupons for free subscriptions.

!

AGENDA

There are risks and costs to action. But they are far less than the long-range risks of comfortable inaction.
JOHN F. KENNEDY

Who Are You?

► List your features and their many benefits.
► Identify one or two prime benefits that you provide to people or companies that use your services.
► What is your positioning compared to your competitors, and compared to people taking no action?

With Whom Do You Want to Work?

► What new segments or target markets does it make sense for you to investigate?
► Can you create a niche that gives you an "unfair" advantage?

What Are You Doing Now?

► What are you doing to actively enhance relationships with clients and prospects? (The subsequent chapters will help you with this.)
► Have you committed time and attention to regularly deal with questions such as these?

CHAPTER FOUR

ADVERTISING

You Pays Your Money and You Takes Your Chances!

> *I know that half my advertising is wasted—*
> *I just don't know which half.*
> JOHN WANAMAKER

The first thing most people think about to get more business is usually advertising. Buying an ad is an easy way to take action, and there are lots of people selling ads to you. Unfortunately, for most advertising, Wanamaker's famous quote still holds today. And the percentage of advertising that works is probably *less than 50 percent* for most services.

You'll probably remember from Chapter One that advertising is defined as impersonal, mass-media, paid approaches to marketing. It's the impersonal and paid aspects that I hate.

My emphasis is on relationships and cost-effectiveness. I'd love advertising if I could be sure that it was cost-effective in producing business and building relationships.

FOR WHAT SERVICES DO ADS REALLY WORK?

People prefer to have referrals for services, but they will respond to advertising in some cases. For example, people may not want to ask for a referral for therapists (unless they travel in circles where it's expected that everyone will have a therapist!).

The more tangible your service, the more likely that advertising will work for you. For instance, plumbing, bookkeeping, hauling, and dentistry can have success with ads.

If people don't know where to get referrals for your service, they will look for information in the Yellow Pages, or notice ads in the newspaper,

Test Before Spending

Perhaps the simplest way to create cost-effective advertising is to test, test, test inexpensively.

Test by getting free publicity in different media and seeing how much response you generate. Test different headlines. Test different appeals. Test ads of different sizes. There's even a way to get other people to do your testing for you.

One smart publisher was looking for places to advertise his books. He wrote dozens of advertisers, like himself, from all the media he was considering. He asked them how well their ads did and offered to share, in return, his experience. He also asked for other suggestions. He got some new places to advertise and saved wasting money on ads in a number of places that did poorly.

on television, and so on. Personal-injury attorneys seem to advertise a lot on television, divorce lawyers specializing in men as clients advertise in the newspaper sports section, and so forth.

You Have to Track Results

Another reason that I don't like advertising is because it is often difficult to track its effectiveness. Advertising results *can* be tracked, particularly with pay-for-performance arrangements online. But the effects of advertising are often hard to measure, and many people don't even try.

If you don't know where your clients are coming from, you can't tell if your advertising is working. If you're advertising in a lot of places, you must ask people where they saw the ad. Or you need coupons or other ways of coding the ads to track results from each source.

Image Advertising

One of the worst concepts for most service providers is *image advertising*. I want you to see results from all your marketing, especially methods that cost you money such as advertising. Put in its most basic way, image advertising is the opposite of this.

Image advertising says that it is worthwhile to spend money without seeing any results because you are building "brand awareness" or your image in people's minds. While image enhancement can result from good advertising in the long run, it reminds me of the expression that in the long run we're all dead! I urge you to aim for immediate results from any marketing expenditure. (As just mentioned, to do this you must track results.) Good advertising will give you results now *plus* long-term image building.

TOO MANY TYPES OF ADVERTISING

Unless your services are something that people understand well, such as swimming pool maintenance, construction, or tax preparation, I don't recommend advertising as your first choice. As the subtitle of this chapter says, "you pays your money and you takes your chances" with advertising. I prefer to only spend money *after* I know that an ad will work! (There is a way to find this out.)

Where can you advertise? You can advertise through:

- television
- radio
- online
- newspapers
- trade magazines
- billboards
- Val-Pac and similar group coupon mailers to specific zip codes
- Yellow Pages
- the newsletters of groups you belong to or serve, such as the chamber of commerce, or trade groups

If you are really set on advertising, you could advertise on:

- billboards (outdoor)
- bus stop shelters
- the sides of your own vehicle if you're in the "trades" (if you work in the city don't forget the top, too, which can be seen from high-rise buildings)
- the sides of taxicabs and buses
- anywhere else that someone can think of selling you a space (perhaps the strangest one was a firm that was setting up small advertising placards in restrooms!)

I can dismiss most of the above forms of advertising for professional services, out of hand. They just don't fit a professional image, although I do like the "chutzpah" shown by the boy wearing the signboards. (And I've since seen a number of real people who did something similar and got job leads that way.)

By the way, the book cover illustration shown here is also an example of street-smart marketing, or "ambush marketing," as discussed later in this chapter. The publisher used an author's name, "Alger," to capitalize on the many similar Horatio Alger books.

EXAMPLES OF ADVERTISING MEDIA

Here are a few advertising methods as examples of the way you need to analyze possibilities.

Most people selling you advertising will tell you how well their product reaches people. Some will tell you how low their "CPM" is. This means cost per thousand people theoretically reached (such as subscribers to the newspaper). If their CPM is high, they'll tell you about "pass-along readership" (that is, several people read each magazine). Or they'll talk about how well targeted their audience is for your service.

Don't be distracted by their CPM, sales comparison charts, or other fancy material. If they're not willing to guarantee your response—and 95 percent won't—it's all guesswork.

Guaranteed Responses

While guarantees are rare, they're not unknown. For instance, the local coupon mailers who do sets of ten thousand coupons at a time to specific neighborhoods have enough experience to know what services will get a good response.

Once one of my companies was approached by the local Val-Pac salesperson who gave us this guarantee. If our test of ten thousand didn't produce enough profits to cover its cost, Val-Pac would mail more coupons for us free until we made enough to pay. And the company trusted us to measure profits.

Many online sites, including search engines, will sell you "clicks." That is, you only pay for people who actually come to your site. Some sites get paid only when you make sales. For instance, that's the way "associate" programs such as amazon.com's work. (See Chapter Twelve for more on online marketing.)

Newspapers

Advertising in your local newspaper or your weekly business journal can work. Tangible services such as private detectives and bookkeeping need

---

Go Where Your Customers Are

One heating and air-conditioning contractor bought a $450 ad in the program of the local symphony. The owner's logic: The people who go to the symphony own the biggest buildings in town.

to devise a way to get attention by using a good headline and being in the right section. See the discussion on page 74 about laying out space ads for a few ideas.

Editorial-Style Ads

Most ads for professional services should be written like a guest column. These show you in a professional light and may pass as editorial material, which has higher readership and credibility.

Make your ad as close to the look of the medium you're in as the publication will allow you. Use the same type style and headline style that it uses.

One way to achieve this is to make your ad a "letter" to prospects. Explain your services. Educate them. Entertain them. If you can make it interesting, they will be far more likely to read it than another ad.

Write about topics that are important to the people you're trying to reach.

- If you're a dentist, write an article about how to encourage children to brush more often.
- If you're a lawyer, explain how to avoid lengthy litigation.
- If you're in insurance, write about home security or defensive driving for teenagers.
- If you're a Realtor, write about how to buy or sell a house.
- If you're a banker, write about how to get an SBA loan guarantee, or how to save money on car financing.
- If you're an expert witness, advertise in a legal magazine and explain some of the tricks of the trade.
- If you're an accountant, write about how to lower taxes, or make more money in business.
- If you're a landscape architect, tell people what trees do best in your area, or how to grow roses.

Some companies will sell you "stock" newspaper ads you can use. For instance, chiropractors can buy sample columns to put in their local papers explaining their training and services.

On the next page is a sample of one like that.

```
+------------------+
|                  |
|                  |
|      Your        |
|     picture      |
|      here        |
|                  |
|                  |
+------------------+
```

Hi. I'm Elaine Smith. As a chiropractor, I have eight years of training to help you deal with your aches and pains. My education included four years of chiropractic school after college. Our program of study is much like what an M.D. goes through, except we place more emphasis on preventive medicine and holistic health, and we receive a D.C. degree.

In addition to my training for the degree, I do at least one hundred hours a year of continuing education to keep up on the newest techniques and nutritional information. This is in addition to my constant reading of the latest research on pain, bone structure, nutrition, and other topics.

If you have an automobile accident, often there are delayed effects that are like whiplash. By having yourself checked immediately, these can be avoided. If you wake up in the morning with a sore back, you need to do something about it. I don't just deal with your immediate pain, I want to eliminate the causes for you. I can recommend everything from a firmer mattress to an exercise program to strengthen the weak abdominal muscles that can cause back pain.

Some of my clients like to have a quarterly back alignment just to keep themselves in top shape. They say it's like changing the oil in their car regularly—a good way to avoid problems.

If you'd like to find out what I can do, please call and let's discuss the results you're looking for.

To help us get acquainted, I'm happy to offer you one free session if you mention this ad. I'm sure that when you try my services, you'll see how I can be a partner in helping you with your long-term health.

Sincerely,

Elaine Smith, D.C.

Note that by offering a free session *if* they mention the ad, she can track its effectiveness.

Yellow Pages

If your services are simple to understand, such as remodeling or pest control, the Yellow Pages can be an important advertising vehicle for you. Normally, the main Yellow Pages are far more cost-effective than smaller phone books designed for specific groups, because most buyers use only the main Yellow Pages.

If you have a business phone, you get a free listing in the Yellow Pages. This is just one line, so it will attract little business unless you are the only one in your category.

Be Careful About Buying a Big Ad

For most professional services, I don't recommend larger ads unless they simply explain your hours or services.

For services such as plumbing, larger ads can be useful. But don't just be one of a dozen similar ads. If you can't afford to be the biggest, you must do something distinctive. This could be twenty-four-hour service, a 100 percent guarantee, or services that others don't offer.

Yellow Pages Advertising

- According to a study sponsored by the Yellow Pages Publishers Association, people go to the Yellow Pages with an open mind: six out of ten consumers said they did not have a preference when they turned to the Yellow Pages.
- Advantages of a Yellow Pages ad are targeting a specific geographical area and twenty-four-hour-a-day accessibility. Those who use the Yellow Pages are usually ready to make a purchase or gather information about your business. (One study found that eight out of ten consumers contacted a contractor from an ad in the Yellow Pages. Further, 40 percent made a purchase, and another 40 percent said they were likely to do so.)
- Disadvantages are that your ad remains the same for an entire year, and there is a lot of advertising clutter. Your ad will have to stand out to get results.

One reason I don't like advertising in general is that you have to pay first and see if it works later. For the Yellow Pages, the case is even worse. You're stuck with your ad for a year!

My Buddy Makes a Big Mistake

The best example of the wrong way to buy Yellow Pages advertising is a friend of mine who was a printer.

Paul got a "brainstorm" for a new service to offer when his Yellow Pages ad came due. His idea was a rush overnight service designed for people who came to town for trade shows or meetings and forgot their business cards or other printed material.

In order to highlight his new idea, he took a half-page ad that cost him $500 a *month*. (And that was many years ago.)

He very quickly found that the ad didn't work. People from out of town didn't look in the phone book for overnight service. Perhaps they didn't think it existed. Or perhaps they had material sent overnight to them. To add insult to injury, Paul was reminded of his mistake every month when he had to pay his phone bill!

How to Avoid Mistakes Such as This: TEST

If Paul had approached his idea the way you will after reading this book, what would he have done? He would have tested the idea cheaply *before* committing $500 a month to it.

He could have taken an ad out in the local daily paper. Out-of-towners are more likely to look at it than at the Yellow Pages.

But wait! He's a printer. What if he had printed up some flyers explaining the service? Then he could have paid a teenager to pass them out by the local convention center. Rather than relying on mass media, he could have put the offer directly into the hands of his target audience at almost no cost to him. In fact, his idea might still work if carried out this way.

Television

At first glance, I would say television is too expensive and too general. But when I watch old *Perry Mason* reruns at noon on my local television channel, most of the ads seem to be from lawyers offering help with personal injuries from motorcycles or on-the-job accidents. This must be effective for finding people who are home in bed watching television and don't know how to approach a lawyer.

1-800-LAWYER!

They give you 800 numbers and they tell you there is no cost to you unless you get a recovery. They urge you to act now before your rights are taken away by insurance companies and others. They tell you that even if you're at fault and have a police citation, they can still help you with your case.

These are good sales "pitches" or good benefits to customers—no risk, someone who understands their situation, doesn't care if they're guilty or not, and will protect them from scary lawyers and insurance companies! These are the types of concerns that people unfamiliar with lawyers (and that's most people) have.

Can TV Work for You?

It's hard to believe that professionals, such as architects, would get much benefit out of television advertising. But think of contractors. Perhaps there are a lot of people who have something they wouldn't mind repairing or remodeling, and never get around to it.

Local television channels may be effective if your work appeals to many people who are hard to reach. There is also cable television advertising. Here, for as little as $2 a spot, you might be able to buy a small ad, in a very small cable system, that will appear on ESPN, TNT, and other major channels on that cable. More common prices would be $10 to $100 a spot, depending on the size of the cable system and how hungry it is.

Radio

Few services use radio advertising. The most common example that comes to mind is the companies that say they help inventors bring their products to market. It must work because they've been doing it for years, despite the fact that most of them are scams.

Another successful radio advertiser was Franklin Bank. It and others have used radio to make fun of competitors' fees and impersonal service (*positioning* themselves against the "big boys"); for instance, "Push #4 if you want us to jack you around some more."

More than television, radio allows you to better target your audience because of the multiple channels. (As defined in Chapter Three, this means that certain kinds of people listen to certain kinds of stations.) Jazz might have an upscale audience; classical music might have an older upscale audience; rock and roll would appeal to younger people; and so forth. You can pick the kind of people you want to reach pretty well by picking a particular radio station. As television fragments into more and more cable stations, you'll be able to target audiences better with television commercials as well.

Online Advertising

There are a lot of Web sites and e-zines that take advertising, and professionals can pay to receive various consulting job leads from a number of sites. In my experience, you'll generate more interest by writing in most of the places that want you to advertise (see Chapter Seven on publicity). Most of the lead sources are questionable as well.

Try to experiment with free listings in your area or field. For instance, Craigslist.org is big in the San Francisco area and is spreading to other cities. One marketing consultant got two of her first four jobs there (at discounted rates). And one lawyer continues to offer his services for barter there, which means he is getting some results.

Specialty Advertising

Specialty advertising is when you put your name on items that have some value to people, such as calendars and pens.

You can find providers listed in the Yellow Pages under "Advertising Specialties." There are catalogues full of material from tennis balls to beach towels. There is a whole industry of people who will sell you clever items with your information printed on them. You may also have been solicited in the mail for pens, datebooks, or calendars.

Pens and calendars are useful enough that most people you give them to will keep them around. But they don't notice your name very often. Better items are novel enough to get attention, and useful enough to be kept; for instance, unusual letter openers or refrigerator magnets.

Perhaps the best use of a specialty-type item was by a plumber. He distributed a sticker to go on the home phone. It had a list of emergency numbers such as police, fire, poison control, doctor, and *plumber*! Right on the phone is a great place to be when people only need you once every few years. I've also seen service labels on heating systems or hot tub controls, right where you need them when something breaks.

Trade Coupons

Specialty ad items such as pens don't qualify as "mass media." There are other such hands-on methods of advertising in a local area.

It can often be very effective to put a small coupon (perhaps a third of an $8\frac{1}{2} \times 11$-inch piece of paper) on the counters of some of your local merchants or in the offices of other professional colleagues. You could put a coupon good for a free twenty-minute consultation in the waiting room of a local dentist, bank, or other business, or even the local convenience store, if appropriate for your service.

You ask others to put the coupons in their offices, and you offer to do the same for them. You could end up having coupons or flyers in twenty different places. These become implied testimonials and referrals from the people putting them out. I know one person who has coupons all over, yet few of those displaying his have gotten around to creating a coupon for him to give out.

THERE ARE UNMET NEEDS OUT THERE

As mentioned earlier, some surveys have suggested that for every person who goes to the dentist, there are seven people who need to go but don't get around to it.

Specialty Advertising Ideas

Make Your Prospects and Customers the Stars

A printing company in Franklin, New Jersey, came up with a great promotional item. It printed up "baseball" cards for businesses in its community. Each card featured a business *and* illustrated some printing capabilities such as embossing or thermography. This is a classic example of the old rule that nothing appeals to people more than themselves. You don't have to be a printer to create a collectible that will keep you in your customers' minds.

Most Popular Promotional Products

Wearables (T-shirts, baseball caps, sunglasses)	19.7%
Writing instruments	13.4%
Glassware and ceramics	10.8%
Desk, office, and business accessories	9.2%
Calendars	8.7%
Recognition awards, trophies, jewelry	8.5%
Sporting goods, leisure products	7.2%

Perhaps the same thing is true for doctors, bookkeepers, landscapers, and others. So, while mass-marketing media such as TV and radio should only be considered after you've tried other more cost-effective and image-congruent methods, it is possible that such advertising can be effective in tapping a broad audience.

LAYING OUT AD SPACE

If you're advertising in the Yellow Pages, newspapers, or other print media, you're buying space.

The design of these ads is usually created free for you by the newspaper or Yellow Pages salespeople. To some extent, you get what you pay for with them! But if you know what you're looking for and make them perform the way you want, you can often get an ad that will attract more business than your competitors' ads.

If you can have an ad half the size of your competitors, that draws just as well, you'll have a competitive advantage over them. (See also the section on graphics at the end of Chapter Five.)

Small-Ad Approaches

The way to create a small ad that pulls well is to use a small amount of "reverse" type and other dark areas. For instance, have a dark bar across the top, with reverse type for the headline. You can also put a box around the ad, and a tie between the bar and the ad itself. Below are a couple of examples.

I WANT TO DO YOUR YARDWORK . . .

. . . while you play with the kids, curl up with a good book, visit with your friends. Your time is precious. Let me pull your weeds.

Dependable • Reasonable Rates
Call Linda at 555-5555

We take your computer files from any tape or disk to any tape or disk for any computer. Also . . . scanning, list rentals, and mailing label printouts.

Data Conversion for LESS

CEO LISTS
415/924 - 1612

Bigger Ad Styles

For bigger ads, the headline should take up one-quarter to one-half of the ad. If your headline doesn't get their attention, people won't stop to look at the rest of the ad. Then make a clear statement of your benefits to the reader. Keep it simple.

One common mistake is to cram as much into the ad as you can fit. After all, you're paying for all the space, why not use it? For the small ads pictured on page 74 a little clutter is expected. But for larger ads, blank space both attracts the eye and highlights the other material.

HEADLINES

Headlines are key to the success of much of your written material.

When you're creating an ad, the headline is absolutely the most important element. It must get people's attention and entice them to read the ad. Many times, people glance at the headline and, unless it grabs their interest, they read no further. This means that all the rest of the ad is wasted.

Guides for Headlines

There are a lot of rules that can be applied to writing headlines. Perhaps the most important is to speak to people's interests. Headlines should convey benefits to the readers rather than highlight you or your features.

One way to get attention is to combine words in an unusual way, such "A Tuesday drink." If they catch attention, headlines can get people to stop for a second to consider your ad.

You can use a contrast approach; for example, "It takes a tough man to make a tender chicken." Or a rhyming approach, as in "Winston tastes good, like a cigarette should."

You can ask people questions and you can test them: "How good a parent are you?" "Do you make these mistakes in English?" These were classic headlines that worked well. Offer news in your headline. Or you can make people a big promise: "I want you to have this, while there is time."

Magic Words for Headlines

A classic Yale University study found these words to be attention getters:

■ new	■ avoid	■ mother	■ proof
■ now	■ stop	■ unique	■ last chance
■ at last	■ reduce	■ money off	■ 100 %
■ finally	■ fast	■ save	■ latest
■ free	■ easy	■ direct from	■ sale
■ amazing	■ introducing	■ economy	■ discount
■ how to	■ announcing	■ bargain	■ special
■ suddenly	■ revealed	■ breakthrough	
■ never	■ magic	■ guarantee	

Because many of these "magic words" are overused, they can have a feel of sales hype. But some are worth considering as you look for ways to get attention with your headlines.

You can challenge people: "If you can find a better car, buy it." (Lee Iacocca, for Chrysler.)

Other Headline Ideas

You can appeal to people's different needs with different kinds of head-lines. Those "ultimate" needs include: to be accepted; to have love; to have mental stimulation, comfort, convenience, friendship; to have fun; to satisfy curiosity; to build up ego; to gain respect, family togetherness, health, security; and to acquire things. (See also Chapter Three on "ridiculous extreme benefits.")

Copy Classic Headlines

Perhaps the best way to think about headlines is to have models to copy. It's much easier to write a headline this way than to start from scratch.

Let's take some examples of headlines from years ago. Below are fifteen all-time great headlines that did well in various tests and are considered classics in their fields. The funny thing is that they are for everything from farm materials to piano lessons. Yet all can be adapted to almost any service.

For each headline, I've given some examples of how it could be applied to various services. And I've left space for you to write a similar headline for yourself. This takes a bit of a knack; you have to let yourself go a little. You can't always write a headline exactly like the example, but you can write a similar one.

1. "The Secret to Making People Like You"

   The Secret to _____

Everyone wants "secret" knowledge. Here, you would talk about the secret of your prime benefit. The Secret to Getting Your Taxes Done Early. The Secret of Never Having a Lawsuit. The Secret of Having Your Neighbors Envy Your Yard. The Secret to Financial Security. The Secret of Fresh Vegetables. The Secret to Great Entertaining.

It doesn't matter what your service is, there could be a so-called secret to whatever benefit you offer.

2. "A Little Mistake That Cost a Farmer $3,000 a Year"

A Little Mistake That Cost a _____ $_____ per _____

People want to avoid mistakes. A Little Mistake That Cost a Homeowner (or Renter) $10,000 a Year. Perhaps it's a mistake that cost them a million-dollar lawsuit. There doesn't have to be a time reference. Perhaps it's a mistake during a speech that cost them embarrassment, or an interview mistake that cost them a job.

People are worried about mistakes and part of your service should help people avoid them.

3. "Advice to Wives Whose Husbands Don't Save Money—by a Wife"

Advice to a_____Whose_____ by a _____

People believe other people who have been through what they have. For instance, advice to parents whose children disobey—by a parent whose child went to this family therapist and become an obedient child. This headline could convey advice to homeowners, lawyers, or business owners who have a particular problem, by someone who is like them, providing a testimonial for you about how you helped with the problem.

4. "Are You Ever Tongue-Tied at a Party?"

Do You Ever Have a _____ Problem?

This is focusing on a problem and uses a question. Do You Ever Worry About Your Looks? (for a grooming consultant). Do You Ever Worry About Being Sued? Do You Ever Do Something That Might Be Construed as Sexist?

Everyone has some problem. This headline is designed to target your audience by attracting people with a particular need or worry.

5. "A New Discovery That Saved a Florist's Business"

A New Discovery That _____

Maybe your headline can promise a new discovery that cuts construction costs. A New Discovery That Avoids Litigation. A New Discovery That Gets You All the Clients You Need. A New Discovery That Gives You More Leisure Time.

Whatever you deal in, there should be some new ideas your prospects haven't used. You could say, "A New Idea" or "A New Way." It doesn't have to be a technical discovery.

6. "How to Win Friends and Influence People"

How to _____ and _____

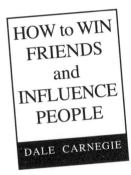

This is the classic Dale Carnegie book title. These are two big promises. For instance, How to Win More Cases in Less Time, How to Save Money and Look Better, or How to Have a Better-Looking Yard with Less Work.

7. "Who Else Wants Softer Hands for Less Money?"

Who Else Wants_____ for _____ ?

This headline may have been written for dishwashing soap or hand cream. It combines a question with a double, apparently conflicting, promise.

The general question implies that there are lots of others who have achieved this benefit. It has a built-in implied testimonial. Who Else Wants to Get Their Bookkeeping Done in a Half-Hour a Week? Who Else Wants Better Fingernails at Less Cost? Who Else Wants a 100,000-Mile Warranty Included in the Price? Who Else Wants Less Work and More Money?

8. "Do You Make These Mistakes in English?" (followed by a test)

Do You Make These Mistakes in _____?

People love to read about themselves. This headline also appeals to people's fears. Showing them where they stand now positions you as the expert, and by implication says you can help them. For instance, Do You Make These Mistakes with Your Employees (or computers, tax records, home maintenance, and so on)?

9. "Why Some Foods 'Explode' in your Stomach"

Why Some _____   _____

At first glance, this headline looks hard to work with. I don't know what this was written for originally, but it has a bit of a mystery to it.

Without worrying about the mystery, we can simply plug in a benefit that you offer. For instance: Why Some Companies Never Get Sued. Why Some People Never Have Accidents. Why Some Construction Companies Have Workers' Comp Premiums at Lower Rates. Why Some Yards Need Less Water. Why Some People Always Look Good.

10. "Hands That Look Lovelier in Twenty-Four Hours—
    or Your Money Back"

_____ — or Your Money Back

Again, we're back to dishwashing soap or cold cream. Here's a clear promise with a guarantee added. Get More Clients This Week or Your Money Back. Win More Cases This Year or Your Money Back. Impress Your Friends Next Week or Your Money Back. You should be able to do something similar.

11. "You Can Laugh at Money Worries—If You Follow This
    Simple Plan"

You Can Laugh at _____ —If You Follow This Simple Plan

Or combining it with number 7, you could also say,

You, *Too*, Can Laugh at Money Worries—If You Follow This
Simple Plan

This implies that you have lots of cases of people you've helped. Again, it's a big promise. It is also a promise connected to a worry. You Too Can Laugh at Lawsuits—If You Follow This Simple Plan. You Can Laugh at Retirement Worries—If You Use Us as Your Financial Planner. You Can Laugh at Recessions—If You Follow This Simple Marketing Plan. This headline promises a step-by-step plan to make it come true.

12. **"Why Some People Almost Always Make Money in the Stock Market"**

Why Some People Almost Always _____

This is an interesting promise that suggests that you can join the group of "some people" with inside knowledge. Yet, it's conservative at another level because of the phrase "almost always."

Why Some People Almost Never Face Lawsuits. Why Some Restaurants Are Almost Always Full. Why Some Gardeners Almost Always Enjoy Good Crops. The word *almost* qualifies the big promise. But the promise is more credible because of it.

13. **"When Doctors Have a Headache, Here's What They Do"**

When _____, They _____

When Lawyers Get Sued, They Consult Us. When Consultants Have a Problem, They Bring Me In. When Accountants Need Advice, They Come to Me. When Bankers Need Money, They Borrow from Us.

14. **"Five Farm Problems—Which Do You Want to Overcome?"**

Five _____ Problems—Which Do You Want to Overcome?

It could be five problems in public speaking; five problems doing your bookkeeping; five problems in making sales; five problems hiring people; three problems keeping your lawn healthy—anything.

Of course, most people will want to overcome *all* the problems. This headline lets you show a range of skills and services, without looking scattered (shotgun marketing). And it lets the prospects focus on what they want if they only have one problem.

15. **"They Laughed When I Sat Down at the Piano . . . and Then I Began to Play"**

This is perhaps the greatest classic. This headline has also been used with *computer* replacing *piano*. It is dealing with fear of ridicule, and fear of performance, and promises terrific lessons that allow you to overcome them. It also takes a story form and provides a firsthand testimonial.

You might change it to say, They Didn't Believe I Could Build My Business . . . Until They Saw the Results. They Laughed When I Said My Building Would Have the Most Expensive Rents in Town . . . Until They Saw My Bankbook. They Laughed Out Loud When I Said I Was Going to Cut Hospital Costs . . . Until I Won the Association Award.

Summary

The previous section gave fifteen different headlines and numerous variations, but there are lots of other possible headlines that use these principles. And there are lots of different ways of thinking about what headlines can do.

For instance, headlines can be *direct,* telling people your offer immediately. They can be *indirect* to arouse curiosity. A *command* headline can tell people to act now. *Question* headlines will involve the reader. *Reason* headlines provide specific reasons (benefits) why people should read your ad: "Four Reasons to Talk with Us About Your Service Costs." *Testimonial* headlines provide an endorsement of your benefit by a real person. The *news* headline promises something new. And the *how-to* headline promises step-by-step guidance on how to achieve a benefit.

Of course, the best headline seems to be directly about the people to whom you're trying to appeal. David Oglivy tells a famous story about an ad man who had a client, "Joe Smith," who didn't like long, wordy ads. The client said that people read only a brief headline, and glance at a picture.

The ad man bet him that he could write a full-page ad of small type and the man would read every word. He won the bet by simply saying that his headline would be: "Joe Smith, This Ad Is the Untold Story About Your Life and Accomplishments."

The more personal you can make your headline to your target audience members and their concerns, the better.

BIG BARGAINS ON ADVERTISING

If you're purchasing advertising, you should know that "rate cards" are often a fiction rather than a fact. You should also know about remainder space and something called "per inquiry" or "per order" (PI or PO).

Rate cards supposedly tell you how much an inch of space or a minute of airtime costs. You'll often see discounts per unit for buying more total time or space. But what salespeople usually won't tell you is that they often cut their own rates if you negotiate a little.

One way they do this is to throw in extras. For instance, they double the number of radio spots you get if you buy this week. Or they give you space in a special section if you put an ad in the regular newspaper.

Talk to others who advertise to find out what kinds of deals they've seen. Negotiating often takes a "tough" attitude. Ad salespeople don't always think win/win. They have been known to lie about what's possible.

Remainder Time or Space

When a radio or television station has passed the time of a potential commercial that isn't played, the time has no value to them. Similarly, once a magazine or newspaper is printed, it can't make any more money from advertising. Therefore, sometimes it will sell, or "remainder," this space at a very low cost.

With remainder space, you prepare an ad that is ready to use. You send it to the media with a note that states: "If you ever have any remainder space (time), I'd love to test the effectiveness of advertising with you. Because ads for my services don't do well in most media, I can't afford to test using your rate card. If you ever have some unsold, cancelled, or remainder space at the last minute, please consider this letter a contract to purchase one ad (ten spots, and so on) at a rate of _____. Just send proof of publication (notes of play time) along with your invoice."

If you call the media and make this offer, 95 percent will say they never heard of this or never do it. But up to 20 percent will run it when they have it in their hands and their alternative is to get no revenue from the unused time or space. I know I've accepted offers such as this when I owned a card deck (as described on page 85).

Find the Lowest Rates

An interesting way to discover what the lowest actual rates are is to find out what politicians are paying near election time. There are often laws which say that politicians must be charged the lowest rate quoted to any advertiser within, say, forty-five days of the election. Ask your local political campaign volunteer, or friends at the chamber of commerce, Rotary, Moose, and so on. Or maybe the media will tell you themselves. Even if they explain why you're not getting that rate, it puts you in a stronger negotiating position.

Sell First, Pay Later

So-called per inquiry and per order are even better deals than remainder space. They are now widely available online, which is putting pressure on other media to use them.

Ad Involvement

Levi's and other advertisers have increased customer involvement by having people vote online for the ad they like most. For instance, to participate in a sweepstakes for the Super Bowl, consumers had to register, which gave Levi's more market information.

!

If you're not sure about how effective your ad will be, some media will run a commercial for which they are paid only if people respond; thus, the per order or per inquiry name. In general, the media run the commercial at their expense. As the responses come in, they charge you and forward them to you. Of course, if you don't get payment with the order (per inquiry), you can't be certain that customers will pay you.

Pay Only for What Works

For instance, here is how it might work on a TV station. You call the station and ask about per inquiry or per order ads.

They'll usually deny any knowledge of such a thing. But if you watch the station and they have commercials late at night selling every record ever made, slicer dicers, or knives that cut through steel, you're in. Normally all the orders for these products will go to the same 800 number in Atlanta, or wherever the station is based. This is another giveaway.

The reason that PI/PO all go to the same place is that this is how the station gets paid. Since they get only a deposit up front, they need to know how many orders come in so they don't have to take your word for it. You don't care, because you're only paying for the number of orders or inquiries that they send you.

This approach is a way for stations to get some revenues from time that would otherwise go unused. There is also a potential advantage for the station. If your ad does very well, they can actually make more money than from their regular rates. But don't begrudge them these rare extra profits. You can always change to running regular commercials if they work that well!

Card Deck PI/PO

Card decks are bundles of postcards, each with an ad for one service or product. You can use PI/PO in national card decks as well. It's a good way to test them. (For more on card decks, see Chapter Five.)

Don't assume that your profits are assured with PI/PO. Our publishing business uses per inquiry because we can't expect people to send money for an expensive newsletter or book that they haven't seen. Once we got responses from two hundred people to whom we sent sample newsletters, and only one subsequent order! That one newsletter sale cost us about $1,000 (at $5 per inquiry). But for another deck at the same time, 10 percent of the people who got samples paid, so we did okay.

There's another thing that can go wrong with PI/PO. It may be profitable for you, but if it doesn't generate enough orders, the media can throw you out in favor of a new advertiser who may attract more orders. Nothing is foolproof. But by knowing about PI/PO, you're ahead of 95 percent of the people who advertise today.

Online PI/PO

As mentioned earlier, it is now common practice for some search engines to allow you to bid for listings in categories. Thus, you are paying for click-throughs to your site (PI). And associate programs like Amazon's pay only for orders (PO). (See Chapter Twelve for more on this topic.)

AMBUSH MARKETING

One advertising approach mentioned earlier is called *ambush marketing*. This is a technique in which one advertiser takes advantage of large promotional possibilities without paying fees. For instance, McDonald's Corporation paid millions of dollars to be the exclusive fast-food sponsor for the Olympic Games. But some of their rivals simply put posters in their windows with scenes similar to the Olympics and signs that said, "We'll be there." Or, rather than becoming a general sponsor, they sponsored an individual team or athlete for a fraction of the price, then advertised that.

Be a Cautious Buyer

Don't let people talk you into advertising until you've taken a serious look at how effective it's likely to be.

Wendy's, for instance, called itself "a proud sponsor of ABC's television coverage of the 1994 Winter Olympics." It used this theme on its napkins and everywhere. It couldn't use the five-ring Olympics symbol. Instead, it used the similar ABC television five-rings symbol.

To the average consumer, Wendy's looked like just as big a sponsor as McDonald's. And a study at Florida State University confirmed that Wendy's got the best of the deal. Ninety-four percent of viewers of its ad thought it was an official sponsor. Even when viewers knew who the official sponsors were, they were still fooled by the ambush ads. And I doubt very much if average consumers care about the distinction.

CONCLUSIONS: ADVERTISING CAN KILL YOU!

It should be clear from this chapter that I don't particularly like advertising. It's one of the least cost-effective ways for many service providers to market. It can kill you if you spend a lot of money on ads that don't work for you.

However, advertising can be important for some services. To the extent that your service is easy to understand, such as lawn maintenance or car repair, advertising may be effective.

If your competitors advertise, you may be able to beat them while spending half as much. Look at the places they advertise and test them carefully to see if this is where they're actually building their businesses.

The mass, impersonal aspect of advertising is the opposite of the personal-niche, one-on-one approach that I'm advocating in this book, but advertising is easier to do than many more personal marketing methods.

Ads Should Start the Selling Process

One way to make your advertising more personal—closer to the first step in building a relationship—is to feature a free "needs assessment" in your ads. Here, you would use the consultant selling approach discussed in Chapter Six. You give people valuable information, whether they use your services or not.

Of course, the opposite of mass and impersonal is personal sales or networking. Since many of you are going to be wary of personal selling, you may be tempted to use advertising. It is very concrete, is easy to do, and is painless except for the expense.

Please don't let your discomfort with personal selling push you toward ineffective and costly advertising. When you read Chapter Six on personal selling, you'll see that it can be a professional, dignified, nonpushy, and even enjoyable way of meeting people and building relationships.

AGENDA

The best time to plant a tree was twenty years ago.
The next best time is today.
Ancient Chinese adage

Test, Test, Test

▶ If you already advertise, make sure you have a way to tell how effective your current efforts are. Either systematically ask people how they heard about you, or code each ad with a different phone number, "department," or offer.

▶ Find a group where you can informally test ads before you use them. Perhaps this will be a regular lunch at a Moose Club, or a networking group that allows you to introduce yourself.

▶ Try to test media by getting free publicity in them to see how much response you receive.

▶ Call or write other advertisers who are using the media you're considering. You'll be surprised at how much they'll tell you about the effectiveness/ineffectiveness of their ads.

Create Better Ads

▶ Develop a list of criteria that you will use to decide where to advertise, such as cost and image congruence. Have your criteria available before the Yellow Pages salesperson calls to tell you that there are only three days left before your ad is due!

► If you advertise, look at your ads with fresh eyes and see if the design and headlines could be improved. Try to get the same impact with a smaller ad.

► If you advertise in the newspaper for a professional service, consider writing an editorial-type ad, as shown in this chapter.

► Write at least fifteen headlines for yourself using the models provided in this chapter. If you don't use them in ads, you can use the best ones on handouts, brochures, and so on.

Make Advertising Pay for Itself

► Try to cut rate cards in half if you advertise, or look for remainder or PI/PO deals.

CHAPTER FIVE

WRITING YOUR WAY TO CLIENTS

Brochures, Sales Letters, and More

> *Give the reader helpful advice; it is about 75 percent*
> *more effective than copy which deals directly with you.*
> DAVID OGILVY
> *Confessions of an Advertising Man*

When most people decide to focus on their marketing, the first thing they often consider is a brochure. Unfortunately, brochures seldom sell you directly. They are expensive and impersonal. Further, they are becoming more and more outdated because of Web sites.

DECIDING WHAT YOU WANT
TO COMMUNICATE

Before you start writing anything, or do any other in-depth marketing, you need to make some strategic decisions.

In Chapter Three, we discussed things such as who you are and your niche. Write down the answers to the following questions and have them in front of you before you try to write a sales letter, brochure, advertisement, or similar materials. (Also see Chapter Fifteen on planning.)

- Who are you trying to reach? (Your target audience.)
- What do you stand for? (Do you have a mission in your business?)
- What's your image?
- What's your USP? (What's different about you?)
- Why should people come to you? (What set of benefits do you provide?)

The Copy Platform

A good way to keep key information in the forefront while you write is called a copy platform. It uses your benefits, unique sales proposition, target audience, and so forth, and answers questions or states them in a way that makes clear what you're offering in your sales material.

Another way of summarizing this is: Who are you talking to? What will you offer them? What evidence supports your claim? What impression do you want to leave them with?

Examples of Copy Propositions

Let's take some examples of copy propositions, the basic part of a copy platform:

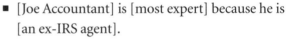
- [Joe Accountant] is [most expert] because he is [an ex-IRS agent].
- [Hospital X] is [the best deal] because it is [non-profit, associated with X university, and so on].
- [Computer programmer] is [the best value] because she is [the most skilled at the XML language], the most technically relevant language for creating your Web site.

To elaborate, here is what the accountant's statement is saying: This particular accountant is the one who can solve your problems because he is an ex-IRS agent, knows how the IRS thinks, knows how to deal with it, and so forth. This is better than just being a CPA, or from a particular school. To make it even stronger, you could talk about your experience with the prospect's industry, how you saved others money, obtained tax refunds, or provided other benefits.

You can fill in the brackets with who you are, what you're best at, what your claim is, and why people can believe that claim. Try it on yourself here:

I am [_____] because I am [_____].

Looked at another way, your goal is to convince a particular target group that your service would provide a benefit because of a proof you offer. Let's lay this out for you to fill in the blanks.

My written material needs to convince [target] that [service] will provide [benefit] because [proof].

This statement may be very similar to the self-introduction you'll develop in Chapter Eight on networking. In ten or twenty words or less, you should have summarized your prime benefit and the kinds of people to whom you appeal.

BROCHURES

Now let's look at brochures and other written sales material.

Do You Need a Brochure?

There's an old saying in marketing that sales literature such as brochures "tells, *not* sells." A brochure can be an add-on to your personal contacts, referrals, and other factors that directly sell your services. It can look professional. It can comfort people. But it will seldom sell by itself.

Many people don't need a brochure but think that they do. Today Web sites are replacing more and more brochures. The main reason for a brochure is if most of your clients expect to see one. The other reason for a brochure is if visual material is very important. If you're an architect, photographer, or contractor, it may be important to show pictures of projects you've completed. However, this needn't be in the form of a brochure. It can be actual 8" × 10" pictures, such as "before" and "after" for contractors.

Alternatives to Brochures

Every customer or client wants specific help. That's why most brochures aren't of much direct selling value. Instead, develop single sheets that speak specifically to one type of industry problem that you've solved. These, along with industry-specific testimonials, will be more convincing than most brochures.

Video, CD, and Computer Brochures

In some fields, video and other new forms of "brochures" are becoming common.

If you have ever been interviewed for a local cable TV show, ask for a master copy of the tape. In fact, it might be worth seeking appearances on some small cable show just to get a tape of yourself. Similarly, you can do an audio "brochure," if you appear on local radio stations. Many people will listen to CDs in their cars.

If you're in the computer or multimedia industry, you may want to put together a sampler on a CD of what you've done. Or your CD could guide people through a series of questions that provide a custom printout for them to consider. The more you can involve people with your material, the better.

If You Want a Brochure

Use your responses to the earlier questions to write your brochure. Who you're trying to reach with the brochure will determine what you put in it, what you want it to look like, or even if you need one at all.

Be Different

One contractor cut sales pieces to 9" × 11" (instead of the typical 8½" × 11"). Odd sizes and colors can make your materials stand out from the crowd.

!

Basic Brochures

As shown in the following illustrations, a simple 8½" × 11", three-fold brochure on inexpensive paper in one color is a modest way to start. As you get feedback or find errors, you can improve it and spend a little more if you find that it's effective for you. It's amazing how much time you can spend writing even a simple brochure.

If you started with a simple 8½" × 11", tri-fold, three-panel brochure, you might be able to produce it at your local copy store or on your computer. A tri-fold fits into a No. 10 envelope, the standard business size. It even makes a good self-mailer, if you leave one panel blank.

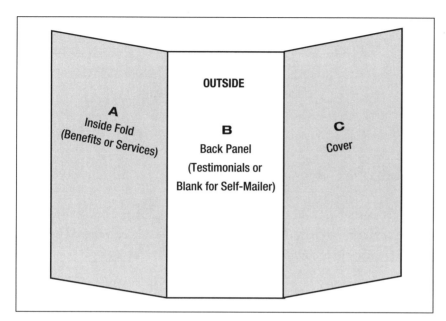

What to Put in Your Brochure

If you could only put one thing in your brochure, it should be the element that most people leave out—testimonials. But let's go through the more traditional "sections" of a brochure.

In a three-fold brochure, you have six separate panels with which to work. A brochure is a sales presentation on paper. You start with an introduction, then include benefits, services, references, and an invitation to act. A common three-panel configuration is shown below, but there are many options.

On the front panel (C), you typically have your name, the name of your service, or some other brief headline or descriptive material about what you do. You don't try to fill this space. You want to say one or two things that get people's attention and interest. For example:

Carla's Landscaping

We Do It Right, We Do It Fast, and
We Guarantee Our Work in Writing

or

Jim's Bookkeeping
Bookkeeping blues?—End them with us!
We take the hassle off you.

or

Elva Smith, Ph.D.
Short-Term Therapy—Long-Term Results!—Specializing in Phobias

To get started on a brochure, try to fill in ideas for yourself in each section as it is covered here. First, list three possible descriptions or benefits of your service to include on the cover:

1. _____

2. _____

3. _____

When you open the cover, you see two panels: the back of the front panel (D) and the one folded over (A). They can be integrated to create an overall picture, or each of them can have a separate headline covering matters such as testimonials, past clients, services offered, background, and so forth. I prefer to see something that shows benefits to the readers, so it might be services offered or testimonials from people you have helped.

When you open to the last panel (F), you now see the three inside panels (D, E, F). Again, they can be integrated designwise so that they work together.

Include your phone number prominently in at least two places. Ideally it should be on either the front or back panel so your prospect can locate the number easily without opening the brochure.

The two panels on the right could have one headline on a bar across the top; or, they could cover separate points. One might be a reply card or coupon requesting more information, a free report, or a free phone consultation. If your address and phone number are on the coupon (or the back of it), make sure they are elsewhere so that prospects can locate you even if that panel is removed.

If your brochure is not a self-mailer, the back panel can have some of your best material, such as testimonials or a brief description of your benefits. If people never open a brochure, they still tend to look at the front and back.

Fancier Brochures

More expensive brochures are usually created as booklets of various sizes with photos and graphics.

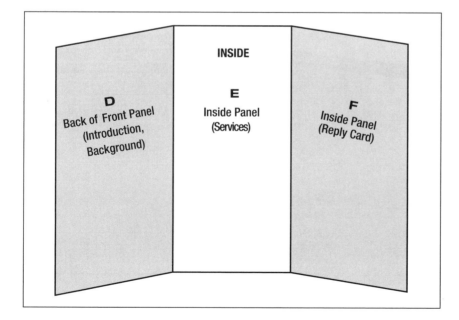

Another interesting format that looks expensive but can be done cost-effectively is the folder brochure shown below. You use 9" × 12" glossy, colored folders with pockets in them. The folders alone can cost you about a dollar each, but you can buy blank ones at the stationery store, particularly at discount stores, quite inexpensively. Then you could create a nice label for them, one that is customized on a laser printer and that can look very fancy. Inside, you put articles you've written, your résumé, testimonial sheets, philosophy, photographs or slides, and services offered. You can also include a personal letter.

There are two nice things about this format. First, you can change what's inside, depending on who you're talking to, or, over time, as your services and experience change. Second, you can photocopy many of the components inside very inexpensively. You don't have to preprint thousands of all the pages like a traditional brochure. Even copying or printing in color can be inexpensive today if you shop around or if your computer has a good color printer.

There is another custom effect with this format at no extra cost: Just design and print your inside sheets so that they can be cut to different heights. When people open the folder, they will see a tiered effect, each with a headline saying exactly what it covers. This looks impressive and

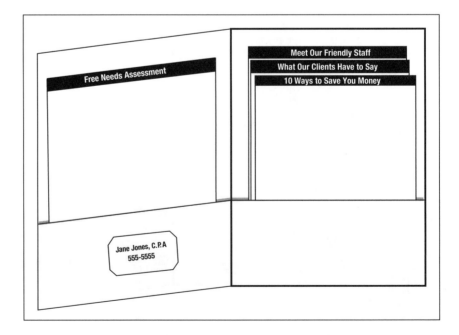

helps the reader see what's enclosed at a glance. You get a great effect at a relatively low cost. Plus, you have the flexibility of changing what is inside. Most folders also have a couple of slits die-cut in one of the pockets to place a business card.

You can also use these folders for old-fashioned press kits, when you need to include other material in addition to a press release. (See Chapter Seven on publicity.)

FLYERS

Perhaps the cheapest form of written sales material is a flyer. You could call flyers the simplest brochures.

Usually, a flyer is a single sheet of paper that you staple to a telephone pole or tape to a bus shelter. It can also be as small as a filing card to put on a grocery store bulletin board, or your business card displayed at your local printer or other businesses.

When you're working with small material such as this, you need to use a very simple message. For instance, on a flyer, the entire top half of the flyer might be devoted to a one- or two-word headline to get people's attention. Then, when they stop to look more closely, they can read the fine print, and perhaps tear off a detachable tab to take with them to remind them of your phone number.

Of course, flyers don't fit most professional services, or an expensive image, unless they're done very well. But you might use them on bulletin boards for seminars you're doing.

ADVANTAGES OF WRITTEN SALES MATERIAL

Next, we'll cover written sales letters. If you'll approach them as a personal expression, you'll be much more effective with both prospects and current customers.

With any written material, you have time. You can analyze it, think about it, control it, edit it. When you're speaking to someone in person or on the phone, you don't have time to control your communication this well. In a verbal conversation on the phone or in person, research suggests that recipients are going to miss the majority of the content. When you put something in writing, others have time to study it and understand the complete message.

As you can see, I like written material. I like to read and write, and I like the control of being able to analyze my words before they go out. It can do a number of things for you:

- It has a physical substantiality that can reassure people.
- It can cover technical details that require written explanations.
- It can use pictures, diagrams, and other visual aids.
- It can represent you when you're not there.
- It can be mailed to people to clear the way for a personal call.
- It can remind people of what you said.
- It can be a work sample that shows your expertise.

SALES LETTERS

The written word can sometimes convey a depth of meaning and feeling even better than in-person contact. Sales letters are a way to communicate with clients, at your convenience and theirs. Approach written marketing material as you do personal letters.

The modern-day form of letters is computer e-mail messages. They're faster and cheaper than regular letters. You can write them any time of the day or night. Recipients can read them and respond at their convenience.

You should write to people whenever possible. Let's start with a personal letter or e-mail. Ideally, you want all your sales letters to seem personal to the recipients.

Keep It Simple

As you start writing, remember the old basics about writing, whether a graduate dissertation or a sales letter; that is, 1) tell people what you are going to say; 2) say it; 3) tell them what you've said. It's not a bad approach to give people an overview of what's coming, then say it, and then summarize what you've said. Even a short letter can do this.

Everyone Likes Personal Letters

Your best sales tool is a often a sincere personal letter. Try to make it sound like you're speaking out loud. Sometimes dictating the letter can achieve this. Then edit it for further clarity.

Everybody reads personal letters. If you have something to say that is specifically for that person, you should write him or her a personal letter. While it's much more expensive per person to write a letter than to run an ad, it's also much more effective.

Let's take an example. You met someone at an event last night, and you follow up with a three-line personal e-mail. Or, if you have more to say, you type a half-page letter on your letterhead, send it along with an enclosure or two, and tell the person you're looking forward to seeing her again.

Computers let you create a number of "personal" letters that you keep on your hard disk, and then customize for each person or mailing. Good writing is mostly editing and rewriting. You have plenty of time to develop a letter that reflects your personality, is enthusiastic, and speaks to the interests of the people receiving it.

Keep in Touch

Think of a reason to write to your best customers once a month. When you offer a new service, send personal letters instead of generic announcements or press releases.

The Custom Form Letter

I use a number of different types of form letters designed to look personal to the recipient.

One I call the *custom form letter*. I save letters on my computer that deal with questions that could come up repeatedly. For instance, someone might ask me about my experience in a specific area. When I get a similar question from someone else, I'm able to pull up the letter in the computer, write a few sentences specific to that person, then give him a page or two of "personal" response. I can do this very quickly because most of the letter has already been thought out and written. I give a detailed, fast response, which suggests that my service might be equally good!

The Custom*ized* Form Letter

My custom form letter is distinguished from what I call the *customized* form letter.

Six Ways to Write Better

1. Only write when you have something to say.
2. Write the words as if you were speaking them.
3. Use short words, short sentences, and short paragraphs.
4. Have a personality. Don't hide yourself behind formal third-person language.
5. Remember your audience. Think of your readers as busy people with better things to do than read your prose.
6. Learn to edit. Good writing is mostly good reworking. Spit out ideas and then rewrite. Don't use writer's block as an excuse—just write something, then fix it up.

Here, you write a good letter, but it's clear that it's a form letter because you copy it and have it addressed to a generic category. For instance, we have an academic journal that publishes technical papers. I've written a few letters which I addressed, "Dear Fellow Researcher." I pick people who have done research I like, and send them a letter about our journal, why they should subscribe or why they should submit their articles. It's interesting and relevant to them, so they read it. But it's clearly a form letter. In the letter, sometimes I will even say, "I'm sending this letter to fifty people who have recently written articles which I like."

The key difference, the customization, is that, at the bottom, I sign it in blue ink so they'll know it's a personal signature, and I add a personal P.S. noting something about each one's article.

For instance, I say, "I liked your article on self-esteem," or whatever the topic was. This shows the recipient that I actually know her article and didn't just get her name from a general list. It takes an impersonal letter and makes it very personal. Your comment could be "I also lived in Chicago for a while." You just need something to personalize the letter to show recipients you know who they are specifically.

Junk Mail

So-called junk mail involves sending out large mailings to many people you don't know. Only those of you who have services that anyone could use—such as car repair, dentistry, carpet cleaning, and similar services—should consider this approach.

Junk mail is recognizable because of the bulk mail postage, address labels, and "teaser" copy on the outside of the envelope which tries to get you to open it. It's disliked largely because it is not specific and personal. (See Chapter Twelve regarding the online equivalent of junk mail—spam.)

To get an education in mass mailings, all you have to do is save your junk mail for a few days. This will give you a lot of ideas you could use.

Not all mail you receive will be good examples to copy. If you receive the same mailing several times a year, it is probably profitable for the mailer. Features that make "good" junk mail include:

- "teaser" copy on the envelope that makes people want to open the letter
- a great opening line
- getting to the point quickly
- multiple items in the envelope
- a P.S. that draws people back to the letter
- a clear, simple way to act now

Contrary to what you might think, long letters are more effective than short letters. However, this is *only* if you write well and the recipient is interested in the topic.

Whether you use junk mail or personal letters, the key is to make the mailing relevant to the people receiving it. As discussed in Chapter Three, keep their needs in mind, not your features.

Junk Mail Versus Custom Mail: Relative Results

If you were to send junk mail, with bulk-rate postage, form letters, several inserts, and so forth, selling your latest book or videotape, you'd be lucky to get about one-half of 1 percent of the recipients to send you money. If you write a "customized form letter" or, even better, a "custom form letter," you might get 20 to 30 percent. The more personal you make your letter, even if it's a form letter, the more effective it's likely to be. But this means you have to know something about the people to whom you're writing.

"Personal" Advertisements

It's also possible to use a personal letter style when writing an ad. The advertising chapter (Chapter Four) gave one example.

In the box below is a brilliant example of how a totally impersonal product can benefit from this approach.

Not only does the writer build credibility and get through your "B.S." detectors, but he deals with the most difficult aspect of buying a new thermostat. Few people like electricity, and no one has any interest in installing a thermostat by himself. Almost as an afterthought, the writer explains to you that it's no problem whatsoever.

With this major objection finessed, he has to show you why you'd care about this thermostat. In the rest of the ad (not shown), he gives you the feeling that he researches products and buys only if they're a good deal and a good product. This is great personal writing for an impersonal product. And, yes, I did buy one. (It's still working, twenty-five years later.)

[*Here is an attention-getting headline for something relatively boring, like a thermostat. Look at the way he opens.*]

THE "LOVE-HATE" THERMOSTAT
You'll Love the Way We Hated It Until—
an Amazing Thing Happened

It had no digital readout, an ugly case,
and a stupid name. It almost made us sick.

You're probably expecting a typical sales pitch, but get ready for a shock. Instead of trying to tell you what a great product the Magic-Stat Thermostat is, we're going to tear it apart unmercifully.

When we first saw the Magic-Stat, we took one look at the name and said, "Yuk." We took one look at the plastic case and said, "How cheap looking." And when we looked for the digital readout, it didn't have one. So, before the salesman even showed us how it worked, we were totally turned off.

"REAL LOSER"

So, there it was—at first blush, a real loser. But, wait. We did find one good feature—a feature that led us to a discovery. The Magic-Stat installs in a few minutes, and no serviceman is required. Thermostat wires from your wall follow standard color codes, so when you install a Magic-Stat, you attach the red wire to the red location, and the white to the white location. That's playschool stuff. And it's safe. Conventional thermostats installed over the last twenty years generally are only 24 volts, so you can either turn off the power or work with "live wires" without fear.

The ad on the facing page was a full-page spread in the old JS&A catalogue. It's a classic by Joseph Sugarman, best known later for selling blue sunglasses on TV. He's a great writer.

TYPES OF PROOF

One of the biggest problems you have in your marketing is proving that what you say is true: that you can actually deliver the promised benefits. People are increasingly skeptical as they are bombarded with advertising and sales baloney. You need to work hard in all your marketing to build trust and come across as credible.

People Are Afraid

Remember that the main reason people don't use your services when they have a need for them, and can afford you, is because they're afraid.

They're afraid that you won't be able to do what you say; that you'll take advantage of them; that they won't get their money's worth. They're afraid of making a mistake or of looking stupid; afraid that you don't really care about them and you only want their money.

In general, written material can reassure people about your stability. More specifically, some written material such as testimonials becomes a proof of your claims. For instance, testimonials reassure people that you've helped others like them.

Twenty-Five Ways to Prove Your Claims

I believe there are only a certain number of types of proof that exist for you to use. I think I've listed below all the types available in one form or another and that this is the most complete list available anywhere. Some are better than others and some overlap.

Think of each of your benefits or claims. You can try to attach each kind of proof to them.

"Objective" Evidence

Better Testimonials

Testimonials need to be specific to be effective. A good rule of thumb is to have at least one testimonial that covers each benefit described in your marketing materials.

!

- *Research evidence.* This could be scientific evidence that you find in the library from studies in business and psychology. It could be informal research, talking to ten to twenty people, or asking people for a show of hands.
- *Comparison data.* Perhaps there are data available about how good you are compared to other people; for instance, winning the "best" award for your field as mentioned in Chapter Eight on networking.
- *Total amount of evidence.* Sometimes you don't have one type of proof that is strong, but you can stack one thing on top of another so that people have no doubt that it's true (for instance, several of the types of proof covered here).

Self-Evident (Face Validity)

- *Logical argument.* You can convince people that it's simply logical that you're not going to steal their $25, when your normal service costs $100 or $10,000. Why would you risk anything for such a small amount of money? Avis's positioning statement, "We're number 2. We try harder," probably fits here.
- *The amount of risk people are taking.* Minimize their perceptions of the risk by showing them again, logically, that even if you failed totally, they're not taking much risk. This can be a convincing argument.
- *You have no reason to lie.* This is a variation of a logical argument, but it specifically deals with people's fears.
- *You want their future business.* This is a form of logical argument. For instance, you show people that you don't make money the first time you do business with them. You have to do a good job, to get the profitable continuing business and referrals.
- *Type of person.* It's believable that architects know something about house design, or photographers about portraits. People often don't doubt your capabilities.
- *The type of promise.* Some promises are pretty obvious or secure. For instance, you promise they don't risk their deposit in a real estate transaction because it is kept in an escrow account at the bank.

Testimonials

- *Direct user testimonials.* This is perceived as one of the two best kinds of proof, from people just like your prospects.
- *Testimonials from celebrities.* These are not worth as much as they used to be. Many public figures have gone down in popular esteem, and if people think a public figure is doing it only for the money, they discount it.
- *Your customer list.* This implies both testimonials and a track record.
- *Referrals from sources others know and trust.* These are perceived as "best" proof.
- *Expert testimonials.* This would be one doctor vouching for another.
- *Government agency testimonials.* This could also be an electrical testing institute, for example, or some other impartial expert institution.

Evidence About You

- *Your credentials.* For example, if you have a CPA, Ph.D., engineering degree, or have written a book. These suggest certain capabilities.
- *Your employees.* Experience or skill requirements to work for you.
- *Your track record.* The fact that you've been in business a long time, your size (big for stability, small for personal service), bank references, or other evidence of your stability.
- *Features to prove it.* For instance, your project management documents show that you know how to organize a job.
- *Specialization.* The fact that you work for lots of clients like your prospects and know their industry or issues.
- *Memberships.* For instance, in the Better Business Bureau, the Psychologists Association, Accountants Association, and other groups, imply that you're a respectable person; people are not complaining about you.
- *Institutional affiliations.* Like your credentials, if you're at Harvard or Stanford University, people assume you're good. If you have other impressive-sounding affiliations, perhaps even being the chamber of commerce president, this gives you an edge.

- *Marketing materials.* If you have complex marketing materials it is a small bit of evidence that you are well financed and likely to stay around. Likewise, high-quality material suggests that you are a high-quality provider.

Guarantees

Guarantees are worth a section by themselves. They are underused, yet highly valued if you can make them credible.

- *Strong guarantees.* Surprisingly enough, many service providers can offer a 100 percent money-back guarantee. So few customers will use this to cheat you that it's usually not much of a risk, but it looks very strong.
- *Free samples.* A brief sample of your services is a bit like a guarantee since users can't lose anything but time. (There is more on this topic in the next section.)

Of course, in many cases, it will be more powerful to combine several of these types of proof to build your credibility.

More on Free Samples

I've already mentioned that a big problem selling services is that many of them—such as law and accounting—are intangible. The client doesn't know how to judge quality. You may be willing to sit down with prospects for a free introductory meeting, which amounts to a free sample. However, some "tire kickers" will abuse that.

There are more different types of samples than you might think. See if some of these would work for you:

- successful cases explained
- a seminar you give
- before-and-after pictures (for contractor, landscaper, and so on)
- a booklet of tips in your field

- a resource guide
- your newsletter
- an information kit
- a reference list of articles
- the results of a survey
- an article you've written
- a tape of one of your talks
- a needs analysis sheet
- a checklist
- a flowchart showing solution alternatives
- handouts from a talk by you
- a brief analysis of a prospect's document

One person who uses the approach of giving away a free sample offers to analyze a sales letter free. He applies a checklist/analysis sheet covering fifty areas (for example, headlines, sentence length, benefits, focus). He then offers to help customers improve the noted weaknesses for a fee. About 50 percent of the prospects take him up on the free offer and many eventually hire him. That would be an unusually high response rate, but it suggests that this approach can work.

YOUR IMAGE

The image your written material conveys should be appropriate for the audience with which you are communicating.

If you're trying to reach bankers and attorneys, your material should appear expensive in a quiet, dignified way. Look at the written material your audience uses to get ideas for what will be the best fit. For instance, for bankers, embossed, two-color, corporate-looking cards will be a good fit. This material will be more expensive than average.

An expensive brochure could make other audiences feel that you're too pricey. They would prefer someone more down to earth. Remember that you're trying to "speak" to people with your material when you can't be there. It should accurately represent who you are. Let's look at some possible images you could use:

- Your image could be high-tech, particularly if you're a computer consultant and use online databases or other cutting-edge technologies.
- Your image could be New Age or environmentally conscious.
- Your image could be inexpensive and down to earth.
- Your image could be expensive, high-quality, or good value.

Consistency of image is part of what it means to have integrated marketing. Everything you do contributes to your image, and should be in agreement: how you dress, how your office is, what kind of car you drive, and your written material. For instance, if your image is expensive or high quality or high tech, you'd usually use more complex graphics and more expensive paper. If your image is New Age, you might use warmer colors and 100 percent recycled paper.

Be Interesting

For many services an eccentric touch can add to your memorability, without losing customers. The following philosophy was posted in a restaurant and caught Tom Peters's eye.

RESTAURANT PERSONAL PHILOSOPHY

In our restaurant you will find atmosphere and character.
Friendly and witty staff.
A half-crazy owner, and real food.
The kitchen is in open view to the customers,
and you are welcome to inspect it.
The cockroaches left me a long time ago.
The only animals remaining are my cats, Jeffrey and Luigi.
Otherwise I am left with a bunch of paranoid human beings.

Peters said, "Valerio's [restaurant] had marvelous food, but mostly the place was a kick. Valerio's had spirit, character, quirkiness, and personality."

LOOK AT OTHERS' MATERIAL

Don't be shy. Go out and find brochures and written materials from competitors. See what they look like and what they are claiming. Be sure that you are competitive. Find material with a look and colors you like from services unrelated to yours. Whether you do it yourself or hire help, having a model to follow can save you time and money.

It always breaks my heart when people spend a lot of money on printed material, then something changes and they're stuck with five thousand copies of a four-color glossy brochure. This is one reason I recommend less expensive brochures, particularly for your initial attempts.

Know Your Competition

Have family and friends save clippings and marketing material for you. Try to evaluate what works and what doesn't for your competitors.

OTHER SALES TOOLS

Let's look at other types of written material that you may want to create.

Postcards

Postcards are appropriate for some services. They're inexpensive, give you first-class delivery, and can be used to clean up your mailing lists at no charge by adding "address service requested" below the return address.

Postcards are almost always read. If you have a quick, simple message or interesting picture, postcards can be useful as a way of keeping in touch. They can be personalized. If you are on vacation or pick up an interesting postcard, you can use it to send a note saying, "Hi. Haven't seen you for a while. Just thought I'd drop you a note."

If you want a bigger message space, for the same postage as a single postcard, you can send a double, or even a triple postcard. This gives you the advantage of sending a card with a portion that prospects and clients can tear off and return to you.

My Favorite Postcards
An idea I've recommended to people for twenty years is to use foreign stamps on postcards or envelopes.

Postcards Contact More People in Less Time

A postcard doesn't have to be opened—the message gets through at first glance. It's short and to the point: "Enjoyed talking with you today. Hope we can work together in the future," or whatever. (Put your logo on the card so it's immediately recognizable or use interesting pictures.) Some companies preprint cards for thank-yous and other items.

They always get attention. They don't even have to be mailed from a foreign location. You can simply add foreign stamps as you would Christmas Seals. The postal service doesn't mind as long as you pay the U.S. postage. But if you can get them mailed from overseas, it's even more impressive, particularly if you have some clever tie-in to the country from which you are mailing them.

I've received three good postcards that I use as examples. The first two postcards I particularly like (because they embody my advice) are the one below mailed from Monte Carlo and an "imitator." The Monte Carlo front side has a nice color picture. The message was printed in blue (to look like handwriting). It's a cute message. Of course, what the sender means is "Please write a check, use your credit, and let us charge you some interest. You could be in Europe tomorrow. Turn your dreams into reality." This is clever, catchy, and colorful.

After reading the first edition of this book, Don Shapland mailed me a postcard of Yosemite National Park. He'd sent these to the postmaster

An aerial view of Monte Carlo, famed city of Monaco and jewel of the Riviera.

It's as beautiful as they say! "Having a wonderful time. Wish you were here." And you can be... here or anywhere you've ever dreamed of vacationing.

Just use your line of credit from Boston Safe Deposit & Trust Company. Simply write a check against your available credit for tickets to the Riviera, Rio, the Virgin Islands... anywhere. Current low interest rates (and low airfares) make now a great time to do it! Need more credit for a long, leisurely trip? Just apply for an increase by calling 1 800-343-4101, toll free. (Or call with any questions.)

Turn your dreams into realities with your credit line from Boston Safe Deposit and Trust Company. Enjoy!
Kathleen Burke

R. Crandall
Dr
, CA 9
U.S.A.

IMPRIMÉ
PAR AVION
AO

there to mail for him. He got a lot of impact with his real clients and prospects without leaving home.

Another postcard advertised a new service. It's a dry-cleaning box the company installs near your house, with a lock on it. It's novel enough that a postcard with a picture of the box is very useful. Then, in a few words, the card can explain it. (You hang your dry cleaning in the box. Employees then come with a key, pick it up, clean it, and return it to the box.) For busy people who don't want to stop by the dry cleaners, it's a great service.

Card Decks

There's another kind of postcard mentioned in the last chapter. A set of postcards called a *card deck* comes bundled together in a wrapper. These can be useful if you want to reach a national audience. (Also see Chapter Four.)

The mailer uses plastic or foil to wrap sets of twenty to one hundred postcards. One side has a return address to one advertiser, with postage paid; the other side has the sales message. For two to three cents apiece, you can reach 100,000 people at a time. While you seldom get a 1 percent response, it's a way to reach a lot of people in a particular field who read a particular magazine (or whatever the basis for the mailing is).

Your Business Card

Your business card is the smallest bit of written material that represents you. Your card conveys an image.

Cards can vary from dull, centered, lawyerlike cards, to better-designed ones, to artistic and radical cards.

A lot more variations are possible than most people ever consider.

- You can print your philosophy or services on the back.
- You can print useful information from your field on the back to encourage people to keep your card, such as a ruler, postal rates, architectural definitions, or Edward Deming's fourteen quality rules.
- You can have a folded card that is a mini-brochure.

Four Tips for Effective Business Cards

You want people to notice your card, and—most important—you want them to keep it.

1. Stay with a horizontal design (it fits into more people's storage systems).
2. Make sure your phone number is large enough to be easily read and that it includes the area code.
3. Choose an ink color that can be photocopied or faxed (blue, orange, and brown are poor choices).
4. Use your logo if you have one.

!

Humor Works

The head of a British company passes out his business card which measures only 1" × 2". In addition to his name and phone number, the card says, "The lack of business from you has made this economy-sized card necessary." It gets a laugh out of people, and nobody forgets it. Business is doing very well.

!

- You can print your card as the cover of a blank booklet to give people notepaper.
- You can precut your card to fit in a Rolodex system.
- You can print your card on unusual material. I've seen brass and plastic and heard of others.

The possibilities for creativity are almost endless if an unusual card fits your image.

Look at Your Card Today

Even if you're not ready to redesign your card today, take a look at it now.

Many people let their cards get out of date. For instance, your fax number, e-mail, or Web site address may not be on your card. You can get simple cards for less than $20 per thousand at discount stores such as Office Depot or Costco, so there's no excuse not to make temporary improvements while you're thinking about a fancier version.

GRAPHICS

If you're creating written material, the way it looks can be very important.

The ancient Greeks articulated five elements for good design, which still hold true today. They are:

1. *Order.* The images are organized, not overly busy, easy to follow.
2. *Balance.* This shows stability and safety, but if everything is exactly balanced on the page, it can also be boring.
3. *Contrast.* This is a yin-yang, using complementary colors or contrasting elements.
4. *Unity.* The overall piece should look like it's whole.
5. *Harmony.* A summary of the overall artistic impression.

Some of the new designs that are popular, as I write this, are extremely busy, colorful, and wild. In some ways, they are disharmonious and hard to read. But at the same time, as you begin to get used to the style, it creates its own consistent aesthetic impression.

Here are a few general rules with which to evaluate your graphics.

- Don't use too many typefaces per piece of paper. Try to keep them to two—one for the headline and one for the body.
- Your headline should usually be set in a sans serif typeface such as Helvetica, and your main copy should be a serif typeface (such as Times Roman).
- Create a focal point for the page, usually top left or middle.
- Organize your material so that people get the general idea just by looking at the headings or subheadings.

DON'T OVERINVEST IN PRINTED MATERIAL

Don't get carried away with creating elegant written material. It can create an image for you, but it won't usually sell for you. Its major purpose is to get potential customers to speak to you personally. It should get you an appointment so you can start a relationship.

Written material can build your credibility, particularly articles or newsletters by you that show off your expertise. Testimonials also build your credibility. Written material can also suggest that you are here to stay, particularly if it's expensive looking or complex. But remember that good written material can only open the door for your real sales efforts.

AGENDA

*Take time to deliberate, but when the time for action
has arrived, stop thinking and go in.*
NAPOLEON BONAPARTE

Who Are You?

► State your "copy proposition" in one sentence (from p. 91).
► In one sentence, state how you are different from other people in your area (your positioning or image).

To Do Today

► Look at your business card and see if it needs updating, such as adding fax or e-mail numbers. Can you create different cards for different services or target audiences?
► Gather copies of all articles you've written, articles about you, or other written material that represents your approach in some way.
► Write three personal letters to clients, prospects, or possible referral sources. Commit to doing this daily and you may have a marketing program.

Projects This Week

► Collect the testimonials you have available and summarize other types of proof you have to show that you're good. How can you gather more types of proof than you have available now?
► Look for a unique postcard that people will remember when you send them notes.

CHAPTER SIX

HOW TO LIKE PERSONAL SELLING

Turning Selling from Sleazy to Satisfying

> *I love selling because it gives me a chance to meet*
> *different types of people, some of whom will buy from me.*
> *Essentially, I get paid to make new friends.*
> JACK SWEENEY
> Sales Consultant

Let me be superclear here. Selling as traditionally done and taught is often sleazy, especially for services! And if you are uncomfortable with selling, you will not be effective and will feel bad about it as well.

I know you didn't go into business in order to become a salesperson. In this chapter, I'm going to show you how to sell in a nontraditional way that helps others *and* your business. As my friend Jack Sweeney says, selling your services can be looked at as a way to make new friends.

Done the old, wrong way, selling is the last of the traditional, weak methods of marketing for service providers (advertising, brochures, and sales) covered in this chapter. Done right, as I'll show you here, selling is the first chapter in a sequence of powerful and professional marketing methods covered in this book that can support you your entire career.

Everyone Sells

Don Cvietusa of Silicon Valley Bank says everyone in the bank should think of themselves as helping with marketing. Even operations people can "make a sale."

!

SELLING IS EVERYWHERE

While sales can be done on the phone, online, or at a seminar, usually selling is considered a face-to-face activity. When you sell services, any time you talk to someone, you are a salesperson at some level.

If you think about it, we all sell every day. Sell should not be a "four-letter word" in your mind. We sell our ideas to other people or "charm" other people into liking us. We sell our kids into behaving well (or at least we try!). You may even have to sell yourself on getting out of bed on Saturday.

Your Selling Isn't Sleazy

> To reach full realization of the importance of marketing requires overcoming a deep-rooted social prejudice against "selling" as ignoble and parasitical.
>
> Peter F. Drucker
> *The Practice of*
> *Management*

Selling is not tricking people or forcing something on them that they don't want or need. The official definition of sales is that you are offering something to prospects that meets their needs when they have the means to pay for it.

If your service meets people's needs, and you're not pushy about showing people how you can help them, then you're *helping* people by selling. *If you're not sleazy, then your selling isn't either.*

Think of Realtors as an example. The good ones don't sell a particular house. They use their resources to help you find a property that meets your needs. They don't care which house you buy. They are supportive, not pushy.

Why You Don't Like Personal Selling

Don't Be Afraid of Prospects

You know more than they do about your company. And you should know how you can help them. Fears that are genuine should stimulate you to deal with areas of weakness. Fears that aren't genuine waste your time and cause you needless anxiety.

What you don't like about your stereotype of selling shows good instincts. Selling is normally approached in a selfish, pushy, offensive way. Pushy salespeople are not concerned with their customers' needs. But I'm going to show you how you can handle *your* selling in an honest way that you won't be ashamed of.

The other thing most of us hate about sales is the idea of being rejected. But if you provide a good service at a good value, and help people meet important needs, then you shouldn't be shy about telling others what you do and how you might help them. If they're not interested, they're not rejecting you. They either don't have a need or aren't ready to act.

A SALES MODEL

Selling is far more than face-to-face communication about your services. In fact, that's the least part of it. In my book on sales, we break the process down into five general areas:

1. building relationships
2. analyzing needs
3. knowing customers' industries
4. generating creative solutions
5. helping your customers succeed

1. Building Relationships at Higher Levels

This entire book talks about the importance of building relationships in all your marketing.

Here, I'll point out that there are different types of relationships you can have with your clients. Your goal should be to climb to the top of the relationship hierarchy. You can begin to build these relationships at the higher levels even before you do business.

When you are a *vendor*, you are a commodity. Dry cleaners, Realtors, accountants, and many others fall into this position when they don't differentiate themselves from their competitors. Contrary to Peter Drucker's advice, vendors are selling what they have, *not* working on clients' needs. *Solution providers* have a skill that they want to apply. They still aren't focused on what the customer needs.

> True marketing starts out . . . with the customer, his demographics, his realities, his needs, his values. It does not ask, "What do we want to sell?" It asks," "What does the customer want to buy?"
>
> Peter F. Drucker
> *The Practice of Management*

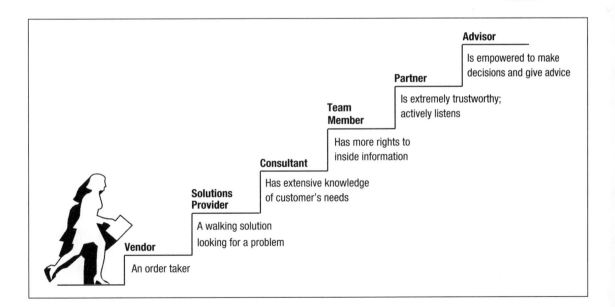

The *consultant* level is the beginning of a long-lasting relationship. You are applying your expertise to understand and solve client problems. (We will discuss more on this and the higher levels shortly.)

A *team member* has transcended the barrier of being an outsider. You know more about your clients' processes and are trusted. If you used to work for the client, you often start at this level.

The term *partner* is much used, but seldom attained. Here you have proven that you have the clients' interests at heart. You are privy to high-level information, and do more than you are asked to do. You treat each client's business as if it were your own.

Advisor includes all the other levels, plus the ability to act independently for your client. You take responsibility for his or her business, and often act as a mentor.

While there are many ways to describe relationships between you and your clients, this hierarchy gives you some goals to shoot for. While you can't be at the highest levels with every client, you will build the best business—and enjoy yourself the most—when you have clients who trust you at the top levels.

SPIN Selling™

Different questions are best at different times to advance the sale. The sequence in which they are asked gives you the information to develop key questions. The SPIN acronym gives you the type of questions and the order:

1. **S**ituation
2. **P**roblem
3. **I**mplication
4. **N**eed-payoff

Neil Rackham
SPIN Selling

2. Analyzing Needs

In order to analyze prospects' and clients' needs, you need a repeatable method. Obvious examples are checklists or a series of questions, followed by action steps.

For instance, one insurance agent has trained thousands of others to use about ninety brief questions on clients' finances. The form takes a prospect nine minutes. It helps clients understand their own needs, qualifies them, demonstrates the agent's expertise, and starts the relationship off at the consultant level. And it immediately screens out people who have no needs.

Needs analysis questions can start with the general situation, but should move quickly to the prospect's unique circumstances. They should cover needs, wants, and concerns, including what the prospect requires to make decisions. In one case, a needs analysis was so valuable for a large-ticket purchase that the salesperson *charged* prospects to apply it and make a recommendation about what they should buy. That's a good goal—for your needs analysis to be worth buying by itself!

To perform a needs analysis, you should be much better at asking questions, listening, and analyzing than at presenting. This gets you away from old-fashioned selling situations with their stereotypical "arm twisting" and pressure.

3. Knowing Customers' Industries

When you specialize in clients' industries, they know you're already up to speed. They don't have to pay for your education or for beginner's mistakes.

Not all the ways you can help improve your clients' profits will come from your direct services. Some may come from connections you make for them in their industries. This is one advantage of specializing in a niche (as discussed in Chapter Three). You not only serve customers better, but you give and receive stronger referrals that are more relevant to you and your clients.

4. Creativity

Creativity helps you at two stages of the sales relationship. First, it makes it easier to come to prospects' attention and convince them that you are worth investing their time. If you look and act like every other "salesperson," you won't stand out. People spend time *avoiding* "average" salespeople, not building relationships with them.

The mere fact that you do something different early in the relationship—such as a needs analysis—suggests that you may offer more customized, one-to-one solutions. Clients need new approaches, and you do too if you are to avoid being a commodity.

The second area where creativity serves you and your clients is in producing new and better solutions. If you offer something no one else does, you (and your customers) have a unique advantage.

You may also be more creative in customizing solutions specifically for clients' needs. Some people define the ultimate in expertise as knowing all there is to know. This means you know the state of existing "art" in your field. I would argue that knowing *how to create new solutions* is more important to your expertise. Don't just apply what has been done before;

> Any business enterprise has only two basic functions: marketing and innovation.
>
> Peter F. Drucker
> *The Practice of Management*

create customized solutions for clients. Of course, this is also the opposite of the "vendor" at the bottom of the relationship hierarchy.

5. Helping Your Customers Succeed

You've probably heard the old example that someone only buys a 1-inch drill in order to obtain a 1-inch hole. The drill is the feature, the hole the benefit. However, this example doesn't go far enough. People have a further reason they want the hole. As discussed in Chapter Three, you need to know more about the benefits of your benefits.

The simplest way to help your customers is to know more about who *their* customers are. For instance, many consultants do free sessions for their customers' customers. This builds goodwill for your customers.

While your customers may need your services, remember that they only want these services to attain *their* goals. Their ultimate goal is to succeed. There is more to the definition of success than money. You need to discover the dimensions of success your customers care about. By keeping their goals in mind, you will realize that there are other ways besides your services that you can help your customers.

In the area of profits, when you give customers your business or a referral, or when you connect them to a referral source, you help them succeed.

But your clients want other things besides business. They may want public recognition (you could nominate them for an award or an elected office). They may want to be invited to exclusive events or parties to impress their families. Ultimately, they may want help selling their businesses. These are just examples. To build relationships, it's up to you to learn the range of what your clients want.

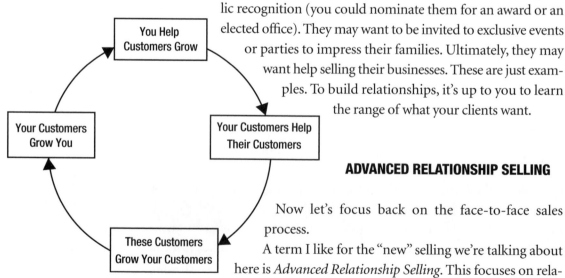

ADVANCED RELATIONSHIP SELLING

Now let's focus back on the face-to-face sales process.

A term I like for the "new" selling we're talking about here is *Advanced Relationship Selling*. This focuses on relationships and is in clear contrast to the old, high-pressure, basic "selling 101" that most people still teach.

The techniques for how to sell in a way that is not pushy have been around for a long time. Unfortunately, traditional sales training is almost backward for selling services in a professional, dignified, nonsleazy way. Instead, it has continued to teach people how to give presentations, to overcome objections, and to close sales. (More about that shortly.)

One new term that I've applied to sales is *Santa Claus Selling*. It conveys the spirit of the kind of selling you can be proud of.

In the film, *Miracle on 34th Street*, Kris Kringle, Macy's Santa Claus, was told by the toy department manager to push certain toys on which the store was overstocked. Instead, he sent people to Bloomingdale's or other department stores if these stores had a better doll or fire engine of a particular type. People were so impressed when Santa didn't just plug Macy's stuff that they became more loyal customers, spread the word to friends, and the company received lots of publicity.

In brief, if you "sell" like Kris Kringle, you will treat your clients and prospects the way they want to be treated, and you will be proud of your selling efforts. Be a trusted advisor to help people get the best they can. Don't sell them something they don't need, including your services.

Actually, by putting clients first this way, you don't give up much. Many times they are so appreciative of your efforts on their behalf that they hire you even if you've told them that there are other people who are better. They trust you now and want you looking out for their interests, rather than having to invest in building a relationship with someone else who may not care as much about them.

The Pros Have Always Done It This Way

The most effective people in any profession have always used this sincere approach that builds trust with clients. It's funny that many attorneys, accountants, architects, and other professionals in large firms talk as if they don't believe in selling. In fact, if the founders of their firms hadn't been able to sell, there wouldn't be large firms today!

Top professionals ("rainmakers") have always gotten along with clients and brought in business. They don't do it by calling strangers. They don't look like they're selling, and often they don't feel like they're selling. They are letting people know what they do, impressing people with their demeanor and knowledge, and making themselves accessible.

They do it by calling existing customers and keeping relationships alive; by writing articles, giving speeches, and following up with contacts; by building relationships with referral sources. Or they do it by meeting new people at trade organizations, church, or the country club. Then when people have a need, they don't hesitate to call.

This is a "nonsales" sales approach that even the most antimarketing professional should feel comfortable carrying out.

Consultative Selling™

There will, of course, be many cases where you are talking to people with whom you would like to do business. So they know you are selling at some level. As suggested in earlier chapters, the real key is to approach others *not* as a salesperson trying to make a sale, but as a consultant trying to help.

Despite the fact that most sales training is still wrong, there are several approaches that do not train salespeople to be pushy and selfish. The longest established one is Mack Hanan's trademarked *Consultative Selling*. There are whole books about this approach and how its inventor recommends it be done. I will summarize my version here.

Start at the Beginning
Try to design a consulting approach that starts before you ever meet with prospects. For instance, the first thing that Elan Software Corporation does is send inquirers a needs-analysis survey. It focuses on how the prospect company handles things now and how they'd like to change—not on what Elan's software does. (Put in more common marketing parlance, Elan asks what benefits are wanted; it doesn't list its features.)

Prospects appreciate this approach. It helps them clarify what they need, even if they don't buy from Elan. It sets up a consulting relationship from the beginning. It can educate prospects to unrecognized needs. And the good questions allow customers to conclude on their own that Elan knows what it's doing.

It's Simple—Act Like a Consultant

Think of yourself as a consultant who is being paid to help prospects make intelligent decisions on how best to meet their needs. If your services can't meet their needs or can't meet them completely, you would then recommend other approaches. If you can use this approach sincerely, you'll feel better about yourself and you'll do better in the long term.

The most impressive thing you can do quickly to show people you are not a hard-sell type is to recommend that people *not* buy from you.

I recommend starting every sales proposal with some things that you *can't* do, and offering specific recommendations that will help your prospects meet those needs elsewhere. Good referrals to other sources show them that you really have their best interests at heart.

You build great credibility when you point out things you can't do. This is the consulting role. It helps convince prospects that you're not just trying desperately to sell something for your own benefit.

By giving them free consulting advice of high value, you create the start of a real relationship. Think how much credibility this gives to the things you say that you *can* help them with!

Never try to sell to someone who doesn't need your service. You may be able to educate people to needs they hadn't been aware of, but never shove things down their throats.

Most Companies Won't Do It

Unfortunately, most service providers do not understand the value of using a consulting approach. For instance, "mystery shoppers" went to fifty large banks around the country. Many banks pitched investments to them without bothering to ask about their situation and goals in life. According to Prophet Market Research and Consulting, "The climate at some banks is not unlike the auto industry in the 1970s."

To counter that, one bank is setting standards for what types of risks different types of investors should take. If its brokers sell something inappropriate, the computer kicks it out and the broker's commission is docked or the customer is allowed to undo the trade. If this approach is enforced, it won't take long for the brokers to refocus their behavior on what is good for the customers.

Needs Analysis

1. Your issues
2. Main concerns
3. How can we help?
4. What do your customers care about

Marketing Should Build Relationships

When you use Consultative Selling to benefit clients, it leads to word-of-mouth publicity (as in *Miracle on 34th Street*), which leads to community goodwill, repeat business, and so on.

Don't just sell what you have to offer. Salespeople who want to build relationships with people give their best advice honestly, even when that advice says prospects don't need their services.

FAKE CONSULTATIVE SELLING

A lot of lip service is given to selling like a consultant as described above. Unfortunately, most people who say they advocate such approaches seem to fall back on old-fashioned manipulative selling at some point. Almost all sales books now talk about building relationships, but here are some quotes from them that contradict their lip service.

- "Develop strategies and tactics to get others to say 'yes'"
- "Convince others that your product is exactly what they need"
- "Outsmart prospects' objections"
- "After you ask a closing question, Shut Up! The next person who speaks loses."

These strategies aren't advice for consultants, partners, or advisors with their customers' interests uppermost in their minds! They're remnants of the old hard-sell approach.

TRADITIONAL SALES TRAINING

In order to better understand why the sales approach I'm advocating is so different, let's look at traditional selling in more detail.

First, I'll show you what a traditional approach to sales looks like and the steps that "they" say you should go through to follow it. Then I'll illustrate how to modify them to sell services in a nonpushy manner.

Before the Meeting

Before you meet with someone face-to-face, you should do three things: *prospecting, qualifying,* and *research.*

Prospecting is finding people who are likely to have a need for what you offer. Sometimes prospects who haven't been confirmed are called "suspects." You *suspect* they need your service. They become real prospects when you've done the qualifying and research stages.

Qualifying is making sure that prospects see a potential need and have the means to pay for it. By the way, this is one reason why selling shouldn't be pushy. There's no point in trying to sell to someone who's not a qualified prospect.

Before you meet prospects, you do as much *research* as you can about their situation. The ideal case is that you have an informant or are very familiar with their organization. You know what their real problems are and you know the political issues that will have to be negotiated.

The best sales approach is often based on such inside knowledge. You give presentations that lead people to conclude that you can help them with a problem that you've never mentioned directly. This way, they don't feel like you're trying to sell them. They feel that they've identified your capabilities that can meet their needs. It's much more credible when they "discover" you than when you tell them you can help them.

Top Five Sales Mistakes

In surveys, customers list these problems with salespeople.

1. Selling to someone who doesn't need your services
2. Deception
3. Talking too much and not asking questions
4. Insincerity
5. Not building the relationship

The Sales Meeting

You've done your homework ahead of time. Now you have the face-to-face sales meeting.

Qualifying Questions

The first step is qualifying questions. Even though you've tried to qualify prospects ahead of time, and presumably have, it never hurts to reconfirm. You confirm that the client is the decision maker. You confirm that the client recognizes a need and has the means to pay for it.

Qualifying questions can be phrased many ways, such as by asking clients if they have room for improvement in this area, if they have a budget to spend on service in this area, and similar ideas. You can often just ask them outright. Do they have the need? Do they have the means to pay for it?

If a prospect says, "Oh, no. You should be talking to Sandra, down the hall," you just thank him, say you enjoyed meeting him, hope that you can work together on something else, and go down the hall and see if you can make an appointment with Sandra.

It's good to start with qualifying questions for two reasons. It gets prospects in the habit of answering questions. And it helps you understand the situation before you go into your presentation.

The Presentation

The second step in traditional sales training is that you give a presentation. Traditional presentation training tends to be product oriented. That's one reason it is usually the wrong approach for services.

The presentation is sometimes called a "dog-and-pony show." You try to wow prospects with your abilities, knowledge, and skills. You tell them about your capabilities and you impress them so that they want to work with you.

The Proposition

The third step is the proposition. It's very much like a romantic proposition! After you've given your presentation and wowed potential clients, you have to suggest, "Well, let's get into bed together." You might suggest they hire your services on a trial basis, or that you make a bid to take care of their problem.

Handling Objections

The next step, handling objections, is somewhat ironic. In traditional sales training, "they" have so little confidence that your presentation will be convincing that they train you to expect a series of objections.

Sometimes these objections will amount to the same ones you'd get in a romantic situation: "I don't know you well enough now to get into bed with you." Other times they'll be very traditional: "I don't know if we have the budget this year."

Often, the stated objections will not be the true objections. For instance, "I need to think about it" doesn't tell you why they're not convinced now.

You Need to Have Answers to Objections. If you've built a real relationship and trust, you may not have specific objections. In fact, you gain more credibility by having already dealt with them before people bring them up.

If you know your area, you should be aware of all the possible objections before you meet with people, and you should have worked out answers. For instance, if they're worried about price, you might have guarantees or trial periods, or you talk about value.

If prospects want to know if you'll do what you say you'll do, you might have references and testimonials.

If you haven't thought of all the objections and haven't worked out all the answers, then your early sales calls are simply practice. After a while, you'll be able to categorize all the possible objections. If you can't come up with good answers for them, you should get input from clients, friends, consultants, and other people in your area.

The Ultimate Advice on Objections. For help handling objections, even ask the people who aren't going to buy from you!

Many times you can change the entire tone of a presentation this way. You can turn it from adversarial to joint problem solving, as it should be. You say, "What could I have done that would have made you comfortable working with me?" You'll not only get good advice, but sometimes you'll reopen the door for a sale.

Old-fashioned sales training handles objections like balls being thrown at you in cricket. If you can bat them all away, eventually the prospect runs out and you "win" the sale. That's too adversarial, but you do need to understand objections in order to put people's fears to rest so they can be comfortable building a relationship with you.

Closing the Sale

The final part of the traditional sales technique is closing the sale.

There are hundreds of different techniques to close the sale. Some are very cute—for instance, the "puppy-dog close." If you have a product, like a puppy, you send it home with the prospect. It's so lovable, they get used to it, the kids love it, and they don't want to send it back.

No Simple Answers

Don't give simple answers to objections. When people raise objections, they are saying, "Yes, but . . . " If you give a quick answer, another objection will often emerge. Find out what is behind the objection. Think twice and speak once. Objections are often not what they appear to be.

This doesn't work directly for services, but a variation could be that you give them a free, or very inexpensive, sample that gets them "hooked" on what you can do for them.

Closing Is What We Don't Like About Sales
Closing really exemplifies the hard-sell tactics that most of us despise about sales.

One of my favorite ways to illustrate this is the "half-nelson" close. Sometimes in the sales process, the person you're trying to sell asks a question, such as "Can you do it by a certain time?" The half-nelson close suggests that you don't rush to say yes. First ask, "*If* I can do that for you, are you ready to buy?"

This close is named after a wrestling hold where you stand behind another person and put your arm up under her arm and over to her neck. You can force her neck down and even break it if you are strong enough. The ironic point concerning high-pressure sales is the reason you use a *half* nelson with only one arm, instead of a *full* nelson with both arms. It is so the client has her right arm free to sign the contract!

This is the old-fashioned adversarial approach to sales, but it's still around. A cartoon with this idea, like the one on the facing page, appeared in a recent sales magazine. Sadly, it's not a joke; it's how some people still think!

There's a large school of selling that believes that if you push hard enough some people will sign up just to get rid of you, or because they're weak spined and can't take the pressure. This idea exemplifies the worst of sales for most of us, but it is alive and well in traditional selling.

Summary of Traditional Selling

As you can see, there are several aspects of traditional sales training that don't fit with the relationship-oriented, Santa Claus, consulting, professional approach that I advocate. But, surprisingly, it doesn't take much to modify it. You *can* be a friendly consultant instead of a hard-sell pest!

YOUR ADVANCED RELATIONSHIP SELLING

Let's go back to the beginning of the traditional sales approach. All the work you do before meeting with people is fine.

The more *research*, the more *prospecting*, and the more *qualifying* you do, the less time you waste (of theirs and yours). The prework is important so that you're not trying to sell to people who shouldn't be buying Your preparation ahead of time also shows your professionalis:

I talked with the in-house attorney for a large company that w hiring a law firm. Management was very unhappy that the thr large firms chosen to give presentations did just that—a lot of talk about *their* firms. Not one had taken the time to research the company's history of litigation. Not one asked intelligent questions about needs—they all just gave a *sales* presentation.

Expect Multiple Contacts

Old sales is designed for "one-call closing." It tries to make the sale in one meeting. That can work with impulse purchases and small sales. But research shows that the average large sale is made on the sixth contact. And the average salesperson quits after two!

It's even worse than that for big professional sales. Remember, the best clients are usually changing from another provider. That's a big step for them. The average legal client might have twelve contacts with you before he is comfortable hiring you. And the average lawyer usually quits *before* the first contact. He decides that it's too hard, so he never gets started!

Of course, there are occasional prospects who are ready to make a quick decision. But you should start building relationships and trust long before any business is likely with most prospects.

Most of your contacts won't be traditional sales calls. Prospects may meet you at a seminar, receive your newsletter, or belong to your club. You just need to be advancing the relationship.

A New Sales Tool

To prove to prospective clients that you can handle their jobs, develop a file of past cases. Include how you initially won the job. Be specific about hesitations the clients had. Outline the steps you took to meet the objections and include quantifiable results.

!

At the first "official" sales call, unless prospects are ready to buy, you should keep the pressure off them by just getting acquainted with their needs. Then you should plan on doing research, and talking to them further before any "sales" effort.

A "New" First Step in Person: Building Rapport

As the first step, even traditional salespeople automatically spend some time building rapport. People don't want you to come in the door and abruptly start selling "at them." If you can put the relationship on a personal basis, people will be more interested in working with you.

Good salespeople instinctively look around the office and make some comments, such as "Oh, I see you bowl," or "I see you're from the University of Michigan." They schmooze. They have a conversation. They try to find points of similarity. They know that people like similar others.

This opening social rapport may be the most important step of the entire sales process. Yet it's often overlooked by people who are awkward about selling, thus making their presentations even worse.

It's not unusual in a sales call to spend half an hour socializing and ten minutes deciding how you might work together.

Occasionally you'll run into people who don't want to take time to socialize. You say, "Hi. How are you? Do you mind if I set my briefcase down here?" and they'll say, "Let's get to it. Sit there and tell me what you've got." That's okay. You've acknowledged them, and you've given them control of the situation. They want a less social approach. But you've still taken a social moment to let them define the context.

Qualifying Questions

The first step in the traditional sales approach—qualifying questions—is excellent as your second step.

You need to make sure that your customer is qualified. Questions get his or her mind thinking about the company's needs and considering you as a possibility to help.

More Questions: Needs Analysis

The next step is another place where we part company with the old-fashioned sales approach.

Rather than giving a presentation and a song and dance about your capabilities, you should be finding out more about the prospect's situation. And you should be finding out what she or he really cares about within the general situation. You should be asking questions. There's an old saying in sales that you have two ears and one mouth and you should use them in that proportion!

Building Sales Rapport

Spend some time getting to know your customers. If you are in their offices, look for pictures, plaques, magazines, and other bookcase items that tell you something about their interests. Show an interest in the items and get them talking about themselves.

Some salespeople misuse this technique by sounding like they are interrogating a prisoner. Set the stage by telling the person that you're not there to sell, that you're there to get acquainted so you'll understand his company's needs. This will put him at ease and allow a more normal relationship to begin.

An Example

Let's say you are an expert witness and you're trying to sell your services to lawyers. The questions you'd ask would be designed to elicit a greater understanding of what a case was about, but also to understand their minds and how they liked to approach cases.

Your questions would be of such high quality that they would subtly show the attorneys that you understood the issues that were important. You "speak their language." You demonstrate how they can learn from you and you help them feel comfortable trusting the fate of their clients in your hands.

Questions are a way of demonstrating your knowledge. And they're also a much better way of building rapport than just telling people things. They get the other person talking.

Relate Their Questions to Their Needs

Sometimes people will react to your asking questions. They'll say, "Enough about me. Tell me about your experience." Then you respond to their request. You tell them about your expertise and you say, "How do you use this kind of experience?" or "What do you need in your situation related to this issue?" So, generally you come back to questioning them without being evasive.

Your questions may occur over considerable time as the relationship builds.

How to Ask Better Sales Questions

Good selling involves asking the right questions and listening to the answers. Here are some tips for asking more effective sales questions:

- Does the question challenge the prospect to think in a new way?
- Does the question make you seem more knowledgeable than competitors?
- Does the question build rapport by having a prospect share something he or she is proud of?
- Does the question generate a response the prospect never thought of before?

Jeffrey Gitomer
The Sales Bible

The Nonproposition: Offer Them What They Asked For

The questions may be your whole presentation, or there may be a formal presentation at some point. At the end, you summarize by saying, "If I understand correctly, you have a case coming up where you need several expert witnesses to establish A and B. And you believe that, if you can show it this way, you will win for your client." Prospects should agree because you should be restating what they've told you.

Then you tell them, "Well, I can't help you in area A, but I can give you a strong referral to someone who might be useful to you there." (Sometimes this might be someone they know by reputation, so it will confirm your good judgment.)

Now you can say, with more credibility, that you do have unrivaled credentials in area B. "I've testified successfully in a number of cases. I'm comfortable taking the approach that you prefer, and I've used it in XYZ cases. If you'd like, I can keep my schedule flexible so I could be available at your convenience."

If you've properly understood the situation, in the ideal case, the prospect should essentially proposition you by saying, "Can you be available? It sounds like we understand each other." Therefore, there should be no real objections; just a joint problem-solving atmosphere where you're trying to coordinate things to mutual advantage.

Similarly, there's no closing pressure. There should be a sense of wanting to work with you, and satisfaction with having met the "right" person.

Some service providers take this low-pressure approach too far. They never really tell people that they would like to do business together. You do need to tell people you want to earn their business.

It's flattering to many people to be asked for their business. The late Stanley Marcus, of Neiman-Marcus department store fame, told me that he decided not to buy anything one year unless someone *asked him* to make the purchase. He missed out on his new Cadillac for the year and many other items because no one *asked* for the sale.

After the Meeting

The last step is one that even some good salespeople overlook. Whether the sale is made or not, you should follow up within a couple of days.

When they've made a positive decision, people have what's called "buyer's remorse." They begin to second-guess themselves and to see other alternatives. If you call them or drop them a note a day or two later, they will believe you more than they did when they agreed to hire you.

When they agreed to hire you, you had a reason to lie to them—to get them to sign the contract. But after the fact, you don't have a reason to deceive them.

Tell clients, "I really enjoyed meeting you. I think we're going to be able to take care of your problem the way you want. I'll see you next week (or whenever) and, by the way, here's an article I wrote in this area that may be of some interest to you." Now you're reassuring them.

Call Even When You Don't Get the Job

If you haven't made the sale, by calling prospects back you're telling them that you're still interested in the relationship, even if it doesn't pay you in the short term. This also builds your sincerity.

You're telling them that you don't take it as a defeat and that you do expect to work with them in the future. Many times, if they hired someone else, that person will neglect the relationship once the contract is signed and leave room for you later on. Your goal should be to build a better relationship with prospects than the person who got the first job!

My Friend Jack

Jack Sweeney, the sales pro quoted at the beginning of this chapter, typically tells prospects at the first meeting that he has no interest in making a sale then. He wants to get acquainted and find out about their situation.

The second meeting might be to deliver some articles to them or some research material. He'll outline ideas that might be helpful to their marketing. In his case, he might present research and statistics on advertising, how different ways to advertise could be cost-effective, and similar items.

At a third meeting, Jack might present a brief plan to improve prospects' marketing or an idea to test.

Examples Sell

Specific examples of what you can do for people are very convincing. For instance, Ken Baker, marketing director of Freeman-White, a North Carolina architectural firm, says, "Examples help our architects build relationships with their listeners and hit the key points in the strongest possible manner."

Start Small

Don't ignore small jobs. The best way to prove yourself and your company is with a preliminary job. Do some small work (even a subcontract). This is the ultimate way to start a relationship.

Then there may be several more meetings over time: dropping in, responding to questions, bringing them more material. Jack might not even ask for the sale until the fourth, fifth, or sixth meeting. If they say, "No, our budget this year doesn't allow it," no problem. He keeps in touch with them.

By the time the next fiscal year comes around, Jack's an old friend rather than a salesperson.

Think Long-Term Relationships

In one case, a software consulting firm built a relationship long-distance. Employees never even met a distant prospect until *after* many contacts. First, needs were determined by phone. Then an evaluation copy of software was sent. Included was a *Harvard Business Review* article on the company's type of educational software. Next there were multiple calls over months, without pressure, to find out when the prospect wanted more information.

Finally, there was a meeting and a software demonstration. This was followed by sending further material showing how a problem could be solved. Only then was a proposal for a system put together (and the sale made).

Old Hard Sell	New Consulting Sell
Before the Meeting	
Prospecting	
Qualifying	
Research	
In-Person Meeting	
Qualifying Questions	Building Rapport
Presentation	Qualifying Questions
Proposition	More Questions
Handling Objections	Offer What They Asked For
Closing the Sale	Mutual Problem Solving
After the Meeting	
Little Contact	Continuing Follow-Up

Rather than a long sales cycle being a disadvantage, it can help you in several ways. It discourages your old-fashioned "quick-sell" competition. It lets you understand prospects better. You have more time to build stronger relationships. It lets prospects become more emotionally comfortable with the idea of working with you. You can even start to treat them like customers (such as by inviting them to customer seminars). This can make them want to become *real* customers.

Be Patient

The average sale is made after the fifth call. The average person quits after two.

Selling to a Group

A long sales cycle can also be useful when a committee is making the purchase decision. If that is the case, it is even more important that you work to extend your relationships within the client or prospect firm.

Normally, you will develop at least one advocate within the client firm who wants to hire you. There may also be a variety of other people who will be affected by the purchase of your services; for instance, the buyer could be different from the user. There may also be technical and managerial positions involved.

Some sales systems develop names for various purchase influencers. The important thing is not what they are called, but that you are aware of such internal issues. For example, your advocate may need help dealing with people who support your competition.

It is your job not to be dependent on one advocate to make a sale. You should seek out meetings with all involved parties. A good rule of thumb is to never go in front of a decision committee without first having tried to talk with each of the members separately. Take advantage of the longer time it takes a committee structure to make a sale. Forge your relationships as widely as possible for support immediately, and for future sales.

OTHER WAYS TO THINK ABOUT SALES

Sales as a Numbers Game

Something that may help you handle sales mentally is to look at it as a numbers game. If it takes twenty phone calls to make one appointment, literally draw up a list of twenty prospects and check them off as you phone down the list. Don't worry about the nineteen nonappointments or take them personally. (Remember, Thomas Edison said that his nine thousand failures to develop a lightbulb were what created his successful attempt.) If it takes five appointments to make one sale, simply say that every rejection is getting you that much closer to a sale.

Some people even sincerely thank people for turning them down. They say, "My statistics have shown that I am rejected five times before I make a sale and, since my average sale is $8,000, I figure that every rejection is worth more than $1,000 to me. In fact, if you have any friends who you think would reject me, I'd love to have their names." This creates a totally different atmosphere, with some humor.

It's not unusual to then get referrals from people who don't buy from you and never will buy from you. They can give you names of people who are more likely to buy, either in their company or other companies.

Many people who don't buy will still like you. They can become ongoing referral sources. And some will give you referrals whether they like you or not.

Sales as Education

Like marketing in general, another way to look at the sales process is as education.

Because you have a chance to get around and work with different companies, you're in a position to learn more than people who spend all their time in one company or one job. Many good service providers are quick learners, enjoy variety, and are likely to build their knowledge base far faster than other people.

Education and Fear Selling

Looked at from a negative point of view, some professionals, particularly in accounting, law, or insurance, might raise the fear level of prospects.

They educate prospects to all the dangers that can hurt them if they don't do their taxes on time, draft their contracts properly, or buy enough insurance for their families. Similarly, a dental marketing approach might raise people's fears about untreated gum disease and the terrible long-term effects on tooth loss.

Education Is a Professional Approach

The educational approach is a nonpushy, relationship-building, helpful, consulting approach. People learn something every time they meet you.

All good salespeople are "cross-pollinators." They bring around new industry information, jokes, and so forth. By taking a professional-educator approach, you can build people's skills and help them perform their jobs better. You're essentially acting as a free mentor, or consultant.

RELATIONSHIPS, RELATIONSHIPS, RELATIONSHIPS

Most of your selling time should be spent building relationships in the industries or specialties relevant to your services.

It won't all be building relationships with your prospects. It's often more effective to build relationships with their advisors, with their customers, with their suppliers, or with others who may end up referring you to them.

When you meet people at networking groups, at charity functions, or on the boards of organizations, you're selling yourself. But what you're really looking for are business friends, people who will be comfortable with you and become referral sources or clients.

The Best Business Is Personal

You need to draw your own line between your social and business lives. Meeting people in nonbusiness contexts can be the best way to start a business relationship, and business contacts can become social friends.

In the movie *The Godfather*, the Godfather says, "All business is personal." I think you should try to build your business relationships "socially." If you meet someone month after month at a particular group or on a board, the relationship is one-dimensional. Until you've had a cup of coffee together, visited his or her office, or played tennis, the relationship will stagnate. You need to look for ways to break through.

Some people do this with entertaining. Perhaps you can throw parties or take people to ball games. Other people do it with persistence and variety. Perhaps you send them clippings regularly, put them on your newsletter list, and see them at different kinds of groups.

People also build relationships by asking advice. For certain kinds of prospects, it can be quite disarming to ask them for their "two cents'

> **P**osition yourself as number two to every prospect on your list [where you can't be number one]. If you're standing second in line, in enough lines, sooner or later you're going to move up to number one. And the amazing thing is that no one else ever uses this strategy.
>
> Harvey Mackay

Advance the Relationship

People agree to see you again because they want to learn something new, their needs have changed, or they enjoy talking with you. Don't repeat the same approach. Bring new information.

!

worth." It flatters prospects that you're interested in their opinions. And, as a bonus, they'll often come up with good ideas for you!

Circulate with Others

In order to find prospects and referral sources, you must be in circulation.

There's a saying that luck is "preparation meeting opportunity." To have extra luck finding clients, you must be in contact with new people and in repeated contact with acquaintances.

Whether you do this by phone, e-mail, or in person, the wider the variety of people you meet, the more chance you have of finding the ones with whom you can do business. And the deeper the relationship with each of these people, the more chance of doing business together.

Depending on your skills, interests, and opportunities for contact with people, you have to balance the quantity and quality of the relationships you create.

Hopefully, you can screen a lot of people to play the numbers game for quantity. Then develop relationships in more depth with those who are responsive to you and seem to have interests and needs in your area. You should eventually get more business *and* new friends from your efforts.

Making the Emotional Sale

1. *Comfort Level* Customers must feel that you're "their kind of folks." You must "click" with their way of thinking.
2. *Identification* You must identify with the customers' problems and concerns. And they must feel that you understand "where they are coming from."
3. *Competence* Customers must believe you're capable of solving their problems.
4. *Price* Finally, and absolutely last in consideration, is price. If you've dealt with their other concerns, you should be able to get the work at your price.

!

HAVING OTHERS SELL FOR YOU: LEVERAGING YOURSELF

There are at least two ways to have others directly sell your services for you. (A third one is covered in Chapter Nine.)

Hiring Salespeople

For most of you, others can't represent you as well as you can. But others may be more willing to go out and sell than you are.

Many engineering, law, and construction firms have full-time marketing or sales staff. They have a combination of sales and technical skills so that they can go out and talk to prospects and clients. Often they are technical workers who discovered that they enjoyed selling. Many consulting firms also have principals who specialize more in selling new clients than in delivering the services.

Often salespeople are not well respected within professional firms, so they don't stay long. Marketing directors can have similar problems. If you use salespeople, you should set up a positive environment for them. This will benefit their performance for you.

Hiring arrangements can vary a lot. In one case, a woman consultant represents one CPA. She receives a small wage plus expenses for a wider range of marketing work from PR to direct mail. Then she gets a percentage of the business she generates over three years, going from 15 percent the first year to 10 percent the third year (if there is one).

A Group Agent

The second approach is using group sales agents. There are many cases where someone has represented a group of service providers.

Each arrangement is unique, but here are a few specific cases and their approximate financial arrangements. In one, a man represents several business services. These include a printer, a marketing consultant, and a number of business consultants who specialize in different problems. He gets paid from 10 percent to 50 percent by the different consultants, depending on the job and whether it is completely sold. On the printing, he gets his bid, minus what the printer charges him, with a minimum of 10 percent. With some of the consultants, he gets an additional 10 percent of the first year's billing on clients the service providers sign up from his leads.

In another case, a salesperson wants to sell her own services as an office organizer and pays for her time while making sales calls by offering the complementary services of others.

For instance, if you are calling on small businesses, you could offer printing, bookkeeping, marketing, legal assistance, and so on in one sales call. The salesperson will usually start with a type of business with which she is very familiar.

Receptionists as "Salespeople"

In many companies, whoever answers your phone or greets people in your office may be your best salesperson!

Clients may interact more with them than with you. Think about the difference you feel between a teller at the bank who remembers your name and greets you personally, and the rest. Won't your clients feel better about you if they are greeted personally by people who are genuinely glad to see them?

To get these happy results, hire right, train right, and reward people for positive comments from clients.

!

If you do this, try to have at least one "product" (such as office supplies or printing) that most people need. Then the other services that aren't used as often can be carried.

Determining proper payment for such sales agents is difficult. Anyone who can't pay a 10 percent commission shouldn't be in business. Because services should have a high repeat factor, I'd favor up to 50 percent of the first job. Any business you get this way is a bonus to you, and you can afford to be generous.

REMEMBER YOUR TARGETS

No matter how effective other people are at selling for you, you'll still be selling yourself sometimes. A useful tool is a "Ten-Most-Wanted List."

Especially if you're using the advantages of a niche strategy, where you specialize to dominate an area, gathering information *ahead of time* about specific clients or referral sources you'd like to have is very valuable. Create a specific list of such targets and build a file on each one. Then seek out places you're likely to meet them. If you bump into them unexpectedly, you'll be better prepared to make a good impression.

SUMMARY

Business = Social

This chapter has talked about sales as relationships. Follow my—and the Godfather's—advice: Get personal!

Approach sales relationships like social relationships, with strategies to make new business friends. This may seem unnatural at first, but the same thing would apply to your social network if you had to start from the beginning. If you were dropped into a new city without contacts, making friends would be just as unnatural.

I believe that if you think about where you found your last five purely social friends, you'll see that you did not work to develop them; they emerged naturally. Most of us meet people at work, in the neighborhood, or in activities that we do. And most of us probably haven't made systematic efforts to meet a wide variety of new people. We've allowed our friendship circles to stagnate.

Try approaching marketing as part of your social activity. It will become a way of broadening your social circle. Whether you do business with people or not, by broadening your circle you'll have more fun. You'll try new activities and meet new people, no matter what the business outcome. And the occasional ones who hire you will finance your improved social life!

Business from Agencies

There are agencies in some industries, such as computer consulting, who will get jobs for consultants or engineers, take approximately half the money, and create a constant flow of business.

AGENDA

If you really want to do something, you'll find a way;
If you don't, you'll find an excuse.
FORBES magazine

Building Relationships

- ▶ Decide on several ways you can build your relationships with clients.
- ▶ Talk with clients about things you can do for them, such as helping their clients or bringing them contacts.
- ▶ Develop some creative ways to stand out in your prospects' and clients' minds.
- ▶ Make sure that you're in touch with current clients between bills.
- ▶ Get in touch with people you've made presentations to who haven't hired you in the past.

Delivering on Your Promises

▶ Develop a process for customizing your services better for each client.

▶ Set up a system to educate yourself on your customers' industries (such as reading trade magazines or going to groups).

▶ Develop a list of people to whom you're comfortable referring clients. Then talk with the people on your list to make sure that you're on their lists too!

Implement a Better Sales Process

▶ Develop a needs analysis form or checklist that will help prospects, and you, understand their situations better.

▶ Develop your questioning and listening skills.

▶ Develop a list of objections that prospects might have to hiring you, and build the answers into your new "presentation" questions.

▶ List ways to make your negotiations about new jobs more win/win for you and the prospect.

▶ Agree to suspend your dislike of selling for one month. Commit to contacting one new prospect a day.

CHAPTER SEVEN

FREE PUBLICITY

How to Exploit the Media for Fun and Profit

> *Publicity is the most cost-effective marketing tool.*
> DANIEL S. JANAL
> *Publicity Builder*

Chapter One mentioned that the simplest way to think about publicity (or PR, for public relations) is as free advertising. While it *can be* very cost-effective, like any tool, it must be used correctly for the best effect.

Publicity is formally defined as free mass-media exposure; however, some of the exposure available, such as online discussion groups, is almost personal.

One great publicity item about you can launch a new enterprise. Regular articles by you can build your credibility and a steady flow of business. If you get a story about yourself in the same location in which you placed an ad of the same size, I estimate that the story will be five to ten times more effective in getting you business. And I'll show you how it can be even more effective *after* the fact than when it comes out!

Publicity is one of the best marketing tools for services. However, because its effects are seldom immediate, publicity is most valuable to the established organization. And like other marketing methods, the best way to get publicity is to set up a regular schedule for contacting the media. (See Chapter Fifteen for more on implementation.)

In the case of your services, any mention of your name or any visibility you achieve will help you in the long run. There is a saying that there is no such thing as bad publicity. However, if investigative journalists such as the *60 Minutes* TV show come calling, I would think twice about granting an interview!

Now let's get right down to the details of getting publicity for you and your services.

MAJOR WAYS TO GET PUBLICITY

If you happen to win a big award, the media may seek you out. However, up to 90 percent of what you read, see, or hear in the media comes from people and companies contacting the media, rather than the media finding them. So *you'll* have to make the effort if you want regular publicity.

The first thing most people think of to get regular publicity is to write a column for a newspaper or trade magazine. While a column can be valuable, it is surprisingly hard to obtain unless you have connections. There are usually lots of people jockeying for the same space. I don't consider it productive enough to be a major method, although I'll give you a few suggestions later on how to try for one.

I'll cover nine major approaches to getting publicity, from letters to the editor to doing research, plus many details and examples of how to accomplish them. Some of them are guaranteed; if you apply them regularly, you will receive coverage that you didn't have before. Others depend on the response of the media people you contact.

It takes a two-step process to reap the benefits of publicity. You have to sell the media on your story and then, when it appears, it helps sell you to your ultimate customers. As discussed later, journalists are a difficult group to sell to, so it pays to know what you're doing.

Letters to the Editor

Write Letters

"Letters to the Editor" is the second most read part of the paper. Apparently people like to see what other real people are saying, or see if they recognize someone's name.

As mentioned in Chapter Two, there's a simple, almost surefire, way to gain visibility for your name. The "smallest" type of publicity is letters to the editor.

While radio and television have their "letters," it's easiest to think about print media. In national magazines and publications, it's rather hard to get published. When looking at *USA Today, Newsweek, Fortune, Time,* and similar big publications, your odds are maybe 2 to 10 percent—which still isn't too bad. *People* magazine says it publishes fewer than 10 percent of the letters it receives; *U.S. News & World Report* says the rate is 3 to 5 percent, with five hundred to six hundred submissions weekly. *USA Today* is about the same.

Sports Illustrated editors say one of the easiest ways to get a letter published is to have a personal association with a story subject, so the letter adds a personal touch to a story already covered. For example, I had a letter published in *Inc.* magazine that added some additional tips to an article it published (and I got a small job from it).

Your Odds Are Good

In some online discussion groups, almost everything gets published. In your local newspaper, the odds of getting your letter to the editor published are often 50 to 95 percent, depending on space. And remember from Chapter Two that you can send a similar letter out many different times, and many different letters to the same paper.

Getting your name attached to a published letter won't make you famous, but it will remind your friends and clients that you exist. You'll know by the comments of people who come up to you and tell you they saw your letter. And it will lay the foundation for other people becoming familiar with your name.

Trade Magazines

If your services are business to business, you're best off sending letters to trade magazines that your clients read. In your own trade magazines and newsletters, you may build your stature in your field or obtain professional referrals. In your clients' trade magazines, you have a chance to directly attract business. Letters are a subtle form of self-promotion, as well as easier to get published than a column.

Your First Assignment for This Chapter

So, what do you want to write about today? You can write a letter reacting to something that's appeared in the paper. It may be something in the news, an editorial by the paper itself, or a response to another letter. Look at the paper a little more carefully than usual. If a columnist's comment or a news item strikes a chord for you, go for it!

Most letters to the editor are published on the editorial page, of course. But some columnists will also publish responses within their columns. So, you have multiple targets in any newspaper, and to a lesser degree, in magazines and other media. In the Appendix for this chapter are several sample letters to the editor. They're about generic issues that could apply in almost any community. One of my seminar attendees took me up on this challenge and wrote a letter to the paper about a local road issue. Not only did it get published, but it generated two responses and a response to the responses from him!

Don't Send One Letter, Send Several

Don't forget that you can send variations of the same letter to multiple outlets. For instance, in most areas, you'll have small papers, a large regional paper, and weekly papers.

It Doesn't Even Have to Directly Relate

Your letter to the media doesn't have to be about something that's appeared. You can write about almost anything. Just remember that your objective in writing the letter is not so much to express your opinion as to gain visibility. So, review letters carefully to judge how they will come across to the readers you want to reach.

A valuable approach is to become an advocate for something. If your letter relates to your occupation, it allows you to tell people what you do, and it also gives you a credential and a reason for taking a position.

If you're a dentist, and you write a letter advocating dental hygiene, it will look a little self-serving. A letter saying that costs of dental services are too high will get more attention, and you'll be seen as unbiased and fair. Lawyers are another group that can criticize themselves. This gets a lot of attention because of people's negative attitudes toward attorneys.

"Op-Ed" Pieces

Op-ed stands for opposite the editorial page. Here, papers normally place guest columns by local experts. They allow you more words than a letter (one or two thousand), and often include your picture. If you write a long, articulate letter in reaction to an editorial, and the paper knows you from other letters, it will sometimes offer you an op-ed piece. For instance, my local paper once ran a column about the wonders of hand-writing analysis. I wrote an article which the paper published pointing out that no available data supported handwriting analysis as scientifically accurate. Naturally, this upset the handwriting "expert" on whom the original article was based, so the "expert" and I had a few more back-and-forths on this issue.

BIG MEDIA EXPOSURE

Now, let's look at more sophisticated ways to get publicity in the media.

The first thing you should know is that different media present different degrees of difficulty to you. The bigger the newspaper, Web site, television station, or radio station, the more people want publicity in it, and the harder it will be for you to gain access. So start with the smaller units. The easiest ones are your local weekly newspapers and association newsletters.

In general, I think you're better off doing most PR work yourself, despite the fact that I offer PR services. I've known many companies that paid $5,000 a month and got only a little publicity. There are a few PR firms that charge fees only for actual publicity attained for you, but they are hard to find (and 95 percent of firms act insulted if you ask them about results-based performance). However, good firms will work harder if they aren't getting results, so they do perform.

If you were to hire a professional public relations firm for anywhere from $1,000 to $10,000 a month, it would use some of the following techniques to get you publicity. The first sign of a good PR firm, like any marketing company, is that before employees start, they first interview you closely and observe your business. They would be looking for what's called a "hook," something to tie a story to, something the media would find interesting, novel, or newsworthy. (They'll want to know your USP, positioning, or uniqueness.)

Tie to a Trend

If something is happening in the news today, such as a new tax law, the media is open to an accountant commenting on how it would apply to local readers. After the World Trade Tower destruction on 9/11/01, many professionals offered insights into psychological aspects of people's reactions, economic aspects, and similar things.

Fast Reactions

Sometimes tying to a trend requires you to act fast. I'll talk mainly about newspapers, but let's look at an example from the radio right now.

A computer consultant was listening to a talk show on his car radio. The host said that the guest for the next hour would be a computer consultant who would take callers' questions about computers. As the hour approached, the host became nervous and said, "My consultant isn't here; I don't know what I'll do, since I don't know anything about computers."

As the hour opened, the host admitted that the show's computer consultant was not there, and he didn't, in fact, know what he would do.

PR Pays

Public relations returns $2 to $3 for every dollar invested, according to fifty-two CEOs surveyed by the International Association of Business Communicators.

Our computer consultant screeched to the nearest phone booth, called the host, introduced himself as a computer consultant, and said he would be happy to help out on the air, either talking to the host or answering listeners' questions. The host was grateful, and the consultant turned out to be very good. Not only did he get a full hour on the air, replacing the missing consultant, but he became a favorite of that host and radio station, and appeared many subsequent times. This PR coup required quick wits and reactions to immediate events.

"Trends" Where You Can Take Your Time

There are also hundreds of trends or events you can tie to that are predictable long in advance. For instance, every year brings Thanksgiving, Easter, Christmas, Mother's Day, Father's Day, tax deadlines, and other dates. Many of the minor holidays were, in fact, created by groups simply to get free publicity (or even by Hallmark Cards!). And the media doesn't mind since they like things to which to tie stories. They're there, so why not use them?

For instance, March is National Nutrition Month. One publicist created a radio tour for Dr. Tad, who sold nutritional products. He went up the East Coast doing interviews on many radio shows. His publicist says he reached over five million listeners and sold over $30,000 worth of products.

Your "trend" doesn't have to be linked to a date. Issues such as dieting are always in season. Doug Markham was a chiropractor and nutritionist. He got lots of publicity, including on CNN, from a news release to radio and TV titled "Eating Fat Does Not Make You Fat." This simply bounced off the popularity of dieting and those who promote low-fat products and diets. By taking on traditional wisdom, he drew attention to himself.

Another example of an undated trend was used by a musician. Like many people, he was angry about those who use cell phones in crowded areas. After being trapped on a long bus ride next to an inane phone conversation, Jim Stone dashed off a song attacking cell phones. (One of many lines was "I'd like to take your cell phone and slice it up with a knife, or better yet with a chain saw into little megabytes.") He received lots of publicity from it, including a picture and story in the local paper. Another group obtained publicity from having a book on the Ten Worst-Selling List on Amazon.com. You can create many such lists that are limited only by your creativity.

In today's media-driven culture, tying publicity to a movie works nicely. You can get advance information on when new movies are coming out in order to prepare ahead of time, or wait until you see the movie and react quickly. Marilynn Mobley wrote a humorous article about the business lessons from *Monsters, Inc.*, a popular movie in 2001. Then she received further publicity by writing about her experience in an online e-zine.

Getting PR Is Not Mission Impossible

"Your job, if you choose to accept it," is to prepare yourself now for New Year's, Mother's Day, Father's Day, Grandparent's Day, and other predictable events.

Think about this: The media needs your help. Take the Super Bowl. The media has done "guacamole use during the Super Bowl," "wives of the Super Bowl," and "cities of the Super Bowl." They're dying for a new angle! If you can talk about tax revenues generated by the Super Bowl, they probably would love to interview an accountant or economist!

There are a number of calendars or other sources available, such as *Chase's Calendar of Events*, which list national weeks, days, and months. There is a day, week, or month for almost every occupation or event you could dream of. If there isn't one, several people have found it easy to get their local mayor or governor to declare one for them!

Even without having your own week declared, it's easy to think of publicity that could go with various holidays. A few ideas are listed in Table 7.1, on the next page and more are listed in the Appendix.

Use Trivia

Another way to get publicity was illustrated by the National Pork Producers Council. It used interesting, unusual, and entertaining facts that are not well known for a press release (that was picked up nationally) during National Pork Producers Week.

It turns out that pork had been the most important meat in America in the early 1800s, before the railroads made it possible to ship cattle across the country. Pigs can pretty much grow anywhere, forage for themselves,

---

TABLE 7.1 Holiday PR Ideas

Holiday	Service	PR Idea
Christmas	Accountant	Article about how to pay for your Christmas gifts with end-of-year tax strategies.
New Year's	Lawyer	Corporate "resolutions" to avoid legal problems next year.
Super Bowl	Therapist	How a wife can win points with her husband by supporting his obsession with football, briefly. Or, how a husband can indulge his obsession and not upset his wife.
May Day	Contractor	Erect a maypole for a local school festival.
Easter	Anyone	Sponsor an Easter egg hunt for children aged two and under. (Parents go crazy seeing their kids walk past an egg in plain sight.)

(For more examples and ideas, see page 345 of the Appendix.)

---

and eat lots of things. So pork was the key meat. The council said this was illustrated by expressions in the language, such as "pork-barrel politics," "bring home the bacon," "bottom of the barrel," and so forth. It wasn't rocket science, but it was interesting historical trivia. And the national wire service agreed or it wouldn't have been published.

If you're an economist, you can create interesting statistics, such as how large the economy of your area would be compared to the average country in South America. For instance, California would be about the sixth largest economy in the world if it were an independent country. So, it's very likely that your county or region could easily be bigger than the economies of some small countries.

Create Your Own News

By creating something that didn't exist before, you are automatically newsworthy.

You can put together a one-page sheet of tips in your area. These are often called the "ten commandments" in the PR world, because ten is a good number to fit on one page. For example, Jim Untiedt, an insurance agent, published an article in a local business journal on "Ten Ways for a Smart Contractor to Cut Insurance Costs." Other possibilities might include: "Ten Ways to Beautify Your Home on a Budget" (interior designer), "Ten Ways to Keep Records More Easily" (bookkeeping), "Ten Points to Check Before You Sign a Lease" (attorney), and so on. You can use other numbers besides ten, of course.

You can also publish a little booklet, perhaps folding over a few 8½" × 11" pages, with a cover. These may cost you as much as $1 apiece, if you put a nice cover on them. They may cost a few pennies if you copy a single sheet. But now you have something that previously didn't exist. These booklets can even become profitable products, and many consultants, such as the Walk the Talk Company, have sold thousands to clients who give them out to employees or customers.

Many newspapers and newsletters have small sections in which they can note that "Ten Nutrition Tips" are available free from Joe or Sally Trainer, for a self-addressed, stamped envelope. You can also use them as giveaways at talks or through local merchants such as your bank, stores, and so forth.

How About Giving an Award?

Another way to make your own news is to present an award, or create a list. These can be locally, or nationally, oriented. If you work with businesses, you could present an "entrepreneurial" award.

How about a "safety" award? Or "best guest article in the media" about a particular topic? How about *to* the media, for coverage of your area?

You're already familiar with some nationally publicized lists of "best dressed," "worst dressed," and so on. I've seen similar contests for "worst boss," "messiest office," and so forth. Any of these awards give you publicity. And they give you a great reason to call people—to ask for nominees, or tell them they are potential candidates.

If you don't think that your giving an award will be credible, get a charity or trade group to sponsor the presentation with you. If you offer to do most of the work, it has little to lose. After all, it needs publicity too!

Local Bests

If you don't want to create your own award or list, there may be the chance to exploit existing ones.

Many local newspapers, often weeklies, do readers' polls of the "Best of Santa Cruz," "Best of Marin," and so on. Usually, these have to do with shopping and restaurants. But sometimes there are sections on "Best Local People" in any nominated category.

Once, a group even "stuffed the ballot box," so to speak. Its members were part of a networking group that got together every week to give each other sales leads (see Chapter Eight on networking for further explanation of these groups). What simpler way to give each other leads than to vote for each other as the best accounting firm in the county, best wallpaper business, best restaurant, or whatever businesses they happened to represent?

I knew the person who was rated the "best accountant" in the county one year. That's a credential that will add to his credibility forever.

Rigging the ballot is not exactly fair, but actively asking your friends to vote for you, instead of just hoping that a few people write you in, doesn't cost much and may get you something big. (Asking for votes isn't particularly unusual. Each team tries to influence local fans every year in voting for its own players as baseball all-stars too.)

Stunts

In the old days, to get publicity, you would set up some sort of stunt: sitting on flagpoles, holding a race, swallowing goldfish, cramming into a phone booth, whatever. That's a pretty old-fashioned approach to publicity, but surprisingly enough, it still works. The CEO of a dot-com startup, Surpluzz.com, auctioned off his mother as a stunt. When the Russian *Mir* space station crashed to earth, Taco Bell put out a target where it was expected and promised everyone a free taco if *Mir* hit it. And a farmer in Australia mowed two big Xs in his yard to provide *Mir* a target—so it wouldn't hit his house!

Stunts can be ongoing as well as one time. For instance, many companies have offices in odd shapes, such as a shoe. Others, such as New

England Pest Control (with a landmark 58-foot blue termite on its roof), get attention by adding extras to their buildings.

Anyone who wears an unusual costume can be his own stunt while he brings an extra dimension of entertainment to his clients; for instance, the recycled toner people who dress like 1950s FBI agents and leave roses with secretaries. They're an event in a boring workday, not just service providers. Or author Jill Conner Browne, who has created a "women's movement" with her outrageous advice, attire, and encouragement of women to become queens of flair themselves. If you're not a dignified professional, wearing a costume and becoming "Captain Something" can give you ongoing publicity.

One of the most aggressive ways to obtain publicity if you are a little company is to take on a big company. For instance, many software firms have gotten attention attacking big ones. Greg Shaw, a spokesperson for Microsoft, once said, "If you want your company to get attention . . . come down on Microsoft." For the daring, getting sued, or suing, a big company is a similar way to get PR. On the more dignified side, devoting your life to a worthy cause and always speaking out for it will also get you attention.

Photos

Many stunts depend on good photos. Unusual pictures are a kind of visual "stunt." The Associated Press carries a novel picture almost every day. It might be ten thousand bottles photographed from above. It is always an unusual view, something you don't normally see. Perhaps you work with something that would make a good picture.

If you're our dignified professional, the media is bored with head-and-shoulder shots. They'd prefer a more interesting picture of you doing something, such as with one of your clients. A top lawyer for the trucking industry was featured with his collection of model trucks, which were each painted like one of his clients' real trucks. In *Forbes* magazine, there was a picture of a CEO standing on two large rolls of paper his company sold to newspapers.

Use your imagination to stage a great photo (or use your computer special effects). In my collection, Novell's CEO is posed by a triangular stairwell that looks strange; a fashion shot has three of the same shot, one on top of the other, each one smaller than the next; Kendall-Jackson plugs its winery

Bunny Stunt

Live TV, a British cable channel, used a 6-foot bunny costume, named News Bunny, on the air while the news was given. Eventually, one of the wearers changed his name to News Bunny, ran for office, was arrested, and performed other stunts. This idea got lots of publicity for three years before it was abandoned.

with a fake photo of a 3-foot tomato on its gardener's shoulder; a Christian retailer plugs its online site with a picture of people holding laptops, with the people arranged in the shape of a cross; and the Monster.com CEO poses in *Fortune* magazine in the mouth of a giant monster statue.

Including a little fun in your image can add a dimension for your customers, attract attention, and create publicity. Even our dignified professional may find a little clowning inspirational for the staff in a skit at the company meeting.

Giving Talks

In most trade groups and local papers, there are calendars of meetings and seminars. So, another way to get publicity is to give talks. (See Chapter Eleven for more on marketing by public speaking.)

A stockbroker in Texas said he'd never given a talk about stocks to any group, including the Garden Club, where he didn't get some business. That's probably a much higher ratio than most of us would have. Perhaps lots of people have stocks tucked away that they're ready to sell. But whether or not you obtain immediate business, you can burnish your image, gain referrals, and get names for follow-up. Eventually, you'll see results.

When you give the talks, you want to be sure to have a press release for the local calendar—just a few brief lines (as the example on page 155 shows), giving the facts and saying how people can attend.

Start locally, and work your way as high as you like. Ted Garrison speaks at local construction groups and gains consulting work, plus referrals to the national groups. Local Rotary, Lions, and similar groups meet every week (usually dozens in each area), and have speakers for brief talks on all topics. Once you appear at one, you can be referred to others.

Your Own TV Show

You can even become part of the media yourself. Most local cable systems are required to offer a cable access channel. This means that after taking a brief course to qualify yourself as a producer, you can host your own talk show (or anything). Of course, not many people watch this channel, but some do.

March 23, 2004
FOR IMMEDIATE RELEASE

<u>CALENDAR NEWS RELEASE</u>

FOR MORE INFORMATION, CONTACT:
   415/555-5555

CALENDAR RELEASE FOR:
   Events Calendar

WORKSHOP/SEMINAR:
   How to Become a Successful Consultant in Your Own Field

DATE & TIME:
   Saturday, April 13, 9:00 a.m. to 1:00 p.m.

LOCATION:
   College of Marin
   170 Harlan Center
   Kentfield Campus

COST:
   $45.00

REGISTRATION:
   #8452. In person, by mail, or at the door

DESCRIPTION:
   This seminar will cover all you need to know to conduct a consulting
   business, including: defining your product, targeting your market, obtaining that first client, improving referrals, negotiating fee structures and
   agreements, and much more.

GIVEN BY:
   Sally Blew has been a consultant for many years. In addition to teaching
   marketing, she has written many articles on the topic.

In addition to your small audience, you can use copies of your best tapes to promote yourself as a guest to "real" TV shows. And you can offer guest spots to your best referral sources and clients.

I even know of cases where consultants bought time on small regular TV stations and charged guests to appear, thus making a profit while promoting themselves.

The Really Easy Targets

Some trade magazines and professional newsletters are so hard up for material that they'll gladly publish anything you send them! So, if your local county has a newsletter of the association of your occupation, consider contributing regularly, whether you write letters, opinion pieces, or guest columns.

!

Get Referrals and More Publicity

Talks can bring you referrals as easily as business. For instance, Dan Cooper used to give low-cost seminars on doing your own graphics. He didn't get much business after the seminars because these people wanted to do it themselves. But he received many referrals from the people who attended after other people admired *their* new graphics.

At the end of her speeches to business groups, Bette Price offers to write an article on her topic for their trade magazines or internal newsletters. About 20 percent of members of one audience gave her their cards. This gives you the chance for more publicity, for ongoing columns, and a reason to keep in touch with these people or put them on your e-zine list.

Publicity from Donations

Nothing looks more professional than a service provider donating her time and expertise to a charity or other worthy cause. Attorneys and accountants serve on many boards. While you can also discount or donate your services, consultant Troy Waugh points out that you're actually better off charging full fees and donating them back in cash. This puts you on the list of big donors for more publicity and special events (and it encourages full-fee referrals from the group).

Anywhere that you meet people is a chance to gain business and referrals. Many service providers who passionately support a women's group, fight cancer, or raise money for the environment also get lots of business from their efforts. The trick is to pick a group that you love that also has the kinds of people in it who are good prospects for you.

One minor way to gain exposure and try out a group is auctions. There are literally dozens of auctions to which you can donate gift certificates. Perhaps it's a certificate for an hour of services valued at $100. Perhaps it's books or other items you have available.

The public television stations have auctions. There are at least three that broadcast where we are. There are many school auctions. Today, almost every private and public school is raising extra money through parent organizations for the schools. And of course, there are a number of charity auctions.

Gift certificates not only give you publicity, but allow you to prove the value of your services. If you're lucky, the people who bid for them paid enough that they actually have an interest in your services and may employ you further.

Publicity Through Research

My favorite idea for creating publicity while doing useful work is to set up a research project. This is another example of making news, plus it gives you dignified sales contacts.

What I mean by research is easy. It's not formal, scholarly work but gathering useful information in your field. For instance, if you are an economic consultant, you might call twenty of the largest employers in your region every quarter and ask them about their hiring plans or some other factor. This allows you to speak to some fairly important people and gradually they get to know who you are. You pick survey respondents who could do business with you, or be referral sources, as well as give you useful information.

After you gather a few brief responses, you send participants thank-you notes. Then you write up a summary of your results and send them a copy of that. Then you send a copy of your results to the local or trade media, perhaps a press release with a brief story. Often it will be published. The people you are talking to, who are the types you want for your clients, hear from you on the phone or perhaps in person. They get a follow-up note and a copy of the report, and then they may see the report in the media.

When you've done this for a few quarters, you begin to be *the* expert in this field. If anyone has a question about hiring plans in the local area, they call you. You have built your expertise and image, you have gained information usable to you and your clients, and you have built a contact and a reason for staying in touch with some key figures.

This approach is very professional. It shows that you are interested in the latest trends. It can work regardless of your service. For instance, an obscure college, Quinnipiac, used regular political polls (up to forty-four a year) to garner 2,500 news stories, raise enrollments threefold, and become a university. Name recognition also helped raise millions from donors. A public relations firm surveyed some downtown workers about how often

Simple Survey of Hiring Intentions

1. How many full-time employees do you currently have?
2. How many part-time employees?
3. How many full-time employees do you expect to add in the next three months?
4. How many part-time or contract employees will you add?

they ate at their desks. Dubbing them "desk potatoes," the story made *USA Today* and other major papers, giving the PR firm great publicity.

Use your imagination. You'll see that there are a lot of ways you can perform simple research to create knowledge that competitors don't have, become known to people you want to be familiar to, and gain publicity from writing it up.

Use Your Clients

What you want is a feature story about how wonderful you are. But that will happen only occasionally.

So, what do you do? You use your clients!

Let's say that you're a bookkeeper. That's not terribly glamorous. But you may keep the books for a local film production company, for a sky diver, for many interesting enterprises. Now you have a possible story by linking yourself to your interesting client. Of course, to get these items placed, you use the other techniques discussed in this chapter.

One company that does this regularly is DriveSavers. Every time there is a disaster, it has a story about recovering valuable data for clients off hard drives that are melted, crushed, and so on. For further publicity, sometimes it donates part or all of its services to worthy groups. The company also is a good photo opportunity since it uses "clean rooms" and has technicians who look like doctors. Every time a computer virus strikes, antivirus software companies such as Network Associates provide fixes that become newsworthy. And during the dot-com boom, Net Market Partners got great publicity by featuring clients it had helped, such as Capspring, who became case studies and testimonials for the local business journal.

Every client is a possible story. And somewhere in that story, the client will gratefully say, "Without my service provider, I couldn't have been as successful as I was." So, talk to your clients about getting them some publicity. For them, it's an unexpected bonus, and they most likely will be incredibly grateful if you're successful. Even if you are not successful, they will be flattered that you thought they were worth publicity and pleased that you were willing to make the effort for them for free.

IF YOU'RE A DIGNIFIED PROFESSIONAL MARKETING TO CORPORATIONS OR OTHER DIGNIFIED PROFESSIONALS

For some of you, publicity won't seem dignified, or won't seem that useful. The most interesting illustration of professionals' ambivalence about marketing I know was an accounting firm that sent its new marketing director to my seminar on obtaining publicity, and then wondered if trying to obtain publicity was too "pushy"!

Let's deal with the undignified argument first. Your main publicity should be aimed at the trade publications which your clients read. You will write articles and be cited as the expert. That's dignified enough. But don't write off even local publicity.

To anticipate the point in this chapter, one of the things you'll be getting publicity about is public service volunteer work. That fits a professional image. "Big" people appreciate other people who make a contribution to the community.

You will never know where visibility may lead. Sometimes an item that you support the local high school volleyball team will be just the thing to build a social connection to a corporate chief who played volleyball in college, or whose daughter plays high school volleyball now.

Publicize Referral Sources Too

You can also help your referral sources obtain publicity. This is a great way to strengthen your ties.

Perhaps you make them the feature. Or perhaps you use them as a second local expert in a story featuring one of your clients. They should appreciate the fact that you're trying to get them publicity. And if it works out, they should redouble their efforts to give you referrals. (If they don't try to reciprocate, you now know something else important about your relationship!)

And remember, if you're a corporate attorney, judges read the daily paper. Other lawyers read it. And corporate chiefs (like yours) read it. So no matter how dignified and obscure your specialty, local visibility can be of value *and* fit your image. (And your mother will be pleased that you got it!)

HIRING PR HELP

Many firms end up hiring public relations companies to handle publicity for them. Recently, I've consulted with two such companies. One was in management consulting, the other in publishing.

In both cases, the companies were paying about $5,000 a month as a retainer, and both were dissatisfied with the results. It often takes three months for a story to come out; however, results after six months were weak.

A great PR firm will work harder when it doesn't get results, but many just send press releases and don't uncover great "hooks." If your PR firm doesn't act like a marketing consultant at the beginning and make sure it knows your USP or positioning, it's not great. Unfortunately, the majority aren't.

In other chapters, I talk about paying for marketing only when it works—such as per response advertising and pay per click online. It is possible to find public relations firms that will work on a performance basis. When I searched "pay for placement" on Google.com, I found many such firms. You then know exactly what it will cost you to get on a major radio show, or to get a thousand-word article in a magazine; for instance, I've done this sort of work for, say, $500 per article published in a trade magazine.

Dignified Publicity

If your specialty is obscure, or your image dignified, don't give up on using publicity. Go for the helpful technical-expert role in trade publications, and go for the well-rounded-human-being-contributing-to-the-local-community role in local publicity.

APPEALING TO JOURNALISTS

One of the best ways to create publicity for yourself is to do as much of the work as possible for the media. Having been a journalist *and* editor for many years, I can say that journalists feel overworked and underpaid. They know their stories can be valuable for you. Combined with the fact that they see "pitches" every day, and have done hundreds of stories, they are a very difficult, cynical audience to sell yourself to. They have seen it all, so why should they give you the benefit of their coverage?

The short answer is that you have to offer value to them *and* their audience. There is a kind of unspoken understanding that the media is willing to trade publicity about you for benefits for their audience. That might be as simple as "Ten Tips" credited to you that help readers. But if your efforts assist a charity, the media will be even more helpful.

Write Like a Journalist

Journalists need to decide what's newsworthy or interesting about your story (the "hook"). The best thing you can do, particularly for smaller media, is to figure it out for them and write the story the way they would write it.

A rhyme from Rudyard Kipling about the basis of journalism is still the accepted standard.

I keep six honest serving men
(They taught me all I knew);
Their names are What and Why and When,
And How and Where and Who.

Sometimes you see these listed as the "five Ws"; they leave out the "how" for some reason.

Put less poetically, journalists are taught to put these six components (what, where, when, how, why, and who) very early in every article. So, when they're looking at your press release, they want to see who it is, what it's about, and so forth, immediately.

Another way to look at this is that journalists are overwhelmed and/or lazy. So it's hard to get their attention and it helps you to be quick, clear, and have done their work for them.

The best publicity release I ever received as an editor was for one of our computer publications in the construction area. It was so good, you couldn't tell who had sponsored it.

The publicity people had gone out and gotten the head of worldwide construction consulting at a giant consulting firm to author the piece, and a very objective and clear story had been written on the importance of computers in construction. Then, in the middle of the story, a few examples were given. The article said, for instance, that some of the leading programs in different areas are X for project management, Y for accounting, and so forth. Providing multiple examples (or quote sources) gives an item depth, rather than looking like a promotion piece for you. Clearly, it was one of the cited companies that had sponsored the story, but it was so well done that you couldn't determine which one.

What Editors Want

There is another side to this. I participate in studies of editors, and what we like or dislike about press releases.

Most editors are remarkably open to press releases. (Remember the estimates that 90 percent of what you see, hear, and read comes from video, audio, and printed PR.) What editors don't like are press releases that are not appropriate for their audiences or publications. This means you need to identify your release as relevant to editors very quickly.

If you say that you're a local resident, it lets your local paper know that it's relevant to its readers. If you're going for a national trade publication, you should identify yourself as part of that industry.

COMBINING APPROACHES: AN EXAMPLE

Now, let's take the idea of tying to a trend, and give an example of how you would take a journalistic approach to writing up the story.

Every year we know that there are new tax laws, there is April 15th, when taxes are due, and there's the end of the year—the last time you can take certain deductions. If you're an accountant, tax lawyer, or book-keeper, it is natural to prepare comments on the "new" tax law.

How Would a Reporter Write It?

If you are a journalist, to do the story right you might interview representatives of the National Society of CPAs to get their views on the tax laws. You might interview your local politician or someone who is on the committee of the state or federal government who passed the tax law. And you might interview the head of the National Taxpayers' Association, or a client for a different view.

Your story would talk about the new tax law and would contain quotes from people who had different perspectives, such as the CPAs, the Taxpayers' Association, and the legislator. By the way, it's no problem to get quotes from these groups. You know how to find them because it's your field, or you use a library. They cooperate because they want publicity too!

In the middle of the story, a section might say, "Local expert Sally Smith says that in our area, people are going to be more affected by this aspect of the law, and less affected by that aspect of the law, because our area has higher income, lower income, a different kind of business, and other specifics."

That's the way a journalist would write it. If you're the local tax person, that's the way you should write a sophisticated press release.

If you're good enough at it, some of the weekly papers often will publish the article exactly as it is, putting their own names or yours on it. But bigger media, which are harder to crack, will at least feel comfortable with it because it's written the way they would write it. Of course, you've also done their work for them.

The Press Kit

For big-time stories, you may need a full media kit. This used to be sent out in a fancy folder. However, now major media often prefer to get just what they need from your company's Web site. A kit can include a press release, a photo, a set of questions and answers, background on your company, and interviews or statements from several different people. Rather than having to do the work, media representatives get it all from you.

FEATURES AND BRIEF ITEMS

When trying to get publicity, don't overlook the personal things about yourself that may be newsworthy in the Features or Lifestyles sections, rather than Business. This could be a collection or hobby, charity work, background, skills, education, and so forth.

In many local and trade papers, there are columns specifically for brief business items. Here, in just a few lines, they'll note hiring, firing, moving, seminars, and the like. If you've obtained a new big client, it might be mentioned there.

Anytime you have an anniversary, expansion, or change in your business, send in brief items for these columns, and you'll often get good results. For instance, for one of my businesses, we had a notice published about our one-year-anniversary open house. It generated four or five calls, and one of the callers became a client.

COLUMNS AND ARTICLES

In most papers and magazines, there are regular columns by experts in different areas. As already mentioned, this is the first publicity most service providers want to get, but these are actually quite difficult to obtain. It's even harder to become a regular on radio or TV. (However, as mentioned, your local cable franchise probably has a cable access channel where you can produce your own TV show for free.)

One way to get started is to try for single articles (or appearances). For instance, in several of the publishing association newsletters I read, most of the articles are by vendors obviously soliciting business. Find out what is planned in future issues (the editorial calendar) and discuss possible articles with the editor. I know one case where many editors told a professional speaker that they were unlikely to use his articles. But when he sent in a collection on disk, they used many of them. Not only were they well written, but there's nothing more attractive than having prewritten material when a deadline is looming! (Editors can be lazy too.)

As you get to know your local trade media, you will have more opportunities to write a guest or regular column. The biggest opportunity will come in newsletters by organizations, where volunteer editors are always short of material, or with smaller Web sites and e-zines. If you can be counted on to fill a few inches, you often will earn their gratitude and have a constant outlet for your thoughts.

HOW TO APPROACH THE MEDIA

If you're appealing to local media, such as weekly or daily papers, I recommend that you give them a call.

Don't Use Press Releases for Local Items

Press releases are rather impersonal. Most media people receive dozens of them every day, sometimes hundreds. If you have to contact dozens of places, you must use a press release, but it's much better to call each place personally.

Placing stories is just like selling anything else. The more personal the approach, the better your odds. Remember that you may be able to obtain future publicity if you build relationships now.

The absolutely best way to build a relationship for the future is to invite contacts out to lunch if you have a good story. The next best is to visit them by appointment, next best is on the phone, and next a personal letter.

Get Journalists to "Find" You

Journalists are funny creatures. (Being one myself, I can say this without too much bias.) They know that people want to get publicity, so they worry about being exploited. But, at the same time, they depend on people who come to them, because they don't spend much time out in the community looking for stories. And it's expensive to do so; no paper has enough staff to cover its local area well.

This creates a paradox. Journalists like to discover you, and they don't like the feeling that you are simply contacting them to get publicity. So what do you do?

Playing a bit dumb can help. Try acting modest and say, "I don't really know if this is of any use to you, but a friend of mine suggested that I call you," then let them draw it out of you. When they say, "Can you send a press release?" you can say something like, "I can write it up in a couple of pages and send you a note." They'll say that's fine.

Involve the Media

You, the media, and a charity make good cosponsors for events designed to garner publicity. In Milwaukee, a public broadcast TV station had one hundred chairs decorated as a contest for its fund-raising auction. That got it one hundred other people to help with publicity, and lots of creativity and coverage in other media.

!

Get a Referral

If you apply these principles—that reporters are busy or lazy, like to discover things for themselves, and resent being exploited—the absolutely best way to contact them is through a referral.

Someone who knows them says, "By the way, I met an interesting person at a group last night; you might be able to get a good story out of it." Now, they haven't had to do much work and can feel like they found you. They become more eager to do the story.

Being referred is always better than cold-calling, as discussed in Chapter Eight (on networking) and Chapter Fourteen (on referrals).

An extreme case of someone who went even further to gain a "natural" introduction to journalists is given in *Marketing Without Advertising*. An author took a part-time job as a taxicab driver during the American Booksellers Association convention. She only picked up fares from the convention and talked with all passengers. She told them that she was looking for possible reviewers for her book. She met a couple of reviewers directly and got another ten introductions to reviewers by passengers who admired her *chutzpah* and creativity. Most of them later reviewed her book!

Press Releases

While not your most effective way, the classic tool to reach the media is to send a press release or a press kit. (There is a sample of a press release in the Appendix.)

The most interesting press kit we ever got was a large box. The late Stanley Marcus, of Neiman-Marcus, told me that a box will get through to almost anyone. This large box had fourteen different boxes or bags of chocolate chip cookies in it! It was promoting a book with the theme that a proliferation of products in every area in the marketplace means you have to differentiate yourself effectively in order to compete. The cookies got a lot of attention and generated many stories and book reviews.

Just don't get too fancy. Journalists tell negative stories about press releases that arrive full of confetti that falls out and makes a mess all over their desks.

In a survey of editors, 45 percent said they get more than thirty press releases a day. (E-mail has grown the number). About 20 percent said they read more than 50 percent of the releases, and a third said they scan them all. In other words, they really *do* look at them. However, 42 percent said 10 percent or less were actually useful. Remember, editors are looking for something very early on that shows that the release is appropriate for their audience.

Editors suggest that you read their magazines or newspapers and send in custom-tailored information. Be sure to keep your mailing list up to date so your release doesn't go to someone who's no longer there.

Interestingly, editors are not being deluged by phone calls. Sixty-two percent of the editors said they receive five or fewer suggestions for articles each week. While most of the suggestions they receive aren't useful, this is a way to find out what they want.

What Editors Say

In a survey, editors said their favorite basis for doing a feature on a company was an interview with a company executive or other specialist. Eighty-one percent judged the value of interviews positively. They would prefer the person to come to their offices. Next most popular were meetings at trade shows, followed by facility tours and demonstrations. Press conferences were the least popular.

Some of the other tips editors gave were: Write better releases, provide a brief summary, avoid B.S. and hyperbole, be clear and to the point, have a good headline, keep releases to one page, and be sure to date them.

A SAMPLE APPROACH: ASK, DON'T TELL

Once I thought I had a clever idea for publicity for an upholstery business in which I had invested.

Upholstery companies accumulate old pieces of furniture. They generally don't have time to work on them because they are working on paid business. As a special event, I wanted to offer people a free item if they had it reupholstered; that is, if they wanted a chair, they would pay for its reupholstery, and we would give them the chair free!

My Great Idea Flops

I thought it was a great idea. I called one of the local columnists who wrote a short-item column, and told him my idea. He said something like, "It sounds like an advertising item. You probably want to take an ad for that." I thought he was an idiot.

I was so upset about it, I called another newspaper business columnist, and gave him the same information. He told me the same thing!

In disgust, I called back the first one and asked him what would be interesting for an upholstery company's open house. He said consumer education—how to care for fabric, how to tell quality construction or quality upholstery. It sounded really boring and trite to me, but it fit the newspaper's mandate to provide information that serves its readers more than the people it is talking about. And that is, in fact, the press release I wrote. It was then published and got people to come to the company.

TARGETING INDIVIDUAL PEOPLE AT THE PAPER

Most papers have multiple staff. There are a number of columnists and sections in each paper that select their own material. For example, the Business, Feature, and Lifestyle editors all might take a story on "women in business." By seeing what they write about over time, you can design stories that will appeal to each journalist.

Or you may need to get around a particular editor. For instance, my friend Al was head of a sister cities group that linked a city in the United States with one in Japan. The woman in charge of covering community groups told him that she'd only do one story on each group per year (and she was generally a pain in the neck). So Al simply went down the list of other sections. He started with food, of all things. But it turned out that the editor there was eager to have items about Japanese food and recipes, so Al had the possibility of a regular column! You never know.

In our local paper at one point, one columnist was a man who was teaching at the local community college. The way to meet him would have been to take his course at the college.

Another columnist was an older woman who wrote about life issues. Every once in a while, she'd do a column whose basic theme was: "Older, boring woman does something wacky." If you invited her to go to the mud baths or to be "Rolfed," or have her tea leaves read, she would do it and then write a very interesting column about what it was like to be a first-timer.

Give Journalists a Reason to Meet You

Another standard way to meet journalists is to invite them to speak to a group on "how to get publicity." You can do a favor for your group by lining this up, and you'll receive some simple advice.

In my experience with this approach, I've found that "leading journalists to water" isn't enough—that is, having seen your group or having met you, they don't automatically write about you. Just use this approach to flatter them and get acquainted. Then follow up later to build the relationship.

Save Individual Journalists' Names

Look for individual names on stories in the sections that interest you. For instance, in the Business section, there are usually several business reporters. If you send in a general business release, the business editor may or may not like it and assign it to an individual. Trying individuals first gives you more chances of getting published. If the reporters don't respond, you can then try the editors.

Stand Out from the Crowd

One smart publicist, Spoma, used to put her press releases on light-purple paper. When editors said they didn't remember seeing a release, she could say, "It's the one on purple paper," and they could often see it in the pile of white press releases on their desks.

Keep clippings and names of people who write particular business stories. The individual names will give you multiple chances to gain public exposure. By having names, you can make calls to each individual reporter directly, as my friend Al did.

HOW TO USE PUBLICITY CORRECTLY

There's a much-overlooked fact about publicity alluded to earlier. Publicity is worth much more to you *after* it appears than immediately.

People will see your letters to the editor, the stories about you, and the stories in which you are quoted. You might get some calls, business, or recognition from these (as well as people trying to sell you things!). But publicity actually has a much bigger impact after the fact, when it's no longer fresh. That's because you should clip the items, and copy them. Then, you pass them out to people you're talking to about business.

You keep items in your office as part of your portfolio. You can even use clippings to send to the media. Rather than hurting your chances of a new story, past publicity will help them. The media "borrow" from each other all the time. Save radio and TV interviews as well, and provide online links to items about you.

Clippings give you a credential. People feel that if the local media have covered you or published your letters, they must have screened you in some way; that you must be trustworthy and good at what you do. Of

Possible Ideas for Press Releases

Here is the start of a list of possible topics for news releases you might send out now:

- new services you're offering
- major clients you've obtained
- studies you've completed
- office move or expansion
- new use for an existing service
- some unusual service you offer
- a new certification you've gained, or degree you've earned
- a seminar you're giving
- anniversaries of the company or long-term employees
- memberships in associations
- new training programs for employees
- attending a trade show or exhibit
- success stories based on clients
- company visits by famous people
- a new trademark or publication
- speaking engagements
- available handouts
- reprints of your speeches
- travel for assignments
- personal hobbies
- your company contributions to the community, including employees volunteering time
- awards you give your own employees
- retirements
- civic activities
- fund-raising events for the local community
- sponsoring local programs
- available internships with local schools
- scholarships or community exhibits
- projection or trend forecasts

!

Your Own Billboard

It's almost impossible in California to get a billboard on 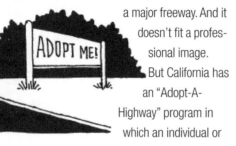 a major freeway. And it doesn't fit a professional image. But California has an "Adopt-A-Highway" program in which an individual or company pays to keep a stretch of highway litter free in exchange for a sign on the highway with the individual's or company's name. (Hawaii and other states have this too.)

An insurance agent used to pass a rival's sign each day on the way home from work. He realized how deeply embedded in his mind this rival's name had become. The agent signed up and got his own stretch of highway.

The recognition factor has increased his business.

Now when he calls a cold prospect to explain who he is, he can say he's "the guy with the sign," and an immediate connection is made.

!

course, none of this is true. But it at least shows that you have been around a little bit and were smart enough to read this book and keep your clippings!

LOCAL "PUBLICITY": DISPLAYS AND COUPONS

Wearing interesting outfits, as mentioned in the section on stunts, can get you publicity, but also garners attention on a personal level. While not technically media, simply getting exposure in the neighborhood around your office or home is of value. This is mainly for small businesses. However, large firms can use variations of this by "sponsoring" a display downtown near their offices.

You may have something that's interesting to other people. For instance, one woman makes gourmet chocolates. She has some custom molds for holidays, such as turkeys and Santa Claus. She casts only a few of these items in chocolate for the appropriate holidays. She'll give one to the local bank, in return for putting a little sign on it that reads, Display by Lila's Chocolates.

If you're a contractor, lawyer, or dentist, this is a little harder. But you may have a personal collection of dolls, books, or coins. There may be room for such displays in the local bank or merchants' windows, with a card that states they are on loan from you, Mr./Ms. Orthodontist. I had a display from my book collection in a local library, for example.

PERSONAL NETWORKING

Serving on boards of charities and meeting people at networking events could be considered personal publicity. We'll cover networking in Chapter Eight, but remember that meeting people directly can create the most basic type of publicity, word of mouth.

Serving on the boards of charities and local organizations, or otherwise volunteering time to help them, does show you off at your best, which is what publicity is meant to do. Volunteering is a chance to meet other people who have a good community attitude. And people who also take time out of their busy schedules to serve on such boards usually give you the benefit of the doubt when they meet you as a fellow board member; they assume that you're the "right" kind of person.

CONCLUSION

You are now in a position to effectively "exploit the media." However, you also understand that, as in all relationships, you must give the media what they want in order to receive the coverage you want. Similarly, many of the new activities you undertake for publicity will serve the community as you contribute your time and efforts to charities or special events.

Start by setting up a systematic program of submitting quick letters and articles. Then develop long-term approaches to major publicity. Soon your name will be out there regularly.

AGENDA

To move the world, we must first move ourselves.
SOCRATES

Quick Publicity

▶ Write a letter to the editor of your local newspaper and a trade publication your clients read.
▶ Go online and contribute to a discussion group or submit a 100-word article to an e-zine.
▶ Check the lists on page 169 and page 346 to see what press releases you could send out now.

► Gather copies of any print publicity you've gotten in the past and make clean copies.

► Donate a gift certificate to a local school or charity.

► Look for unusual pictures that the media would like.

► Become an advocate for something about which you can write.

Medium-Term Publicity

► Work on press releases tied to upcoming holidays or other general trends.

► Create a handout to give away of ten tips in your field.

► Create an award to give out in your field.

► Give a talk at a local Rotary Club and send a press release about it to the business calendar of your local newspaper.

► Talk to interesting clients about getting them publicity.

► Invite a journalist to speak at a group.

► Start creating a list of all possible publications in which you would want publicity.

► If appropriate, think about an outfit and/or persona you could use to attract attention.

► Call the local cable access channel and sign up for and attend the producer's course.

► Add a "press" section to your Web site.

Long-Term Publicity

► Start a research project to collect information from people you want to contact, in a field where you want to be recognized as an expert.

► Start to save clippings of articles from columnists and reporters in media relevant to your area.

CHAPTER EIGHT

NETWORKING

Build Relationships for More Clients

> *Other things being equal, people do business
> with people they like.
> Other things not being equal, they still do business
> with people they like.*
> MARK MCCORMACK,
> *What They Don't Teach You at
> Harvard Business School*

If you're selling services, who you know controls your success more than what you know. Even more, it's who knows you!

This chapter will show you how to improve your networking at least 300 percent. Many people think that networking is a frill they can ignore. They're wrong. Good contacts are what build and sustain your business. Don't put off networking!

"REAL" NETWORKING BUILDS RELATIONSHIPS

This chapter will give you seventeen specific, practical techniques that can each improve your networking substantially if you're not using them now. But don't get carried away with techniques. Keep in mind that the more important goal is to build relationships and make friends. What you need is people who *want* to do business with you.

Networking is a form of personal sales in some ways. You meet people and let them know what you do. Perhaps they give you a try or request further information. You build the relationship to build trust and rapport.

Networking is also about creating referrals. You meet people, they're impressed by you, they tell their friends, and you have a warm invitation to talk about doing business.

The Negative Side of Networking

Networking has both a good and bad reputation. We know that personal contacts are the best way to get business. But book titles such as *How to Work a Room* imply that you're "working" or manipulating people to get something from them.

There are two ways to build a network of customers and friends: retail and wholesale. Retail means the one-at-a-time kind of contacts that are built up through participation in community or social activities. Wholesale means the recognition and acceptance extended by people who don't know you personally but who have heard about you as a speaker, read your articles, or read about you in civic activities in the papers.

Harvey Mackay

People have said they are afraid of being "networked." It's not a correct use of the word, but it means that people who are working the room come up to you, try to quickly assess if they can get anything from you, and then move on if they can't. It is important that you not approach networking this way.

THE POWER OF NETWORKING

The 1993 movie *Six Degrees of Separation* had the premise that everyone is within six people of everyone else in the country or the world.

This is the true power of networking. You can build direct contact with twenty, fifty, one hundred, or perhaps five hundred people. The power of networking begins when you think of all the people *they* know.

It Really Works

Few people know it, but the close connection of everyone to everyone has actually been proven.

Yale social psychologist Stanley Milgram did a study years ago that found that we were within about five links of anyone else in the country, on a first-name basis. Milgram had people on the West Coast try to reach a person on the East Coast. All they were given was the person's name, and the fact that he was a stockbroker in Boston.

The rules were that you had to call people you knew on a first-name basis. Then they had to call people they knew on a first-name basis, and so on, until you reached the stockbroker in Boston.

Most people knew a stockbroker or someone in Boston. Once they were into the target person's geographical or occupational network, it took several links to reach the person.

Jane Fonda Is My Ticket to the Big Time!

On average, people who played and completed Milgram's game did so in only five links. For instance, I'm only three links away from Jane Fonda, and, of course, she knows many famous, powerful people.

This is not to say that Jane Fonda knows me from Adam, but I'm good friends with a psychologist I met through work twenty years ago. Jane Fonda's foster sister once worked for him as an intern. And, of course, she would know how to reach Jane.

The funny thing about this type of networking is that you never know who you're close to until you ask for something or reach out and tell people you have a newsletter, a political interest, or are raising money for a charity. Then you discover that these people know others who may help you.

Tips for Smart Networking

- Know what you want to accomplish when you meet people. When attending a specific event, review your goals or write additional ones.
- Always have business cards in your pocket or purse.
- Reinforce yourself. Write down the results of networking. For instance, after every event, make a note of each conversation you had. You'll be surprised at things you've learned or benefited from. Remember that benefits from networking vary from learning a new joke, to making potential new friends, to business leads.

THE HISTORY OF NETWORKING

"Old-boy networks" have always created a lot of business.

People who knew each other from clubs, school, or early jobs (usually men) steered business and career opportunities to each other throughout their lives. If they knew you, you were assumed to be okay.

The good thing about these classic networks is that people are less likely to take advantage of each other if they know that the others in the "club" might hear about it. The bad thing is that it is hard for newcomers to break into a network.

Networking became popularized in the 1980s by women. They began to analyze their exclusion from the old-boy networks and they systematically set up networking groups. Because they thought it out, their groups tended to be more efficient and more fun.

YOUR NETWORKS

We automatically belong to a number of different networks. We have networks of friends, networks from the schools we attended or schools our children attend, neighborhood networks, job networks, and networks based on spare-time activities. I've even met people who renewed old acquaintances at *grammar school* reunions!

Most of your best contacts will already be in one of your existing networks. In a way, the best marketing you can do is to get the people in your natural networks to want to market for you.

GETTING TO KNOW STRANGERS

Dealing with an "Old-Boy" Network

Existing networks aren't always hostile to non-members, they just aren't always encouraging. Ken Blanchard says, "When you want to be accepted in other people's worlds, you need to make the effort to enter. You've got to show that you're trying to fit in. Show your interest and give it time."

!

Meeting new people with whom you have no connection is much harder, even though some groups are set up to facilitate this. While these groups give "permission" to make contacts with new people, they also make it somewhat artificial and uncomfortable. It's much more natural when you have a leisure activity in common, and you begin to chat about what you do.

The book *What Color Is Your Parachute?*, by Richard Bolles, has been around forever. It introduced a job-search technique that is a classic. He calls it "informational interviewing." This approach is ideal for people who are new in business or to an area or industry. That's your reason to contact strangers. However, you can use other reasons.

In Bolles's method, if you're looking for a job, you contact people and tell them that you're doing some extensive research about their field—and that you are hoping to get some well thought out advice from them to educate yourself. In your case, perhaps you're looking for information in a new area.

Gather Information

Because this is nonthreatening, people don't feel you're selling to them. You interview them about their field, as if you were a reporter. You get their advice on where they think the growth areas are, and so on.

Once You Know Something

You do this with maybe ten, twenty, or thirty people. Now you should understand the needs in this area. You can show people how, by hiring you, they can take care of something that's not being done.

Apply This to Your Service

Pick a specialty you're interested in and research it. Perhaps you're a lawyer starting to work in construction law, an accountant targeting downtown retailers, a printer aiming at ad agencies, a consultant targeting restaurants, a restaurant aiming at singles, or some other case.

Repeat Contacts

After you have a grasp of the field, you call back some of the thirty people with whom you talked in this network. When you first spoke to them, you probably didn't come across as too well informed, either because they were doing all the talking or because you *weren't* too well informed.

Now, you will come across to them as a knowledgeable person in their area. You can tell them, "Based on what you and a number of other people told me, it seems to me that what's needed in this field is someone to do XYZ. Would this apply to your company? I have some ideas I'd like to share with you. Could we talk about how we might create a service contract to meet this need?"

Now You Have Something to Offer

If you do this with different people, about things you truly believe in and have learned about, you stand a much better chance of getting a new client than with advertising or other traditional approaches.

You approach people with a proposition custom-designed for their situation, based on an intimate knowledge of their needs and their field.

> Authors need to invite everyone, including the people they helped with fifth-grade homework!
>
> Elaine Petrocelli
> bookstore owner
> on authors' talks

WHAT NETWORKING CAN DO FOR YOU

Being in contact with other people—new acquaintances or old—can do lots of things for you besides providing direct business or direct referrals.

People in your network can provide for your social needs or be a source of positive thinking, encouragement, and support. They can care about you. They can give you free consulting and referrals.

The fact that others can meet our needs in many ways is why we're called "social animals." And this is another reason you should approach networking as having fun meeting new people, *not* as working to get the most you can from them.

SEVENTEEN WAYS TO NETWORK BETTER

Now, let's look at seventeen ways to improve your networking 100 percent. If you are not already using them, any one of these can double your effectiveness, in terms of people you meet or the impression you make. (But using them all won't improve your networking 1,700 percent!)

1. Keep Track of Who You Know

If you're like me, you "know" a lot more people than you can identify quickly. You may have piles of business cards different places. Or you may lose track of people when you don't see them.

Now is a good time to make sure you have a system, such as a contact manager or database. It will serve as an "extended brain" for you. You'll have more people at your fingertips and be able to keep in touch to better build relationships.

2. Remember Names Better

Our brains tend to remember faces much better than names. There is nothing more embarrassing than recognizing people, but being unable to recall their names. (Actually there *is* something more embarrassing:

On Remembering Names

Harvey Mackay tells a story about how remembering names helped a nonprofit school: "I know the headmaster of a private school who makes it a practice to learn the names of each of the over one thousand kids attending his school. If they're new and he hasn't met them, he learns their names by studying their pictures. On the first day of each year, when the buses arrive to drop off the kids at school, he greets each one by name as he or she gets off the bus. Imagine how reassuring it is to a frightened first-grader, suddenly thrust into strange surroundings, to be recognized immediately by an adult who is in charge of his life. Or to the child's anxious parents who have plunked down $5,000 for tuition. When they ask Junior how it went the first day, they discover that the headmaster of the school has taken a personal interest in their child.

"In the twelve years that headmaster has been at the school, enrollment has more than doubled, the school has moved to a grand new facility that is clearly the finest in the area, and the endowment has been increased sixfold. Not all the result of learning those names, of course, but it certainly didn't hurt to have a headmaster who understood that his performance as a salesperson was as important as his role as an educator."

When they remember your name, and you don't remember theirs!)

Originally, it was thought that visualizing something ridiculous about a face, and connecting it with the name, was the most effective way to remember names.

For instance, if someone's name was Bill Yazinitski, you would transform it to, "Yes, in it I ski." Then you would visualize someone skiing down his nose and jumping out at you. Next, you would imagine dollar bills falling on the snow, so you'd know it was Bill Yazinitski. Actually, just remembering one part of the name—"ski"—often allows you to recall the rest.

Some Easy Ways to Help Remember Names

Make sure you heard the name right in the first place, by repeating it or asking the person to repeat it. Use the name in conversation. Many people say that there's nothing people love more than the sound of their own names. And, by using it, you are helping embed it in your memory. Similarly, writing a name down will often help you remember it, even if you never look at your notes.

The art of memory is the art of attention.

Samuel Johnson

Make a List

Especially if you're part of a large firm, there may be only a limited number of big clients that would be beneficial new business for you. Do your research. Make a list of organizations you want to approach and people who might provide you with contacts. Go to groups to which they belong. Then, when you run into them, you'll be prepared to introduce yourself.

!

3. Pay Attention

When you're meeting a new person, you may observe things that help you build a relationship. For instance, if you're in her office, you may see trophies for tennis, a diploma from a particular university, or other evidence of her family, hobbies, and so forth. These make good points of conversation, which allow you to build a social relationship and get on a more personal standing.

If your conversation proceeds directly into business, you'll never have the rapport that first talking about others and their interests brings.

The ideal case is discovering something in common. Then it becomes natural to talk further and eventually move into talking about business. Similarity makes people less defensive and more open to relationships. They know that you didn't attend the same school they did just so you could sell them something!

If you want to play "crystal ball," you can guess a lot about people by the way they dress, their accents, the way they speak, the way they hold their bodies, the way they look around the room, and other cues.

Once, in a group meeting, a fellow came in, and during introductions he said he was in "real estate." Many people in real estate are salespeople who are not particularly successful, and often work part-time. It turned out that Henry had owned real estate around the country, put together investment packages, and had a very interesting background. By observing his quiet confidence and calm demeanor you could guess that he was a successful person.

4. Project Sincerity

People will also observe you as well. If you flit about in a hyperactive way, only briefly stopping to talk to each person or group, others will decide that you are not a sincere person worth talking to in detail.

A man at one networking group I attended said that he was trying to collect as many cards as possible. So what? I gave him my card, but after he pushed his on me I threw it away. He did not start a conversation; he simply talked minimally to me, took my card, gave me his, and left. Though he had my card, he didn't follow up, so what was the point?

Similarly, there are people who must have taken a course that told them to ask questions of others to be attractive. Unfortunately, some of them approach this like a prisoner interrogation! They run through their questions without telling you about themselves. They violate the psychological rule of reciprocity: that when one person reveals something, the other must reveal something in return.

The point here is to be authentic. Let people know who you are. Use honesty. As someone once said, it will tend to confound the devious and attract people who appreciate the strengths you project.

5. Improve Your Self-Introduction

Most people use what I call a "prisoner-of-war" introduction (perhaps because of some people's "interrogation" techniques). They give their name, rank, and serial number; for example, "I'm Sue Smith. I'm an accountant and work with small businesses." That's about as unrevealing as you can get and still be cordial.

Improving your introduction won't feel natural at first, and it will take you a good deal of time to develop and practice a new one. But it's something you can use forever. People want to know who you are. Even in a social setting, rather than just giving them your name, rank, and serial number, you can briefly give them more information which intrigues them and makes them want to talk with you longer.

What Makes a Better Self-Introduction?

Here are five ways to improve your introduction. You'll have to work to come up with one you are comfortable with and that honestly projects your strengths and personal style. Combine several of them for the strongest possible introduction.

1. Enthusiasm Who wants to talk to someone who doesn't enjoy what he does or who's depressed? Have you ever asked someone how she was feeling, and she actually told you that her knee hurt, her in-laws were in

Be First

Stand near the entrance early in the event so you can see who comes in. Then you can plan with whom you want to talk during the rest of the night.

Your Elevator Speech

Your self-introduction needs to interest people in talking with you and help them remember you. Think about a high-speed elevator—you have only ten to twenty seconds to make an impression.

town, blah, blah, blah? Who cares? Be enthusiastic about what you do, and speak with a positive tone of voice.

2. Show a Sense of Humor People rate humor very highly. Humor does not mean that you're good at telling jokes; it means that you don't take yourself too seriously. Therefore, humor that pokes fun at yourself or your profession often is seen as revealing and very positive, particularly if you're in an intimidating profession, such as law or banking.

3. Reveal Something a Little Personal About Yourself Psychological research shows that people tend to reciprocate. If you say something personal, the other person will tend to respond with something personal. Next, you might reveal a little more, and they reveal more.

This is how friendships get started. If someone doesn't reciprocate, it's often a sign that he or she is not open to relationships, not friendly, or is not the type of person you want to know.

We're not talking about telling people things they can blackmail you with! We're talking about saying something that doesn't sound like you're a prisoner of war.

For instance, revealing that you're a little shy at this kind of networking function is a perfect example. Most people feel a little shy at a cocktail party or in a group where they don't know many others. If you add a little flattery—"I'm always a little uncomfortable meeting new people. You seem very at ease. How do you do it?"—this pulls them into the conversation.

4. Use Trivia Have some bits of trivia about your field or the local area that would be memorable. Everybody likes to learn something interesting as long as it's painless! For instance, earlier there was the example of an economist who might tell you the size of the local economy compared to small countries in the world. A Realtor could have stories about unusual local houses. A financial planner could talk about local companies that were good investments. That's interesting trivia.

5. Build an Implied Testimonial into Your Introduction How do you build a testimonial (or endorsement) into your own introduction? If you are General Motors, you may be able to say, "We're particularly proud this month that the Powers Survey has found our cars to be number one in their marketplace." But since most of you don't have formal market research by independent consumer organizations about how good you are, you'll have to imply a testimonial or build it in yourself. I like the phrase "My clients tell me that . . ."

Combining several of the items above, you could say, "Most people think accounting is rather dull. I have to admit that even I don't like accountant parties, but I really enjoy the work, because my clients tell me that they love my taking the hassle off their hands. They bring in their shoe boxes and don't have to worry about it." That's a little lengthy, but you get the point. "My clients tell me that . . ."— then, you use humor, enthusiasm, and a prime benefit.

The prime benefit (discussed in Chapter Three) should be what people want the most. It might be price, quality, value, or something more subtle, such as not having to worry; for instance, "My clients tell me that they like the fact that I go to bat for them."

It's often effective to combine self-deprecating humor and some of the other techniques. For example, "My clients tell me that they like working with me, despite the fact that I'm a lawyer."

Active Listening Skills

Active listening skills involve more than just listening to what others say. Here are a few guidelines:

- Face the person speaking head-on.
- Pay attention and hold eye contact.
- Lean slightly toward the person.
- Nod and say "uh-huh" occasionally.
- Suspend judgment about what the person is saying.
- Don't be preparing what you want to say.
- "Reflect" what the person says by saying, "Then you're saying that . . ."
- Mirror some of the person's body language; for instance, put your hands in similar positions.
- Agree when you can; don't say, "Yes, but . . . "

The Perfect Introduction?

It might take you a long time to develop the perfect introduction. I've met perhaps one person in a hundred who had a great one. It was often customized and didn't follow a clear formula like those I've given you.

Let's try a few "fill-in-the-blank" structures to see if you can come up with a draft introduction that is brief and comfortable for you. Then you can go on from there.

"Hello, I'm _____. I really enjoy being a _____ because my clients tell me that I _____ ."

"Hi, I help [type of client] accomplish [their goal]." (This often leads naturally to listeners asking what your profession is.)

"Hello, I'm _____. I just heard that [trivia]. No normal person would know stuff like that [self-deprecating humor], but I happen to be a _____ , so I have an interest."

6. Listen More Than You Talk

As discussed in Chapter Six on sales, most people talk too much. Boorish people tend to tell you all about themselves without determining your interest in what they say.

The art of great conversation is—paradoxically—being a good listener. Ask questions that draw out the other person. When it's your turn to talk, be brief. When you talk, you're not learning anything new.

There's one question that is particularly good for both getting to know others and making a positive impression. In the years that I've been going to networking-type groups, only a handful of people have ever asked me this. *Ask people what would be a good referral for them.* This clarifies for you what they really do. And it tells them that you are not just thinking about what you can get from them. It also encourages them to reciprocate and ask you the same question. Which leads us to the next point . . .

Share Humor

Keep a list of truly funny, tasteful jokes for especially helpful, receptive contacts you meet on the phone or in person. This does three things:

1. It establishes you as an individual human being,
2. it brightens up someone's day and gives him "something" for his time, and
3. it establishes rapport through shared laughter.

7. Ask for Referrals

Ask for referrals, even from strangers.

Say, "I've never been to this group before. What kinds of people come?" If they have never attended before either, you have something in common. If they've been there before, they become a source of advice for you. Then, you can ask if there is anyone there to whom you should speak.

If you ask someone for business, he can become defensive. But if you ask for an idea or referral, he's often happy to give you a lead.

If you are an architect talking to a new person, you could ask her if she has any need for design or if she is considering remodeling. But this is fairly aggressive and can make people close up.

It's much better to ask if she knows anyone who uses architects. Then, she can give you a lead. Even if you suspect that people themselves have a need, it's better for *them* to bring it up. Then they've invited you to present to them. Asking for their advice is much less threatening to them.

You can actually obtain multiple referrals from each person. Unless you know that those referred have a strong need for your service, you're better off telling them that "Sally suggested that I call because you'd be a good person to talk to about my field. Could you give me a minute on the phone or in person?" Each contact can actually produce two or three more contacts. Your list of contacts and referrals can get bigger and bigger as you keep going. You'll never run out of leads.

8. Read the "Monday" Business Calendars

As mentioned in Chapter Seven on publicity, in most papers there are calendars of seminars and meetings

Systematically note upcoming seminars and meetings. Better yet, develop a database. Even if you don't visit a group, you'll have the name, the type of people it serves, a contact phone number, meeting place, and so forth. This will be valuable for your future scheduling and some of the next tips.

SAMPLE BUSINESS CALENDAR

■ WEDNESDAY, 11/30

COMMUNITY ENTEPRENEURS ORGANIZATION: The regular monthly meeting of CEO will be held from 7:30 to 9:30 P.M. at 45 San Clemente Dr., Suite 130, Corte Madera, CA. There will be mingling, introductions, and brainstorming. A panel will discuss "How to Start Your Own Business." Cost is $5.00. Call 415/209-9838 for more information.

COLLEGE OF MARIN: A workshop on "Marketing Your Services" will be offered at 170 Harlan Center from 6 to 10 P.M. by Dr. Sally Smith. Cost is $45. Reservations at the door or call 415/555-1612 for information.

---

9. Regularly Visit Groups and Join the Best

Systematically visit the groups you learn about and join the best. These can be industry groups, social groups, leisure groups, or business parties.

Groups are the easiest way to meet a lot of people at one time. Often, they're very stable and supportive; other times, each meeting attracts different people. In running a networking group for more than a decade, I've seen much business done, many friendships made, lots of stimulation, and quite a few speakers. There are many interesting and useful groups out there. (See pages 192 to 195 for a discussion of types of groups.)

Ask!

When you're mingling in a group and want to find a particular type of person, ask. Ask the people at the door, ask the president, ask the speaker. They'll point you to the people in the group who fit your needs.

Casual Visiting Isn't Enough

As a visitor, you'll get only a partial picture of a group. Perhaps one meeting will be enough for you to know if the group is for you; often, it isn't.

If a group looks good, you normally have to ante up something to join. That gets you on the mailing list and may get you discounts on events. Joining won't be enough to open up the "inner secrets" of many groups for you. Sometimes, only time can do this. Normally, someone has to see you several times before he or she feels comfortable with you.

The leaders of groups often look for someone who is willing to contribute. So if a group looks good, volunteer to do something.

Pick something easy. Volunteer to sit at the door and make name tags or make change. I've even done this for a group I was visiting for the first time. It gave me a chance to see who came to the group, and I'm more comfortable with a job to do rather than mingling in a party-type atmosphere.

A related tip is to save nice badges with your name on them. You can also make one yourself by putting your business card in a plastic holder.

This makes a good conversation opener. People will ask you why your badge is different, or why you have one at all if they don't. I keep a badge and business cards in the pockets of all my "dress-up" coats. That way I always have them with me at events.

10. Make Notes on Business Cards

Make notes on business cards from people who interest you.

In Japan, it's not polite to write on people's cards. Cards must be accepted with two hands with a gracious bow. But in America we're much more casual. If you write on them, it's flattering, because people know you're trying to remember them.

I can't tell you the number of times I've come home from meetings with a pocketful of cards, and I've forgotten why I had taken them. So always make a note of the date and meeting, the topics you've discussed, and the reason you kept the person's card. If people push their cards on you, and you have no interest, simply put the cards in another pocket. When you go home, throw away that bunch!

11. Do Research

Research gives you a reason to talk with people in the group and helps you be memorable.

Based on the idea of writing on business cards mentioned above, a friend of mine, Rick Allen, did a survey at a group. He asked people how they felt about others writing on their cards. Fifteen were positive; they felt flattered. The one negative said that some cultures don't like it. People were interested in his "survey" and even brought other people over to talk with him.

If there's something you could ask that fits your style, give it a try. I sometimes do brief questionnaires on titles for books I'm writing. That gives me a lot of input in a short time, and it helps me mingle.

12. Do Cold Calling

Cold calls are calls to people who have no knowledge of you and didn't ask you to call. Typically, you call a list of prospects that you may have purchased or found. However, it can also be much more informal than that.

Schedule calls to suppliers, competitors, and groups you see listed in the paper. It's okay to call people to whom you are not actually selling. Often they can become referral sources.

Potential suppliers will be eager to talk to you because they could do business with you. Surprisingly enough, you can also have fun talking to competitors. Most competitors don't look at it as a "duel to the death." They know that you often have different areas of specialty, and could be referral sources for each other.

In my experience calling strangers, 30 percent of the people will be friendly, 30 percent will be unresponsive, and 40 percent could go either way.

Cold-Calling Examples

Here are few ideas for ways to open conversations on the phone when you're cold calling. This is calling for networking purposes, not to make a direct sale.

1. "Hello, I'm _____. This may seem a bit unusual, but I saw your name and wondered if you'd be willing to talk for a minute. Is now a good time to talk?" Then you go on to say what your call is about and why you thought the person might be interested.

2. I'm _____ . You don't know me, but I've known who you are because [something flattering, like he or she is an expert]. I wondered if you'd be kind enough to give me a couple of minutes of advice on the phone or over coffee." The person will choose the phone now because it is much easier. If the conversation goes well, you offer to take her out to lunch to report about your success with her ideas, or get further advice.

!

Comfortable Strangers

The hard part about cold calling is that you need some way to make your prospect comfortable talking to a stranger—*you.*

Whether calling on the phone or in person, you need a reason to talk to others. Or, put another way, you need a way to make them feel safe and see a benefit in talking to you.

Here's an extreme example of cold contacts. I discovered that wrong numbers give you an acceptable excuse to talk with strangers. Several times, I've received messages with the numbers written down wrong. When I returned the calls, there was no such person there.

I'd apologize and say, "We are a company that does XYZ, and I just picked up this message." A few times, we've gotten into a conversation, and it turned out that the person at the wrong number had some interest in our business. So a new contact was made.

An Extreme Example of Running into People

Here's an extreme example of meeting new people. A dentist's wife would run into people in the market (and I mean, literally, "run into"). She'd bump into them with her cart and cause a tiny accident. This would give her an excuse to apologize for being clumsy or not paying attention. Then she would introduce herself.

Aside from the manipulation involved, this works pretty well and does not hurt anyone. Everyone needs to have their teeth cleaned, but they avoid the dentist. Having this "accidental" introduction allowed her to recruit people for her husband's practice in what seemed to be a natural way.

If you're standing in line in the market and start a conversation, it's almost natural, but still it's clear you're making the effort. But when you bump into someone, it seems so natural that it actually allows conversations to develop better. It gives you an excuse to get the conversation going.

When You're "New"

If you're new in town or to a business, it's a great excuse to call people. That's one time it's acceptable to talk to strangers. It's expected that new-comers will need help and that people will respond. People will try to be friendly if it's not too much effort.

If you say, "I've just moved into town, or started a new business. Can you tell me where XYZ is located?" it's a chance for them to be friendly at little cost. Being "new" allows you to ask "dumb" questions in a comfortable fashion. And when you're new, you're more eager to make contacts, so it's a good time to reach out.

> The first key to networking is to talk to everyone.
>
> Ken Blanchard

Loosen Up to Be More Creative

I give you extreme examples, like the dentist's wife and the wrong numbers, to stimulate your thinking. They may not apply directly to you. But, in order to improve your effectiveness, you must try new things. As the old saying goes, if you do what you've always done, you'll get what you've always gotten.

You wouldn't have bought this book if you had all the clients you wanted (or the right clients). Be creative and come up with things that you are willing to try or adapt.

13. Do It Online

There is a separate chapter (Chapter Twelve) about online marketing. But it's worth mentioning here that most of the things that can improve your networking can be done online. For instance, online is a perfect place to do the last two items covered—research and cold calling.

14. Follow Up

If there's one method that amplifies all the rest, it's to follow up with people you meet. If you attended a meeting last night, you may have met ten or twenty people. But of all the people they've met, *you* could be the only one to follow up with a brief note or phone call.

If you're interested in the person, follow up while the meeting is fresh in both your minds. Invite yourself to drop by her office. Invite her out for coffee. Or just call or send a note that says how much you enjoyed meeting her and are looking forward to seeing her next time.

If you talk with people about their hobbies or a business field, try to follow up with a clipping that relates to their interests. It's also relatively easy to find such material online.

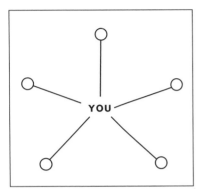

15. Become a "Star"

In the communication field, there are names for different contact/communication networks. One is a star in which you're in the middle. You know everyone in the network, but they don't know each other. By becoming a "star," you're in a position to help everyone with whom you come into contact. And, of course, you learn a lot and benefit too.

16. Give a Lot

The "star" described above is an example of being in a position to both give and receive a lot of information and help. Ultimately, the best way to network is to give a lot to other people. What goes around, comes around.

Jeffrey Lant, in his book *The Unabashed Self-Promoter's Guide*, provides a selfish definition of networking. He sees it like an energy-conservation situation, in which you want to get the most from everyone, and give the least. I think this is not only sociopathic, but stupid. You're much better off generously sharing what you can.

Some people say there are a lot of people out there who aren't "mensches" (they're not "real people"). You can do something for them, but they'll never reciprocate. Be generous in what you give, but stay aware. If someone shows no indications of appreciating or reciprocating, quit giving to them. (See the next section for examples of ways to help others.)

17. Volunteer

Our last networking "method" is to make giving a formal part of your marketing. Volunteer to be on charity or nonprofit boards. Pick a group that stands for something you care about and enjoy. For instance, my oldest son loves coaching girl's softball and has made many contacts as he donates time.

Many groups, from the PTA to local charities, need help. Sometimes they recruit people with legal or accounting expertise to be on their boards.

Other times they recruit people who can give money. But many groups just plain need help. So, if you're willing to make a contribution to your community, this is a way to network with other people who are also willing.

THINGS YOU CAN DO FOR OTHERS

Obvious, but sometimes overlooked, is the fact that the best way to create a network of people who want to do things for you is to do things for them. Many of the things you can do to build relationships are personal. People are often more interested in their hobbies than their work.

Networking expert Sam Wieder points out that there are many distinct business roles you can play that will help others and make them want to help you. Here are my similar "baker's dozen" you may be able to use:

1. *Resource Center.* If you like to collect great business resources (like this book!), share them with others. Audiotapes, videos, books, and business forms are all possible. I do it on the personal side by loaning out movies as well as business material.

2. *Trusted Advisor.* As discussed in Chapter Six on sales, you want to achieve this status with your clients. But you can also be a mentor for new people and others who appreciate your input. Just remember that few people like a critic!

3. *Sounding Board.* Even if you don't have expertise that others can use, you can often act as a test customer. Everybody likes a good listener, and helping people clarify their points is valuable.

4. *Cheerleader.* Sometimes we need people to cheer us on. If you're a positive-type person, being upbeat and cheerful is just what some people need. However, don't force it; some people just like to complain. They don't want to be cheered up!

5. *Bargain Hunter.* When you make a great contact to get something "wholesale" or do the research to choose a big ticket item, you have a resource you can share with others. And you're bringing someone else business while you help your original contact.

Network with People's Advisors

One way to reach top people is through their professional advisors. Your networking can be aimed at them, rather than directly at your target. One large consulting firm builds most of its business by calling other advisors of its clients and suggesting meetings. Since they have clients in common, people almost always agree, which can easily lead to cross-referrals for both of them.

6. *Talent Scout.* Many businesses have a problem finding good employees. Keep an eye out. Often good service providers in one area, such as retail, make good employees in other areas.

7. *Matchmaker.* We all know various people who it would make sense to put together. Keep track and do it.

8. *Reference Librarian.* It's surprising how much basic information people miss. Find out what your contacts need and keep an eye (and a search engine) out for it.

9. *Sympathizer.* Don't get involved with people who do nothing but complain. But many of us appreciate a sympathetic ear when we have problems in business, with teenagers (who doesn't!), and so forth.

10. *Testimonial.* You want those great letters about your services—and so do others. Give generously and it will tend to come back to you.

11. *Marketer.* We all need help with our marketing. When you are interviewed by a journalist, mention other interesting people to them. E-mail makes it easy to pass the word to others when your contact is doing something interesting.

12. *Slave Laborer.* Sometimes we have little jobs facing us that we can't stand, but other people's ugly jobs don't faze us. Look for chances to help people move their offices, clean out that basement, and so on. A lot can be accomplished in an hour or two, and it's often fun to get something done.

13. *Lead Generator.* As mentioned in Chapter Fourteen on referrals, the best way to get referrals is to give them. When you bring prospects to others, they will tend to reciprocate.

DIFFERENT TYPES OF GROUPS

There are many different types of groups in the world that can be used to network. Here are a few, just to give you some ideas.

Trade Groups

Whether you're a lawyer or a window washer, there is a group where you can meet your colleagues. These are great for keeping up on the latest information and building a professional referral network.

Client trade groups are also a strong way to develop a special niche. You could be the only attorney going to a contractors' trade group, or the only consultant volunteering for the board of a manufacturers group.

Trade Shows

Trade shows are usually classified under direct sales, and they are a cost-effective way to gather leads. They are also an excellent place to network. In

---

How to Exhibit Your Services

Many chambers of commerce and trade associations provide opportunities to take a booth or tabletop to exhibit your services. Here are a few tips for a professional *and* effective display.

- Send a mailing to your prospects and clients inviting them to come see you at the event, perhaps even offering tickets.
- Coordinate your efforts with other complementary service providers to either work at your table and share expenses, or to take nearby booths.
- Build a friendly atmosphere. Introduce yourself to the people on either side of you and across the aisle.
- Proclaim your benefit on an attention-getting sign.
- Greet people as they come by your table. The difference between someone who reaches out at a booth and someone who sits back can be *five times* more valuable leads or business cards.
- Provide a handout of ten tips in your area of expertise that people will keep because it's valuable information.
- Have a drawing for a prize. Capture entrants' names from their business cards or entry slips. Give people a reason to come by your booth to pick up the second half of a prize or some other offer.
- Focus. Don't bring all your handouts to the show. Display a list of available titles. Offer to mail them if the prospect will leave you his or her card.
- Follow up the next day with information you've promised the people you met at the show.
- If you can't enjoy a show, don't do it!

!

fact, at slow shows, often more business is done between the exhibitors than with the audience. You don't have to take a booth to use shows. Attending gives you lots of opportunities to network, including with the exhibitors.

While most trade shows are large, even local chambers of commerce now have small yearly exhibits. For instance, Howard's Massage Service took a local booth, paid masseurs, gave away sample massages, and signed up profitable corporate clients (who, in turn, gave massages to employees at work as a fringe benefit).

Service-Oriented Groups

Many groups (such as Lions and Rotary Clubs) have as one of their stated objectives to support worthy causes. This gives groups a reason for meeting and helps them identify with their communities.

Tips Groups

Lots of Potential

One young loan broker traced thirteen clients to one tips group in one year. About six or eight of them were from a Realtor in the group. The rest were either people who were refinancing their own homes, or had friends who wanted to refinance.

When networking started developing as a topic, people created commercial groups whose sole purpose was to meet and give each other business or leads for their businesses.

Some are called "tips" or "leads" groups. Some are run like franchises (BNI, Le Tip, LeadsClub). Some are now run by chambers of commerce for their members. But many groups have evolved on their own.

These groups generally meet weekly for about two hours at breakfast or lunch. They allow only one person representing each type of business.

These groups probably are best for people who sell something concrete, like restaurant equipment salespeople. But some lawyers, accountants, and others get business from them.

The groups are run in slightly different ways, but your assignment at most of them is to bring in a lead every week.

Sometimes the leads are general. Others are out selling their own services. They see a new store opening, and they return with general information such as the location and phone number. It's like having many eyes and ears on the street for you. Other times the rules are that the lead has to be specifically for someone in the group. It is possible in these groups to get direct referrals on a consistent basis.

Virtual Groups

There are an increasing number of "virtual" groups online. There are thousands of interest groups, forums, and discussion groups. You may be able to build relations even better than usual in virtual space because there are no distractions to your message. For instance, FrankelBiz.com is a large online group set up for members to do business with each other.

The Best Groups for Networking: Leisure

Perhaps surprisingly, I think the best groups for *business* networking are leisure activities. Whether you are in the Ferrari Club, the country club, collect stamps, or participate in recreational softball, those are the places to meet people with whom you can have instant rapport. Balance your life a little and add some activity you enjoy. It's the best way to meet a new circle of friends, and friends are the best business and referral contacts.

REMEMBER, IT'S RELATIONSHIPS

While it helps to have specific approaches to use, like the seventeen covered earlier, don't get carried away with "techniques." Your goal is still to build relationships.

Think About How You Make Friends

Normally, you make friends in some natural setting in which you repeatedly see others without any great effort. Perhaps you get to know someone over time at work or a club. You need to find ways to get to know business contacts in a similar, comfortable manner.

When you know other people over time, in a natural setting, you do things for each other. You're pleasant to each other. And if your contacts are mostly positive, you begin to like each other.

A number of other factors, such as similarity, work for you over time. This is probably because we have similar assumptions and are more likely to reinforce each other. That's why salespeople look for points of similarity. It helps the relationship get started on a comfortable basis.

SUMMARY

[You should be] constantly out and about, working hither and thither, via electronic networks, with an ever-changing group of folks from all over.

Tom Peters

What is networking really all about? It's about relationships. It's about making friends. We all want to do business with people we know and trust, people who care about us.

If we're doing business with friends who care about us, they'll take better care of us. They'll give us the benefit of the doubt, and it will be more pleasant to work with them. Similarly, they'll have our interests in mind because the business is only part of the relationship. They won't be tempted to exploit us.

What could be better? Networking helps you make new friends and get new business too!

AGENDA

It's better to do something—even the wrong thing—
than to do nothing at all.
THOMAS WATSON, JR.
IBM

Who Do You Know?

▶ Make a list of all the people you know by name or to say hello to.
▶ Start "filling in the blanks" where you don't know enough about them to make your business a topic of conversation.

▶ Start contacting them, including a form letter at Christmas for people you haven't seen in years. Let them know what you're doing and pave the way for future contacts.

▶ Follow up with someone you met recently who you would like to get to know better.

Gather Information

▶ Start a file of professional and leisure groups you could visit. Use the last few newspaper business calendars as a reference.

▶ Ask someone for referral ideas today.

▶ Ask your friends what groups they attend regularly.

▶ Do an online search to find groups to which you can contribute.

Ready, Set, Mingle!

▶ Work on your new self-introduction for meeting people and telling them what you do.

▶ Visit a group within a week. Join one within a month.

▶ Make yourself a personal name tag. Make copies of it and put them in plastic holders. Keep one in each purse or coat.

▶ Practice active listening skills next time you are in a conversation.

▶ Participate in online chat groups, contribute to e-zines, and so on.

CHAPTER NINE

USING THE TELEPHONE AND FAX

Reach Out and Involve Someone

> *Try calling the most successful people before 8 A.M. at their offices.*
> *They are often the first in and the last to go home.*
> THOMAS J. STANLEY
> *Marketing to the Affluent*

When the telephone was first invented, the experts thought it was a novelty that few would use! Today we know that the telephone—and more modern methods such as e-mail—can be great tools for building relationships, and for your marketing.

While most of you should simply use the phone more often to contact clients and prospects, it can also be used to develop major business. For instance, an investment banker, Platinum Equity, broke the mold by cold calling big companies and asking if they had any divisions they wanted to sell! Six people worked the phones all day long, and Platinum did $2.5 billion in revenue at last count.

WILL YOU USE THE PHONE?

Some people just don't like to use the telephone!

Perhaps they don't mind calling others they know. But they definitely don't like to call people they don't know well. Maybe they're worried about imposing on others. I think I've had people working for us who, if we were giving away $20 bills, wouldn't like to call people and tell them that they'd won!

If you refuse to call people, you can skip this section. The important part that applies to you is simply remembering to use the telephone a little more often to keep in touch with people you are willing to call, such as clients, friends, and referral sources.

Calls Reclaim Customers

Webster Bank set up a phone program to retain customers about to defect. They were successful in getting more than 20 percent to increase their balances or buy other services.

!

IF YOU'LL MAKE CALLS

For those of you who are willing to make more calls, but aren't quite sure what to say, this chapter will help you do it more comfortably *and* effectively—and hopefully motivate you to do it regularly.

Something to Do Right Now

There are probably several people in your professional life you've been meaning to talk to. Call one now, and schedule the rest.

If you're reading this chapter in the middle of the night, call their office answering machines and leave them messages. In a way this is easier than actually talking to people directly. It's faster than talking to them. You can prepare your message, you can leave it, they'll be reminded of you, and they'll appreciate your thinking of them. They may even return your call!

What to Say

If you're not sure what to say when you call people, here are a few possible "openings" for you to consider. The point is just to start a conversation as you would with any friend.

"Hi _____. This is _____. I've been thinking of you recently and I finally just decided to call. I didn't have any particular reason, but I haven't talked to you in a while."

Possible things you could talk about include:

"Would you like to get together sometime?"

"Are you working on anything new since I talked to you last?"

"Will you be going to the trade show coming up?"

Don't Have a "Hidden" Purpose

Don't say you called "just to chat" when people know that you have a specific purpose and any small talk is just killing time until you get to it.

I have some people in my life who only call me when they want something. So no matter how friendly they are in the introduction, I'm simply sitting there waiting to find out what they really called about. Because they never call me when they *don't* want something, I don't think of them as friends.

Perhaps the definition of a real relationship is that you like talking to people or being with them—even when it's for no particular purpose.

Dealing with Voice Mail

Many salespeople consider voice mail a "black hole." Your message goes in, but nothing comes out! Prepare for it. Develop a benefit-oriented message that forces a response. Then tell people when to reach you or ask for a good time to call them.

A TELEPHONE-BASED MARKETING PROGRAM

You can base your entire marketing program on telephone calls. If you make a solid commitment to complete three phone calls a day, this will amount to about a thousand phone calls a year.

I can't imagine a marketing program that wouldn't be impressively improved with that number of calls.

Your problem will become *who* to call. For the first few weeks or even months, you can probably get by calling past customers, current customers, suppliers, competitors, trade associations, and others you know. Then you'll have to start developing lists of new people to call.

Who to Call?

The easy way to get names of new people to call is to have them come to you. Ways to generate this kind of interest include many of the techniques covered in other chapters: talks, seminars, written articles, and publicity which cause people to call you for further information. Then you have a chance to call them back, send them things, and begin to develop a relationship. The phone becomes one of your follow-up tools.

The phone is also a useful tool in combination with mail, fax, e-mail, or other outgoing marketing tools. For example, Boston University increased response to a mailer by 10 percent using recorded message phone calls several weeks before seminars. Live calls would have been more costly, but probably would have been even more effective.

If you take an aggressive approach to referrals, you can also get names and phone numbers of new people from your current friends, customers, and contacts. Calling these referrals is harder than dropping them a letter. But it gives you a chance to better judge their potential. And it's a lot easier than cold calling people to whom you have no introduction.

Cold Calling

There are a lot of suggestions throughout this book for people to call. Eventually, to have a serious phone program, you'll have to use the dreaded "cold calling." This means calling people with whom you have no connection. You'll have to find new lists of people to call who are likely prospects, even though they don't know you. While this is hard, it's a good way to spread your general net of contacts. You shouldn't expect immediate sales from cold calls. You should just try to lay a foundation for future contact, set up a meeting, or possibly get the name of someone else to call.

No one likes to make cold calls. But cold calls are a valuable source of prospects. Use the cold call to determine who makes the decisions, find out their selection criteria, or get the right time to call. Also look for opportunities for further contact—find reasons to stay in touch. Keep the initial contact short. This shows prospective clients that you value their time.

An example of a cold call might be:

"Hello. I'm _____. I saw your name [in the paper, on a speaking program, or wherever]. If you have a minute, I wanted to introduce myself because we have some common interests in _____."

or

"I wanted to introduce myself and ask you a quick question."

Even if the other person does not respond particularly warmly to your call, you've opened the door to a future relationship. You can send them a thank-you note and put them on your newsletter or e-mail list.

Don't Give Up

As mentioned in the sales chapter, the average sale is made after the fifth call and the average salesperson quits after two. Not only do you have to be persistent to build a relationship and trust, but you need to be organized to keep track of when you want to follow up on various leads. If you don't have a computer sales-lead tracker, make sure you have another system with time lines for follow-up cards or calls.

REASONS TO CALL PEOPLE

New in Town or Business?

As mentioned in the networking chapter, people expect newcomers to introduce themselves and they accept it as reasonable. So, if you are just starting, working in a new niche, or new in town, it's a great time to call and introduce yourself.

An example of a simple phone opening if you're new in town would be:

"Hello. I'm _____. I'm new in the area and called to introduce myself [because we are neighbors, or in the same business, I saw your name in the paper, or other reason]. I wondered if you'd like to get together for a cup of coffee sometime, or if you could give me some advice as I start my practice."

Get to the Point

In sales, how you start a call—whether in person or on the phone—is crucial. If the prospects don't know you, the only thing on their minds is what you want. The faster you get to the point, the better. This generally means introducing yourself and the company you represent or the benefit you provide, and asking if the prospect has a moment to talk. Other openings, such as "How are you today?" can make prospects resentful because you're not stating your purpose and they know you don't care how they are.

Why Else Can You Call?

You can call to introduce yourself and see if the person would be interested in being put on your mailing list for your informal newsletter. This is a subtle way of finding out if he or she has enough interest in your service to be a prospect. And this is another way to use a newsletter or e-zine to market (see Chapter Ten).

An example of this might be:

"Hi. I'm _____. I'm a _____ in the area. I just called to introduce myself and see if you had any interest in being put on the mailing list for my free, occasional newsletter on _____."

or

"I just called to introduce myself and find out who would receive information in your company."

This is a much stronger approach than just sending an unsolicited newsletter, not knowing where it's going to end up.

Con Men Build Relationships Too

In calling strangers, we can learn something from "con men." For instance, a two-stage survey approach is regularly used by stockbrokers who are selling dangerously risky stocks.

Usually they get your name from a list of investors. During the first call, they simply say they called to introduce themselves, and to find out if you were interested in hearing about special situations. They say that occasionally they run into great situations and they would then call you at that time. There's no pressure now. (They're simply seeing if you're a prospect.)

Follow their example in this one thing. Keep your calls very low pressure. Just introduce yourself and check people's interests in your area. Not trying to sell also makes the call easier on you.

Three Phone Tips

1. Be prepared when you initiate calls.
2. Don't use a script, it sounds unnatural.
3. But be clear on what your goals are—even if it means writing down key questions.

Charity Calls

A great way to make new contacts, practice cold calling, and help others is to volunteer to make calls for a charity or other organization.

Even if you don't like to sell, you can still be comfortable calling and offering tickets for the United Way auction, or calling past donors and asking them if they'd like to make another contribution. You won't take the rejection personally if people turn you down. In fact, it reflects badly on *them* if they turn down a wonderful charity. You will raise money for the charity and be looked at as brave because you're willing to make phone calls. And you benefit by getting acquainted with new people.

You make contact with more than just the staff and other callers. As part of making the pitch for the charity nonthreatening and low key, you'd introduce yourself, say who you were, and what you did. You'd explain that you'd volunteered to make some phone calls for the charity. If you do this right, the people you call will even *thank* you for volunteering to make calls! It's worked for me. Tell them you were happy to do it, and it's fun for you just meeting new people on the phone.

Once you've introduced yourself this way, you can learn a little about them as you chat. And you have a chance to later drop them a personal note, a newsletter, or something else that extends the relationship if they are prospects of possible referral sources for your services.

Motivate Yourself

If you have trouble motivating yourself to make calls, estimate the business you could get from the person over five years. If it's not large enough to motivate you, move on to the next call.

Research Calls

Another way to use the telephone is to do some general survey work with potential prospects.

A number of people in sales use a *false* research approach to get people talking. It's common enough now that people tend to be a little suspicious if you call and say you're doing a survey. They either don't want to waste their time, or they're suspicious that you'll turn it into a sales call.

You need to develop a way to comfortably call strangers and give them a reason for talking to you. For instance, you can do a very short survey like the type that would be a basis for your publicity (see Chapter Seven). Or you can use telephone surveys as simply a very brief way to get acquainted.

Create five questions or less, perhaps one or two close-ended yes or no questions and a couple of open-ended ones.

If people show an interest in talking in the open-ended questions, then you can end the survey and talk a little further about their interests in your field. Your phone call should be followed up with a thank-you note, a summary of your survey, adding them to your newsletter mailing list, and otherwise making them part of your network. Again, this starts a potential relationship.

An example would be:

"Hi. I'm _____. I'm a _____ in the area. I'm doing a two-minute survey on [topic] for an article I'm preparing. Are you the right person to be asking about this, and do you have two minutes?" Or, "Who in your company should I ask about that topic?"

MAKE A PACKAGE OFFER

Here's how one consultant handled telemarketing. He bought a list, with phone numbers, of companies of a certain size in a specific industry. Because he didn't like cold calling, it took him more than a week to make ten hours of calls. In those ten hours, he got four appointments.

With these four appointments with the decision makers, he was able to actually sell small contracts to three of them, usually to analyze their situations. He had a package approach in which for $3,200, they would get four days of his time. He would come in one day the first week to analyze their situations; then he came in each subsequent week for part of a day, as well as doing work on his reports outside their offices.

Offer a Simple Package

There were at least two clever aspects to what this consultant did.

First, he had a package that they could buy for a limited cost so they weren't risking too much.

Second, he spread his work out over several weeks. This gave him more time to learn about the company and the employees more time to get comfortable with him.

Some of these jobs could work into longer-term situations or other jobs. But let's just look at the economics of the first numbers.

He spent about ten hours on the phone, he got four appointments, and he got three jobs for $3,200 apiece. So he got $9,600 for his ten hours on the phone, plus his regular ninety-six hours of consulting work. Instead of his usual $100 an hour, he had to put in an extra 10 percent-plus on the phone. So he received a big payoff for his time on the phone.

Phone Selling

When trying to reach a particular person by phone, if the person who answers is the right gender, assume it's that person. It saves time and helps to get you through gatekeepers if you start to make your point. If it's not the right person, he or she will correct you and direct your call.

If instead you ask, "Is this Mr. Jones?" you end up answering questions about who's calling, what it's about, or other distractions.

HIRING SOMEONE

This consultant really found it horrible to make calls to strangers. So, he hired someone to make phone calls from her home.

He gave her the same lists of names to call. She was able to make ten hours of calls in just a couple of days. For every ten hours of calls, she was able to set only three appointments instead of the four that he set, because she wasn't an expert in his field. For every three appointments that she set up, he was able to sell only half of them. So, his success ratio was noticeably less. That's understandable.

It Costs Nothing Compared to the Results

But let's look at it another way: It cost him $10 an hour to pay her. This means that each appointment cost him $33.33. His sales cost him $66.66 apiece. So for $67, he got a $3,200 job that might lead to further work. It sounds like an awfully good deal to me! Let's be more pessimistic and say it took five hours to make one appointment ($50 cost). And he only sold 10 percent. Five hundred dollars is still cheap for a foot-in-the-door job.

Inexpensive to Test

To test the use of outside appointment setters, all you have to do is allocate a couple of hundred dollars to try a couple of people out on the phone.

You should write a fifty-word script yourself. Read it out loud to hear how it sounds, then make two or three phone calls—or five or ten. See how it works out when you're actually talking to someone who's responding.

Try callers out for an hour or two on your phone. Let them listen to you, then listen to what they say, and give them a little bit of training. Only then should you let them loose in their own homes with your list. Be sure to check in with them often at the beginning, answer any questions, give them material about your services, and so on. For some service providers, such as consultants, this can be very effective.

Trade with a Friend

There's another way to have other people make calls for you. Trade calls with a friend. This sounds radical but really isn't.

This simple idea could transform your marketing if you apply it. Many of us are not particularly comfortable selling our own services. So in my seminars, I suggest that people pair up and sell for each other.

A lot of people who don't like to sell themselves on the phone don't mind calling for a charity or somebody else. If you have a friend with different services, you could volunteer to call a hundred people for her if she calls a hundred people for you.

There's a detachment about representing others that we don't have for ourselves. Your ego isn't on the line, so it doesn't bother you when people say no. This can work well because each of you is not bothered by any rejection, and each of you painlessly gets a number of leads. If you're a small company, it may even make you look bigger to have someone else calling for you.

When you know that someone else is going to do the "dirty work," you may find yourself energized to get things ready for him. Just remember that you can seldom sell more than an appointment on the phone.

This is an unusual approach, but think about it seriously. It's not that hard if you are both reasonably good on the phone. It really is more comfortable selling someone else, and it could become the basis of your out-going marketing.

The odds are that your buddy will be about half as effective as you in setting appointments that end up buying, and vice versa. However, half-efficiency that is implemented is far more productive than you never making *any* calls for yourself!

Why not proposition a friend about this today? What do you have to lose? If you're in a big firm, senior partners don't have to know that this is how you are getting your new leads!

"JUST THE FAX, MA'AM"

I didn't like fax machines for the first couple of years our publishing business had one. Fax technology is inelegant. The resolution of the page is not as good as a copy machine. It's not as quick as e-mail. All it really does is work!

It also annoyed me that people always wanted to fax me material that I was in no hurry to get, such as press releases!

Build a Relationship via Fax

When it is difficult to reach a customer or sales prospect, the fax machine can be very useful. To improve your credibility, fax newspaper clippings about you or your business, or a copy of a letter to the editor if it relates to your prospect. Keep it brief, perhaps with no cover sheet. You can also fax a note to people to expect your call at a certain time.

!

Whatever I thought, the fax is still a fact of life today. I prefer e-mail, but if you're a "real" business, you send and receive faxes—period.

At its best, the fax is cheaper than a letter and more formal than an e-mail. Instead of dropping people a note, you can fax it knowing they'll receive it quickly.

Cover-Sheet Marketing

If you use a cover sheet with your faxes, it can become a marketing piece for you.

You can go in three directions here. One is to add something humor-ous to be more memorable, such as a cartoon. Rotate funny sayings, quotes, or cartoons regularly to entertain recipients.

The second approach is to add a message about one of your services, such as an upcoming seminar.

The third approach is to give people a bonus, such as a mini-newsletter. (See, for instance, the information on postcard-size newsletters in Chapter Ten.) This could also be a list of your free tips sheets available on request.

Fax-on-Demand Systems

I prefer Web sites, but fax-on-demand systems are still in use. Customers and prospects can dial in and receive documents back automatically on their fax machines. These might be articles you've written on various topics, tips sheets, newsletters, or other items.

These systems can send people an index of what's available. They can be quite fancy. For instance, they can collect credit-card information to sell documents. The technology is always changing, so shop around.

Soliciting by Fax

You can also do the equivalent of direct mail solicitations by fax.

Many directories list fax numbers, and you can rent fax numbers from list brokers. With a fax, you can send a brief marketing message that has more impact than the mail, and is faster and cheaper. If you're trying to reach thousands of fax numbers, there are commercial fax "broadcast" services that can send thousands of faxes out every hour.

The list people's fax numbers come from tells you something about them (for example, the size of their company, club memberships, and so on). This allows you to tailor, or target, your message to them for more impact.

I had a friend, Jim, who conducted business seminars. He faxed three pages describing them to 150 or so law firms and corporate legal departments. This produced a dozen participants every time for him. This is a much higher response than you would expect sending the same material by mail.

There are a few laws against "junk" faxes. Most simply say that you can contact them once, but must let people know how to get off your fax list. Jim's seminar is for lawyers and he's had little negative feedback, and no threats of lawsuits! A conservative approach to the "junk" fax issue would be to fax recipients a note asking if they'd like information. The people who respond will be very good prospects.

CONCLUSION: IT'S STILL RELATIONSHIPS

Using the telephone and fax are simply ways to contact people. The technology may change, but communication is always valuable. The more you communicate, and the more ways, the better for you, your relationships, and your marketing.

AGENDA

*To succeed, jump as quickly at opportunities
as you do at conclusions.*
BEN FRANKLIN

▶ *Call your mother!* If there are some relatives you haven't called in a while, make your first calls to them. They'll appreciate it. You can even tell them that you're reading a book on marketing and working on ideas to get more customers. They may give you an idea about people to call.

Keep in Touch with Clients

▶ Call past clients you haven't talked to in a while.
▶ Call current clients you haven't talked to in a while.
▶ Call people you've been meaning to write. Catch up on responding to inquiries from prospects or customers.

Easy Cold Calls

▶ Call competitors or people in your industry.
▶ Call suppliers.
▶ Volunteer to make calls for a charity.

▶ Develop a fax marketing message to send out.
▶ Create your own script of something about which you could call a stranger.

Get Others Calling for You

▶ Make some test calls yourself to a "cold" list. Then hire someone to set appointments for you.
▶ Proposition a friend about making calls for each other.

CHAPTER TEN

KEEP IN TOUCH

Publish a Newsletter or E-zine

> *Newsletters are . . . the ideal marketing tool to*
> *promote your services.*
> ELAINE FLOYD
> *Marketing with Newsletters*

This chapter shows you how to create a newsletter or online e-zine. And the Appendix gives you material to either use as a model for your first newsletter, or to "lift" and put directly in your newsletter.

While the opening quote may be somewhat optimistic, newsletters are an excellent way to keep your service in your clients' and prospects' minds. Newsletters can build your credibility and image. They should give people free, valuable information while building relationships. And if you do a really good newsletter, it can become a profit center in itself, by your selling subscriptions to it.

Even those of you who still have negative associations when you think of marketing or selling will agree that publishing a newsletter is dignified and professional.

WHY DO A NEWSLETTER?

Always keep in mind the purpose of your newsletter. While it may provide some ego gratification to be able to broadcast your opinions, its real purpose should be to build your image and cause people to want to work with you or refer you.

It should try to represent you when you're not there. It should be your foot in the door to build or maintain relationships. It should get you lots of business!

Good for Starting Relationships

A newsletter is particularly useful to send to people you don't know. It starts a relationship by letting them know that you exist. One consultant sends newsletters for a few months to prospects. By the time he calls them for an appointment, it is a "warm" call and they are usually happy to see him.

In order to get the most out of sending out the newsletter, I highly recommend that you send a brief note—perhaps a Post-it note—personalized for each individual. If you don't know the person, that note might simply be about why you're sending it to her (because you saw her name in a particular place).

TWO WAYS TO OFFER A NEWSLETTER

Generic Newsletters

There are two different ways to obtain a newsletter to send out. One extreme is to buy a newsletter that is franchised to you; that is, another company writes a generic newsletter and sells it to many different businesses. Each of you gets an exclusive territory and receives copies of the general product specially imprinted with your company name.

For instance, in the printing industry, there are many people who send masters of a newsletter to printers. The printers then add their names to the top, print them, and send them to their customers.

Custom Newsletters

The other extreme is to produce the entire newsletter yourself. In between these two extremes would be hiring people to do some of the work for you or getting some of your material from other sources.

Many marketing, advertising, and PR firms will create custom newsletters for you. They generally interview you to get ideas and then compose the newsletter as if it was written by you.

Marketing with Newsletters

The first rule of success is for the newsletter to contain information valuable to the recipient, not promotional information about your services. Here are other tips to keep your customers reading:

- Keep stories short (less than half a page each).
- Write in a personal style so that customers feel that they are hearing from an individual.
- Give customers a person's name to call for more information about each item or your company in general.

This approach can be fairly expensive. However, even a few thousand dollars may not be too much to have a professionally designed, written, printed, and mailed marketing piece that doesn't take much of your time. If you are a larger company, you may even be able to have one newsletter that works for your combined customers, prospects, and employees.

An extreme example of a custom marketing publication is called *Sun,* by the Ray-Ban Sunglass Company. It's produced by the publisher of *Elle, Woman's Day, Road & Track*, and many other magazines. The company is even trying to sell it on the newsstands for $2.50. It looks like a regular magazine and most of the pictures feature celebrities in sunglasses. Of course, part of the cost is offset by the fact that the company is selling ads for other products. You may be able to sell ads in your publication. (Or you may, eventually, be able to franchise your newsletter to other service providers like yourself in other locations.)

E-ZINES, FAXES, AND OTHER FORMATS

E-mail Newsletters

E-mail has made it much easier to send out newsletters, both lowering costs and making production simpler.

E-mail newsletters are less formal than printed newsletters. A friend of mine is getting an excellent response from a typeset, four-color format such as html, but often the newest format is not readable for all recipients. This means that the simplest level, plain text, is acceptable.

The most important thing with e-zines is your subject line and the sender information. People receive so much spam and other material that you want them to know it is from you and what it is about.

The simplest way to do an e-zine is to keep it short—less than three screens. You can include links to fuller stories on your Web site.

Fax Newsletters

Despite predictions of its demise since e-mail was invented, the fax has survived and even prospered.

A fax newsletter allows you the luxury to format your material in a little more detail. It also seems to have an urgency that e-mail doesn't. For instance, one accountant I know sends out a fax letter about inventory issues with an offer to do free phone consultations, but only if recipients call that week.

Other Formats

Newsletters can be effective using many media. CDs, DVDs, and brief wireless messages to pagers or phones are the most common alternatives. For instance, a trucking company sends an audio newsletter to its drivers. While they're driving is an ideal time to listen.

Clearly, videos are best for material where you need to show images. The point is to use the format that is best for your audience and most cost-effective for generating a response.

A NON-NEWSLETTER NEWSLETTER

I want to make it very clear that a newsletter is *not* the best way to keep in touch with people. It is the best *only* when you don't have the time to be in more personal contact.

Your goals are to keep yourself in the minds of others, build your image, and support a relationship. You can also accomplish these goals with "non-newsletter" mailings. Every month, or quarter, you can send a different item in the mail. You could send an article you've written for another publication, or an interesting clipping that you thought would apply to the recipient's business. From the receiver's point of view, these non-newsletter pieces of mail are more personal, and they can be individually customized for each person.

As soon as you begin to produce an official newsletter, it becomes a little less personal. You use a newsletter when you have many people to reach, and you can't write each of them a personal letter (with enclosures that would be valuable to them individually).

Planned Contacts

One accountant subscribes to many trade magazines just to be able to have his secretary clip and send personalized articles for each client.

WHERE TO GET MATERIAL

Often, people are able to easily write the first two or three newsletters because they have a lot of pent-up ideas. After that, writing a newsletter gets harder and harder. It's valuable to develop some consistent sources that you can count on before you start.

Sources of material include:

- press releases
- your own clippings
- clipping services
- academic publications
- the library
- filler services
- government publications
- trade magazines
- online resources
- your customers and employees
- other experts

Press Releases

In your field and the industries you serve, there are probably a lot of press releases. They are sent to publications by suppliers, consultants, and others.

As you become aware of these groups that are trying to gain publicity, ask to be put on their press release lists. Sometimes they'll have items that are interesting to your readers. Other times they will send you items that give you ideas or the names of people to contact.

Reviewing Others' Material
You can also get on the press release lists for new books, videos, audios, seminars, and other material.

There's no obligation to review all the items you receive. But if your newsletter reviews some, you will get a huge pile and many invitations. Looking at one of my offices right now, I see fifty or sixty books that I may or may not find time to even consider reviewing for one of our newsletters.

Computer Clipping

It is possible to set up a simple program that searches through computer databases to give you articles you want. Like any clipping service, most of the items you get won't be just what you need. But with the computer you can refine your "search parameters" to zero in on what you want.

Your Own Clippings

Speaking of reviewing others' material, if you see an interesting article in the *Wall Street Journal*, a trade magazine, or your local paper, you can clip it and put it in your file. You could have a column, section, or page in your newsletter in which you note interesting points from other people. In fact, there are a number of popular commercial newsletters that are essentially digests.

Even if you don't use the items you clip directly, they are a great source of ideas. Any items you clipped caught your eye for a reason. When you write about that reason, you have something for your newsletter.

Clipping Services

There are services you can pay to read publications for you and send you only the material you want.

They look for specific topics, "clip" them, and send items to you. For instance, if you were a consultant working in the customer service field, you would have them send you articles about customer service.

Clipping services can afford to send you custom clips at a small cost because they scan the same publications for many clients.

Most such services cost a minimum of about $100 a month, with some small charge for each item, but there are many possible arrangements. For instance, I used one that cost $5 per clip, *but only for ones I used*. This turned out to be better for me because I have broad interests that are hard to specify precisely. And I also like only paying for what I use! Thomas's Register lists clipping services, and lists are also available online.

Academic Publications

Another source of ideas and free material is college professors. If you have a local college near you where professors are expected to publish (this is usually not a community college), they may be willing to put you on their reprint list. Every time they publish an article in your field in a technical journal, you might write a summary of it in layperson's language, if it's of interest to your readers.

You don't have to limit yourself to local college professors. We're on the press release lists of colleges across the country. And any academic library has lots of technical journals related to your area. If you find a few you like, they will continually have new articles.

The Library

The library is the most obvious source of material. It's amazing to me that so many people don't like or use libraries. The odds are that there's a shelf full of books related to your field, and a number of monthly or quarterly publications. In addition to academic journals and government publications, there will also be popular monthly magazines, computer databases, taped information, and more.

Filler Services

Filler services send you prewritten material that you can use as is or alter to suit yourself. They often include graphics as well as articles. Most of these articles are probably too general to use in your newsletter, but you can sometimes get enough from them to justify the cost. Some are even free.

Government Publications

Perhaps the biggest source of written material is government publications. Even better, the government doesn't allow material it publishes to be copyrighted. Since citizens paid for the material in the first place, we all have the right to reprint it, even under our own names. Many publishing companies make a lot of money republishing government documents, with more interesting covers and better publicity.

You can get lists of government documents and their pricing from the Superintendent of Documents, U.S. Government Printing Office, Washington, DC 20402-9325 (202-783-3238). Through online services you can access census data; view a catalogue of government publications, books, and subscription services; and find information on how to use the free or nearly free government publications and services that are available. Many libraries also have repositories of government documents and information.

Trade Magazines

You can also subscribe to trade publications. Fortunately, most are free.

There are normally a number of free, controlled-circulation trade publications in every industry. Whatever industries your clients come from should have several. I receive about fifty of these free industry publications. If you don't know about them, ask people who are involved in the different industries you serve what they receive.

You can also find them listed in books at the library, such as *Standard Periodicals Guide, SRDS,* and the *Oxbridge Directories of Magazines and Newsletters.*

Online Resources

Of course, the quickest place to find material for your newsletter is online. The best search engines change, but by using a "meta" engine that searches multiple search engines at once, you can find a lot of leads. (At the time of this writing, Google.com is the single search engine I use.)

By experimenting with different searches, you can find many Web sites, e-zines, consultants, books, and other material on any topic. This will give you lots of things to work with, or you can trade articles or get permission to reprint others' material.

You will also find places you can set up links to your site that can bring you Web traffic. And there are directories, ad exchanges, and other resources. (See Chapter Twelve for more on this.)

Your Customers and Employees

Perhaps the most relevant sources of information or ideas for your newsletter are your customers and prospects.

Everybody likes to see their name in print, so including information from and about people you work with serves double duty. It fills your newsletter and flatters people. If you're actively networking, every month prospects and clients will be asking you questions and giving you tips. Much of this information can be captured for your newsletter.

Other Experts

If you don't know anything about a particular topic, or want to involve other people in your newsletter, it's simple enough to interview experts.

Most people won't take the time to write something for you, but they will answer questions over the phone. If you record the conversation and write it as an interview, they can check it to be sure it's accurate, and they may be stimulated to add a few more things. Then you can publish an interview with a leader in your field. These sources can include authors of books you've read, college professors, trade association executives, and government experts.

There will probably be many consultants and related experts who wouldn't mind doing a guest column in your newsletter. This would be counterproductive if they were competitive with you, but it's something to offer them if they are possible referral sources whose interests are complementary to yours.

You're An Expert Too

Eventually, if your newsletter becomes established, things will come full circle. You will become an expert and a source whom others will want to interview for their publications!

TYPES OF ITEMS TO INCLUDE

General topics that could be regular sections or columns in your newsletter are:

- case studies of things your clients did using your services to become more productive, protect their interests, or other benefits
- items about your employees (this does double duty because your employees like to be recognized)
- contributions from readers (many e-zines are composed completely of such contributions)
- ways to use your services
- new services or products in your industry

- quizzes and self-analysis sheets that score your readers on dimensions of interest
- summaries of material from other sources
- trivia
- book reviews
- humor, cartoons
- interviews with experts
- quotes
- short tips
- free items to send for

YOUR IMAGE VERSUS IMMEDIATE BUSINESS

A newsletter is a good general image builder. When you speak to people, they'll often comment on having received it.

That's nice, and it can lead to better relationships and more business in the long run. But most newsletters don't stimulate much direct business immediately. Your object is *not* to produce a great newsletter, but to get more business in the long *and* short terms.

To make your newsletter stimulate business more directly, you have to write items that require people to call you for more details. For a short item, you can add a note to call you for more information, a free checklist, or other material. For instance, Jeffrey Gitomer writes a column on sales for many business journals. He often has an item to send for, which builds his mailing list.

Remember that you don't want your newsletter to be viewed as advertising. And you don't want to tease recipients. If you're writing an article about ways to manage a construction project, have a complete article. But you can mention at the end that you have two or three worksheets available if readers would like to call you.

If you direct them to your Web site, this exposes them to more about you, but it's harder to keep track of who requests what. Work to obtain information about active interests of readers to use as the basis for discussion and possible offers of your services. In every issue, try to have a reason for people to contact you.

PRACTICAL DETAILS

How to Produce a Regular Newsletter

It's amazing how quickly a new month or quarter comes up when you're producing a regular newsletter. The regularity of the demand destroys some people.

The simplest way to produce on a regular basis is to be constantly gathering material, using the methods covered above. Then, when the end of the month or quarter comes and it's time to write your newsletter, you'll have many ideas to develop, or to use directly in your newsletter.

Physical Formats

The most popular size for printed newsletters is one 11" × 17" sheet, folded to make four 8½" × 11" pages. However, this is a lot of space to fill if you don't have good sources established.

Don't hesitate to start small. A consultant in Arizona created a postcard newsletter he sent to his clients. He claimed that he always received an inquiry or two after sending it out. And it's amazing how many little bits of information or interesting quotes he fit on his postcard. (See the Appendix for an example.) As you become more comfortable with your content, you can always expand.

For e-zines, check how many characters wide most screens are and format your e-zine so that it won't split lines differently for different computers. At present, this is about seventy characters in width.

Editorial Calendars

"Real" publications usually have what is called an "editorial calendar": a list of the themes they will cover in each issue for the entire year ahead.

This is interesting as an editorial planner and for discipline. If you can't think of the topics you want to cover in your next year's newsletters, perhaps you're not ready to do one.

!

YOUR EDITORIAL PERSONALITY

When writing your newsletter, there is a subtle factor that can make a big difference in your results.

The most important thing you need to remember is to express a personality. Your newsletter stands for *you*. It's a salesperson when you can't be there. The type of material you put in your newsletter creates an impression of you. Be sure to think about what you're expressing through your choices. The newsletter should reflect your values in a way that is more personal than daily newspapers or trade magazines.

It's also worth taking a chance once in a while to express your personal values, sense of humor, and beliefs. This will help people appreciate your personality before they become acquainted with you. Then, when they work with you, you'll already be a familiar person.

Editorial Voice

The personality I'm talking about is sometimes called editorial "voice." One example of an editorial voice that always impressed me was the old Sebastiani Winery newsletter. It often covered seemingly dull topics—how grapevines were trimmed, or what new machine the winery had acquired to crush the grapes. But it was written with such a sense of love by Sam Sebastiani that you really felt there was a "little old wine maker" out in the field, caring for every aspect of fine wine making. That's what you want to accomplish with your newsletter.

Crusade for Something

Advocate Action

End your articles with "I recommend" or "I suggest." After all, you're the expert and your readers want your advice.

The best way to dramatically make your personality clear is to be a person who stands for something. A law firm could crusade for shareholder rights. A gardener could hate snails. A plastic surgeon could promote higher self-esteem. If you can crusade for something, it makes you memorable, creates publicity, and expresses your values.

Offend Someone?

An extreme way to say this is: If your newsletter doesn't *offend* anyone, you may not be expressing enough personality! For instance, as an accountant or bookkeeper, you might want to take on the IRS. Nobody likes the IRS, so you won't get into too much trouble offending it, as long as you stay within the law. But showing your audience members how to stand up to the IRS will make them see you as a "champion" they can trust to be on their side.

WRITING TIPS

When writing your newsletter, one good approach is to write like you speak. Research shows that people prefer to read at a simple level.

Many years ago the "Fog Index" was created. A high score means your material is very hard to read. In order to get a better score, and be less "foggy," keep your sentences short, your words short, and your paragraphs short. And use more personal than impersonal referents. Hopefully, you'll get an idea of how this is done by reading this book. (See the Appendix for how to calculate "fog.")

Write Headlines That Work

Headlines must attract people's attention so they will read the rest. Some tips for writing better headlines:

- Make sure your headline relates to the specifics of the story. For instance, if you're trying to appeal to CEOs, the headline could be "More Time for Busy CEOs."
- Include an active verb. Instead of "Financial News," use a headline such as "CD Interest Rates Rise."
- Don't be afraid of writing long headlines if they get your message across.
- Consider using words such as *new, free, now,* and *how to.* Numbers are also effective (3 Ways to Cut Legal Costs, 5 Tips to Improve Your Golf Swing, and so on).

Keep It Simple

We're all too busy today to pay full attention when we read most things. Follow the old Texas preacher's advice to "Start fast, get their attention early, and then stop boring when you've hit oil."

In Chapter Seven on publicity, there is some information on how to write like a journalist when you do press releases. (This is to put the Who, What, When, Where, Why, and How in the first paragraph.) It turns out that readers don't particularly like this "inverted-pyramid" approach. However, from it we can take a good rule of thumb: Tell your readers very early in the story why they should read it. Your opening paragraph must say what the story is about and evoke reader interest. Or, in marketing terms, tell your audience the benefits of reading the article.

A last piece of advice for clearer writing in general, and newsletters in particular, is to use a lot of headings and subheads. If these are used correctly, the reader can get the general idea of the article just by reading the bold headings and subheads. (Again, I've tried to use that approach throughout this book.)

Working with Printers

Distribute Generously

Without spamming, send your newsletter out to anyone you can think of. For instance, one professional sends his to "big" names. Many send him notes complimenting him, so it raises his profile and adds status to his subscriber list.

!

If you have only a hundred or so copies of your newsletter to send, it probably would be best to photocopy it or send it by fax or e-mail. You can do it on your stationery, or have a printer do a year's worth of colorful "nameplate" paper with the name of your newsletter. Then you copy the black type onto that for a two-color effect.

When you are ready to go to a printer, and perhaps use two colors throughout your newsletter, I advise you to shop carefully. Your local neighborhood "quick printer" may be twice as expensive as a printer who actually specializes in publications.

When you get to the point of printing, you may want to also pay someone to design the nameplate at the top and the general layout of your pages. These can be used repeatedly, and allow you to develop a specific and professional look for your newsletter.

USE THIS BOOK TO HELP YOU

There is editorial material on general management topics, customer service, quality, cost savings, marketing, sales, health, and so forth, in the Appendix. We're happy to give you these free samples of content. If you own a copy of this book, you are welcome to use any of the Appendix editorial material in your newsletter without credit to us. Please feel free to modify it to suit yourself. (One of my companies sometimes does newsletters for people.)

AGENDA

All the beautiful sentiments in the world weigh less
than a single lovely action.
ROBERT LOWELL

Start Quickly

▶ Start with a "non-newsletter." Send a brief note and a single enclosure
to ten prospects or customers today. (The enclosure could be an article you've written or an idea they'd be interested in from this book.)

▶ Start putting together the list of those to whom you would send an
e-zine or newsletter.

Who Are You?

▶ What do you want the newsletter to stand for?

▶ Is there any issue that you could passionately advocate or attack in
your newsletter to build an appropriate "fighting image"?

Start Gathering Material

▶ Look at the material in the Appendix for this chapter at the end of
the book. Does it contain anything you could use to help you get
your newsletter started?

▶ Start a file of material you might be able to use in producing your
newsletter.

Research Newsletter Topics

▶ Do online searches for material you could use, and ideas about how to do e-zines or newsletters.

▶ Stop by your local public library and college library and see what they have.

▶ Create a draft editorial calendar listing the topics you might feature in your newsletter for the next year. Distinguish among the types of material you might have in every issue (such as humor, case studies, summaries of new laws, or research) and topics that you might cover once a year.

CHAPTER ELEVEN

GIVING TALKS, WORKSHOPS, AND SEMINARS

How to Open Your Mouth and Not Shoot Yourself in the Foot!

> *Help them, don't sell them is the key to selling by seminar.*
> MICHAEL J. ENZER
> *Selling by Seminar*

If you think fast on your feet, giving talks and seminars is an ideal way to promote your services. In this chapter, I'll show you how to increase your opportunities—and abilities—to give people a "product sample" as you show off your expertise.

GETTING STARTED

Stage fright seems to be the biggest concern for people who think about using talks as a major part of their marketing.

You've probably heard that in surveys, people often rank fear of speaking in public *above* fear of death! The major fear in speaking seems to be fear of evaluation. It's natural to be uncomfortable speaking in public. However, if you *are* an expert, your audience is not likely to evaluate you poorly.

Whether or not stage fright concerns you, there are some steps you can take to practice for talks.

HOW TO OVERCOME STAGE FRIGHT AND GET PRACTICE

If you're uncomfortable speaking in front of groups, here are two recommended approaches to overcome your discomfort.

Overcome Speech Phobia

Here are some tips to improve your performance and be less nervous:

- Establish eye contact with a variety of people in the audience.
- Realize that it's normal to be nervous, so be prepared and move ahead anyway.
- Tell stories or give real examples; they're always the most interesting.

Work with Someone Else

First, get someone who likes to speak to do joint presentations with you. The worst case of fear of speaking that I've ever seen was an old partner of mine, Roy. He developed a phobia about public speaking in the army. Roy had given a talk in the 1960s and literally "blacked out" about it afterward. People told him that he'd done fine, but he didn't remember a thing and avoided speaking for over twenty years.

Roy was a real expert in computers. He knew systems of all sizes. I'd seen a course offered on "How to Build Your Own Computer for Under $600." I was giving a lot of seminars at the time and decided this would be a perfect one for Roy.

To make a long story short, I went out with Roy the first few times as we developed the course. He did fine and I barely had to say a word. He went on to give a lot of top-rated courses, alone, for years.

Try setting up a low-key seminar with someone with whom you can do joint referrals. Stick to topics you know inside out. Practice your speech out loud. Time it in advance. You'll do fine.

Practice at Toastmasters

The second approach is to get practice at safe places. Toastmasters clubs are everywhere and are highly recommended. You get a chance to give small practice talks and get advice and feedback from friendly people. You also get to see role models.

Talks at Schools

One place where it isn't too difficult to get practice engagements is a local school or college.

Many high school and college teachers are happy to have some of their workload relieved by having a guest speaker share expertise. It's easy to get these speaking engagements because there are literally hundreds of teachers to approach.

Because teachers are supposed to know something about presentations, this is also a good group of people from whom to get feedback. Just tell them before the speech that you don't give many public talks, and you're very interested in receiving their feedback on ways you can improve. They'll often give you good objective, and supportive, input.

Don't overlook any outlet in getting started. It may not sound too glamorous to give a talk about your occupation to your child's second-grade class, but, as with any networking, you never know what can happen until you get out there.

Teachers may know people to whom they can refer you. Some of the children may go home and tell their parents about you. If you provide a handout, it may find its way to some parents who need your services.

An audience of second-graders is also good for your stage fright. It's hard to be nervous talking to a group of children!

Like everything else, your speaking will improve with practice. The best advice I can give you is to find an audience and start talking.

THREE MARKETS

There are three general markets for giving talks:

1. Self-promoted
2. Talks promoted by other people for the public
3. In-house talks to companies

Self-Promotion

Perhaps the simplest way to get an audience is to self-promote. As mentioned elsewhere, most local papers have a small calendar in which you can put a free listing for a talk. This generally will create some interest and turn out a few bodies.

Talks Can Be Small
If you set things up so that a small audience is enough, then the little, free calendar announcements in the paper can suffice.

Educational Marketing

A large bank found that working women responded to its marketing efforts but weren't actually signing up for services. It added a weekly seminar program that explained various services and products, essentially providing a free sample of financial planning. About half the women who attended signed up for services during the seminar or afterwards.

!

One local business broker regularly put in a notice of a seminar on how to buy or sell a business. The people who wanted to sell businesses never bothered coming to the seminar, but they called him anyway, so he gained a source of new leads. The people who wanted to buy a business would appear at his office, and he'd run a seminar for three or four of them, going through some of the basics. This allowed him to prequalify prospects who might want to buy.

A financial planner mailed out letters to selected neighborhoods offering a free seminar on estate planning. The letters promised benefits such as avoiding probate, increasing cash flow during retirement, and reducing current taxes. He also offered a booklet and a free video. It only took a few prospects signing up for services to make the mailing worthwhile.

Bigger Promotions

If you want to self-promote in a grander way, you can take large ads in the newspaper. But be careful—you may have some trouble taking in enough money to pay your costs unless you're already a known figure.

Many of the local newspapers will cosponsor seminars by experts on topics of interest to their audiences. This can be done with daily papers but is most common with weekly business journals. They will often give you solid publicity and not even want a cut of the door. Banks, office supply stores, chambers of commerce, and others who serve businesses are other potential cosponsors.

Promoting alone is the hard way to go unless you're well known. You can spend a lot on advertising or direct mail without too much return.

Combining Your Efforts

Just as working with others can make speaking easier, it can also help build a larger audience. You gain access to each other's clients and prospects and you have built-in endorsements from the other service providers. This approach also falls into the area of things you could try today. At least you could call a couple of possible cosponsors and see if you can get together to generate some enthusiasm for the idea. (Don't let other people delay you if they're not action oriented!)

For instance, a financial planner could ask a lawyer to speak at an estate-planning seminar. Or you could combine a lawyer, an accountant, and a marketing consultant in a small-business seminar. By combining your efforts you may have more resources available. As an example, one of the group may have a much larger, more conveniently located office in which to hold the seminar.

Another example is Greenbrier & Russel, which uses seminars on a big scale. It is a $20-million computer consulting firm that does about one seminar a month. It gets big-time computer industry players to cohost sessions. Even huge companies such as Microsoft are happy to have access to G&R customers, and such big names draw a lot of attendees. Its seminars have also produced a 12,000-name mailing list for G&R that yields high returns when it sends out sales letters.

How the G&R Computer Consulting Firm Handles Big Players Who Cohost Seminars with It

- G&R picks companies whose software they sell, or whose products complement its services.
- It pitches the fact that it does all the work. Big company reps can just present and walk away with leads.
- When national offices don't respond to its overtures, it enlists the company's local sales force, either to appear or to get cooperation from the head office.
- G&R maintains the host role, introducing all presenters. This helps it keep control and top billing.
- Partners usually put up part of the seminar cost and provide a raffle prize, which also encourages attendees to stay to the end.
- G&R gets a copy of all presentation material ahead of time to coordinate overlaps. It puts handouts together under its cover and logo.
- Breakout sessions allow one-on-one contact and demos. Often enough contracts are signed on-site to pay for the seminar immediately.
- G&R collects an evaluation form at the end that asks about attendees' interests. It gets first choice of all leads and passes on ones it can't handle.

From *Inc.* magazine

A Better "Guest Speaker"

Your customers can give your seminars a spontaneous dimension. Computer Smith, Inc., invited current customers to its seminars. They could provide informal testimonials to prospects in the audience. And at least one customer was also scheduled to speak at each seminar. In just a few minutes, the customer would talk about which services he or she used, providing a testimonial. Customers also answered questions, which could provide lead-ins for the company to cover further in its presentation.

Speaking Where Others Promote

There are literally hundreds of groups where I live, the San Francisco Bay Area, that regularly use unpaid speakers.

There are directories that list many of the groups. If there is no directory in your region, you can start with the phone book. Look under Organizations, Business Groups, and similar headings. In addition to the chambers of commerce, there should be Moose, Lion's, women's groups, sales organizations, and many others.

As discussed in the networking chapter, you can also find people who will tell you which groups are interesting to attend, and at which groups you might be able to speak. Monday Business Calendars will list groups, and you can ask other speakers for leads. The National Speakers' Association also has local chapters of serious speakers who share information (nsaspeaker.org).

Giving It Away Isn't Always Easy

The funny thing about presenting free talks is that they're fairly hard to give away.

Some groups are so disorganized that the speaker coordinators just grab whoever is handy or people they already know. Other groups schedule their entire agendas a year in advance.

With persistence and some personal appearances, you should be able to gradually get talks. One young consultant in our area, Robert, doesn't have a college education, but he speaks well. His name is often in the paper three or four times in the same month, speaking at different groups for free, to promote his various marketing services. He's done hundreds of talks over the years.

There's a bit of the chicken-and-egg problem in giving talks. No group wants to be the one at which you learn.

It helps to have some credentials as a speaker when you approach each new group. That's another area in which your volunteer lectures at schools can help. If you've lectured at local colleges, that is more impressive to most people than speaking to the average group.

"So Easy a Child Can Assemble It"

Getting sponsors to offer your seminars and classes takes persistence, but it is doable. When my oldest son was ten, he took the initiative to become a paid teacher at one of the local recreation districts. He'd seen me work with different colleges. He simply looked at the recreation department catalogue and suggested a course it had never offered.

Essentially, it was a Pee-Wee Baseball training camp for six-year-olds. He got a few friends from Little League to promise to help him, filled out the one-page application, and was accepted. It surprised us that the recreation director accepted his course proposal without checking with his parents!

Don't be disappointed if it's not as easy for you the first time you try it. My record is much worse than my son's 100 percent. But, if a ten-year-old can do it, the odds are greatly in your favor. And they won't check with your parents either!

You Can Make $250 and Up

In most areas, the best monetary return comes through the college and community college extension programs.

Most such extension programs are self-supporting. To sustain your presentation, it must draw enough people for the sponsors to make money. Your course description and self-description are crucial in marketing your course. Usually, ten or fifteen attendees is a minimum for a course to be run.

If you charged $50 apiece, and received half, you would make $250. The course I designed for my ex-partner, on how to build your own computer,

Places to Speak for Money

In our area, one of the local high school districts sponsors extension classes. So do a couple of local YMCAs, two recreation departments, and several community colleges. Going a few miles farther afield, there are many other community colleges and state colleges, as well as commercial groups such as the Learning Annex, which sponsor talks and produce a catalogue.

Groups at the park district or high school–extension level may pay $10 or $20 an hour for a three-hour seminar. At the community college–extension level, they generally pay you 40 to 60 percent of the gross.

!

sometimes drew $2,000 or $3,000 worth of people for a four-hour session at the bigger schools.

A more usual course, such as "How to Market" or "How to Be a Consultant," might draw thirty people at a big school and could be taught in half a day. Thus, you can make from $500 to $1,000 a day at the best schools. At the smaller schools, you might make as little as $100. Even if you work hard, you usually can't make a living from this kind of speaking, but it can be a good income supplement, and get you new clients.

Teaching is also great for networking. I don't use the courses to sell consulting. But I've wished many times that I was able to keep in contact with all the interesting people who've taken my classes. Some speakers even send out a brief newsletter to past students.

National Seminar Providers

If you're ready to "take it on the road," there are national seminar providers, such as the American Management Association and SkillPath. (These companies have generally become less prominent over the last decade.)

They get good speakers presenting canned programs for as little as $200 a time, plus commissions on product sales. (One speaker may do as many as 250 presentations a year.) This is exciting for some people, but it seems like a rugged life to me.

There are also other more specialized course sponsors. Most state bar associations, for instance, require lawyers to take a certain number of courses every year. This is also true of accountants, doctors, and others. Sometimes these courses do not have to be on professionals' technical specialties. A certain number of them can be about related skills, such as business practices.

In-Company Seminars

Seminars in host companies can be very lucrative and pleasant to give, but they're hard to get started.

Some big companies have a lunch program for employees where a wide variety of speakers give free presentations. In areas such as financial planning, these can be samples that allow the employees to look you over, creating future business for you. For instance, one consultant got Cray Research to pay for a free internal class for employees on how to finance children's college educations. The presentation was such a hit that many employees later paid to have plans developed specifically for them.

The best types of seminars to give in companies are training sessions. In these, you present a seminar to ten or twenty executives on, say, how to write a better memo. If they like it, the seminar might spread to all of their offices and managers. For instance, one group eventually trained thousands of managers in the old Chevron Oil Company on clearer business writing.

Getting these kinds of talks depends either on your contacts in big companies or on a marketing program. You need to use all the other techniques in this book to get these internal training sessions, from networking, to phoning human resources people, to sending letters, to giving talks at trade groups, to personal sales.

HOW TO GIVE A GOOD TALK

There are a lot of books on how to be a good speaker. Here are just a few ideas to get you started.

Most people think that their job in a speech is to cover a set of facts, to be entertaining, or both. Actually, the purpose of your speech should be to cover a topic passionately and enthusiastically. For every talk, have a mission (or purpose) that you can state in twenty words or less. This mission should both help the audience and market you.

Keep to a Few Main Points

You should have one central theme. Don't try to cover too much in one talk.

You should be able to list your major points on one page. Have simple points that clarify or elaborate your basic thesis. People don't remember much of what you say verbally, so they usually can't remember more than three main points.

Better Speech Humor

"Warm up your audience with a joke" is common advice. Unfortunately, planned jokes often seem contrived and artificial. It's better to appear spontaneous by making a joke about yourself or something that happens during your speech.

Know Your Audience and You'll Give a Great Speech

- Before you give a speech, find out who your audience is and what its members are interested in. Determine what their expectations of your speech are.
- To prepare, call a few people who will be in the audience to find out what they care about. Use the type of language they would use.
- In the introduction to your speech, try to work in a reference to the current situation. This lets listeners know you're not giving a canned presentation and shows you are relating to them on a personal basis.

An Example

For instance, if you were giving a talk about how to choose a service provider in your area, you might have three general points:

1. Ask friends for referrals.
2. Interview prospects and check for "chemistry."
3. Ask service providers for references.

Under each of these three points, you might have dozens of pieces of advice that elaborate on where to get referrals, how to interview people, and other topics.

THE FOUR KEY ELEMENTS OF A GOOD SPEECH

A good speech should have *content*, useful points that people can take away with them. It should use *stories* or examples. Often this is the main content that people remember. It should project *enthusiasm*. If you aren't enthusiastic about your topic, why should your audience be? Last is a point that many speakers overlook: *personalization*.

1. Content

Fast talkers, those who speak about 190 words a minute, consistently score higher with their audiences in the areas of enthusiasm, honesty, and trustworthiness than speakers who talk slowly.

Robert Half International

You must have reasonable content in your speech. For motivational speakers, this "content" is sometimes not facts that people can take away. It can be inspiration, or even the creation of an emotion in the audience.

By focusing on three clear and simple points, those who don't care about details will be able to understand your general presentation and see your points clearly. Under those three general points, you can include a lot of specific details.

By organizing many details and examples under your main points, you demonstrate your mastery of your topic. This will impress listeners who know more. They will get more from your talk and respect the depth of your knowledge, even if they don't remember all the details either.

The average listener can understand about 500 words per minute. The average speaker speaks at only 100 to 200 words per minute. (Zig Ziglar, a classic sales motivator, says that he has "gusts" of up to 350 words per minute.) This means that if you don't include sufficient content, listeners' minds will have lots of time to wander.

2. Stories

There is something memorable about stories, from childhood on. And there is great credibility in providing real examples of your points, rather than just listing the facts. This is what most people will remember from your talks.

Try to relate your story or example to your audience. Good examples or stories about "themselves" are especially relevant and memorable.

3. Enthusiasm

Enthusiasm may be the most important aspect of speaking.

Recent research from psychology shows that emotions are literally contagious! If you show enthusiasm for your topic, your audience will be more interested. You will enjoy it more, and your listeners will "catch" some of your enthusiasm.

If I had to boil down giving a good speech to one rule, it would be to talk about a subject where you truly believe you have something important to share, and project that enthusiasm to your audience. Your enthusiasm also shows sincerity and gives you great credibility!

Building a Relationship with Audience Members

1. Where are they from?
2. What do they like about their careers?
3. What do they dislike?
4. What types of jobs do they do?
5. Who do they admire?
6. What competitive issues do they face?

4. Personalization

You don't have to change your speech completely to achieve a customized effect. The main change is in the introductory remarks. Then you drop in a few items during the speech that refer to the group to which you're speaking.

The way to customize your presentation is to know the people to whom you are speaking and their interests. One simple way to learn more about your audience members is to mingle with them before the speech.

By speaking with a few, you can pick up a quick sense of the language and "wavelength" on which they are operating.

Other times, you can research your audience ahead of time. Talk to members or officers of a group about the issues that concern them.

NOTES, AD-LIB, OR MEMORIZATION?

You should memorize at least the three to five main points of your speech.

This way, if you begin to tell a story and wander from your main point, you'll be able to bring yourself back. You can also have a file card or piece of paper on the podium as a backup.

For those of you who think well on your feet, you can ad-lib the entire talk from your outline. Some of us have our brains and mouths wired together, so it's easy for us to talk "off the cuff."

This approach to speaking gives a natural, spontaneous feeling to the talk, rather than it seeming like a canned presentation. The audience can tell that you are not simply reciting a memorized speech. The weakness of this approach is that you can stumble a bit or lose your train of thought.

Please Don't Read a Speech

The absolute worst way to present is to read a speech.

If you must read, be sure that the speech is written in a "spoken" mode, not a "written" mode. When you write, the sentences tend to be longer and the thoughts more complex. When you speak, the sentences are shorter, the words simpler, and the thoughts clearer. Reading from a book is the worst possible approach.

If you must read a speech, test it first. Record it and listen carefully to determine if it actually is clear in a spoken mode.

Memorized Speeches Can Be Awkward

The same thing applies to a memorized speech. Be sure it's a *speech*, not a written document. Many times, a single file card will give you key words to help trigger your memory. Or a page of notes, or outline, can be used to combine a memorized and spontaneous approach.

How to Subtly Cue Yourself

Another way to present a speech that provides you with heavy cueing, yet looks very spontaneous to the audience, is to use slides or overheads.

If all the points are on PowerPoint you can work without notes because your notes are on the wall! This allows you to ad-lib a little, but still follow a tight script.

Don't make the mistake of reading your overheads word for word. Restate the points in your own language. People become bored if you read the slides. As you restate, you can occasionally tell a brief story or elaboration that is not on the overheads. This reminds people that you are giving a talk, not simply showing slides.

CONCLUSION: THE ULTIMATE TALK

After you are confident and competent as a speaker, a more daring goal for your talks, workshops, and seminars is to try to change the *behavior* of your audience. Can you offer members something so memorable and compelling that they'll apply it to their lives? This is the ultimate challenge: to motivate people *and* give them a realistic way to take action.

Public Speaking Tips

- Breathe from the diaphragm, and project your voice.
- If using typed notes, use a large, easy-to-read typeface, in narrow, easy-to-read columns.
- Use body language to support your words.
- Use pauses. The audience will process information between your words. Don't fill up dead air with a rush of words.

From *Successful Meetings* magazine

AGENDA

Action is eloquence.

WILLIAM SHAKESPEARE

Choosing Your Topics

▶ Develop a list of five topics on which you could give a knowledge-able talk. Which ones do you really care about?

▶ Create a one-page handout on each topic that you can also use as giveaways, and to generate publicity.

Getting Started

▶ If you're nervous about speaking, visit a local Toastmasters group.

▶ Call a friend about promoting a seminar together.

▶ Offer a mini-seminar in your office that you promote to your existing clients and through free listings in the newspaper.

▶ Contact your local college extension program, YMCA, or recreation department to get its rules for offering courses.

▶ At the next group meeting you go to that has a speaker, find out how the booking was arranged.

▶ Call a local Rotary, Lions, or similar group. There are a lot of them that have a brief speaker every week.

▶ Find a directory of local organizations, or start to create one from the Yellow Pages and newspaper listings of talks.

▶ Don't forget that many seminars are also presented online. Some are free (gemarketingnetwork.com) and some are paid (speakernetnews.com). You can do your own or work with others.

CHAPTER TWELVE

ONLINE MARKETING

Integrated Marketing in Action

> *The Internet allows information to be*
> *distributed worldwide*
> *at basically zero cost.*
> BILL GATES
> Microsoft Corporation

Online marketing success stories are common. The one I like best is from a small, local tile contractor, Bill Furner. Bill said there weren't many contractors online when he started, so he was featured in the media and asked to speak. His site won lots of awards, including a couple from realty sites that could be good referral sources. He called himself "Mr. Tile."

Bill was self-taught on the Mac and his site was self-produced. He did a lot of upscale tile work for hot tubs, kitchens, bathrooms, and so forth. His site featured appealing pictures of his jobs as well as listing resources such as books. Surprisingly, Bill said many people found him online. He credited more than half of his business to his Web site.

Did he get rich beyond his wildest dreams? Absolutely not. But, if the Web can work for a local contractor, it can work for almost anyone.

The goal of this chapter is to give you an overview of online marketing and suggest some ways you can improve your efforts.

STILL GROWING: GOOD AND BAD

When I first wrote a chapter about online marketing and did seminars in the mid-1990s, I had to spend time explaining what the Internet, the Web, and online meant. Despite the "dot-com" bust in 2000, it's no longer necessary to explain the basics.

The technology doesn't matter; it could change completely. The important thing is that more and more people are now in the habit of communicating, looking for information, and buying online. This will continue.

Most people who talk about online marketing are all positive. However, the Web is also messy. As with every other channel, people you want to reach are overexposed to marketing and distracted by "chaff" such as spam. Searching is inefficient and the Web is loaded with hype, outdated information, and small-time scams. This probably will continue as well.

THE "NEW" MARKETING

The Web is a powerful marketing medium. However, while there is new technology involved in making it work, the principles of effective marketing discussed in other chapters still apply.

While at one level, the Web is just one marketing method, at another, you can use all the methods we've discussed on it. You can do advertising, sales, publicity, customer service, research, planning, merchandising, and more online. That's why the subtitle of this chapter is "Integrated Marketing in Action" (see page 250 for a definition).

FOUR BROAD TYPES OF ONLINE MARKETING

While there are hundreds of specific ways to market online, it's useful to remember that there are four major categories of online marketing:

1. Your Web site
2. Other people's Web sites
3. Your outgoing e-mail
4. Searches you do

Your Web Site

While there have been different generations of Web sites, in one way, they are all the same. All Web sites are similar in that they sit somewhere waiting for people to find them. They can be giant depositories of interactive information usable by customers, the press, your employees, and casual browsers. However, *your Web site will not do any marketing for you until you get people to go to it.*

Other People's Web Sites

One way to deal with the problem of people not finding your Web site is to put material on other, better-known Web sites. This can vary from advertising, to affiliate sites, to articles by you that others post on their sites. Advertising on big sites can cost you a lot. Links and many other methods can be free.

Your E-mail

E-mail is still the most common activity people do online. It doesn't matter whether you're sending plain text or video, e-mail is still an outgoing form of communication and communication is marketing.

E-mail can consist of newsletters (e-zines), personal notes to friends and customers, contributions to lists, or spam. The key variables are the same as for direct mail of any sort. The most important factor in your success with e-mail is the quality of your list of recipients.

Searches You Do

This area might be more accurately called research. You can use the Web to gather information about your customers and your competitors. You can find people to link to, or who might become personal referral sources. You can find individuals, companies, or directories to contact by e-mail.

Online searches let you find your contacts and information worldwide. As a research tool, the Web is a wonder that we take for granted. Yesterday I needed to find information on an idea that I wanted to include in this book. It took me only a minute to find the details I needed. You can do the same thing for your customers, as well as find many prospects.

USING THE WEB EFFECTIVELY

In theory, the Web is a great equalizer: An individual or a small company can have as valuable a Web site as a large corporation. In practice, the money of big firms is an advantage, but often their sites are less personal and interesting than smaller sites created with passion.

Many big companies tend to approach online marketing as a medium like television—how many "eyeballs" can they reach for X dollars? More sophisticated large companies are moving toward using technology to customize their interactions with each customer.

Smaller companies often go online just to keep up, or because customers expect it. Despite their lack of sophistication, small companies can achieve more online than larger companies because they are, by necessity, closer to one-to-one relationships with each customer.

Doing business online allows direct contact with customers. This can cut costs, but the greater benefit is simply allowing more people in your company to have direct, unfiltered contact with customers. Everyone in your company can now build relationships directly with customers.

FOURTEEN ADVANTAGES OF ONLINE MARKETING

Online marketing has many advantages that make it appealing.

1. Online Marketing Is Integrated Marketing
Integrated marketing means using multiple methods to reach the same people with a consistent message. Online can be your billboard, your brochure, your catalogue, and your focus group. It gives you a lot of tools and flexibility in your marketing. For instance, Sierra South, a store for those who love the outdoors, replaced its print catalogue with an online newsletter and special online offers. Business has never been better.

2. Online Marketing Can Be Inexpensive
It's easy entry—simple marketing can be done with nothing but your time. And unlike other media, your costs don't necessarily go up as you provide more information or contact more people.

3. Online Is Fast

You can post up-to-date information for your customers and prospects immediately. You can even send it out automatically to your list.

4. Online Is Simple

You can save steps, both for you and your customers.

5. Online Marketing Can Be Customized

Customers can be presented with specific information that is directly aimed at them. For instance, Amazon.com suggests books that fit the buyer's profile.

6. Online Marketing Gives a Lot of Control to Customers

In a world of one-to-one marketing, where customers want personalized service, online marketing leads in this direction easily and naturally.

7. Online Customer Service Improves Service

In addition to giving customers a sense of control, using online approaches can improve service in a number of ways. For instance, more complete information can be made available to customers in a searchable format. And internal intranets can aid all staff in providing customer service.

8. Online Service Cuts Costs

Because online resources encourage self-service, costs of supporting customers can be cut dramatically. For instance, American Express estimated that it saved 60 to 70 percent on the costs of customer contacts, compared to telephone calls!

9. Online Marketing Is Interactive

Much like the personal sales process, you have a chance to get feedback from prospects and buyers.

10. Online Marketing Is Information Rich

Pictures, video, sound, and text can provide more information than any other single marketing medium.

The Homeless Online

While the poor and uneducated tend to not be online, there are exceptions. Schools and libraries make Internet connections widely available, as well as programs that target underserved groups.

A dramatic example of individual initiative to get online occurred in Northern California. Car batteries were being stolen from road maintenance vehicles. Police found the culprit under a freeway overpass: A homeless man had stolen the batteries to power his portable computer and wireless connection to the Net!

!

11. Online Exposes You to a Growing and Diverse Audience

While the Web does not reflect the entire world, many diverse types of people are online. By looking for specific interest groups, you can find representatives of almost any type of person. (See Chapter Three on niche marketing.)

12. Online Marketing Is International

You have immediate access to an international audience, whether for sales, feedback, or ideas.

13. Online Marketing Is a Twenty-Four-Hour Medium

People can respond when they want. If you're trying to run a fast company, this is the tool that will get you there. When someone asks for information, your computer can automatically send him or her a response (using autoresponders), even if you're asleep at the time.

14. Online Marketing Creates a Sense of Community

Through chat rooms, discussion groups, newsletters, and other tools, you can strengthen relationships with customers and build community.

ONLINE MARKETING ALSO HAS DISADVANTAGES

Online marketing is the subject of a lot of hype. The main drawback is that people often expect too much from it. They think if they have a Web site, they won't have to work on their marketing anymore.

If marketing is about building relationships with others, you know that no tool can do it all for you. You can use online methods to enhance your relationships with prospects, customers, and other constituencies such as your employees and community. But if you expect online marketing to be a "magic wand," it will distract you from more effective activities.

SIXTEEN WAYS TO MARKET ONLINE

Now let's look at some of the details of marketing online. There are many specific ways to market online. Here are sixteen of the key ones.

1. Your Signature

When you send a letter, you sign your name and possibly your title. For e-mail, it's traditional to have your name and an additional few lines which can be a mini-ad for what you do. When you post intelligently to a discussion group, or respond to others, they will often want to know more about you.

For instance, a signature could say, "John Smith, Construction Marketing Specialist. We help you impress architects and owners." Your signature should also include a hotlink to your Web page. If your domain name is a great one, this can be a valuable marketing tool on its own.

When a major marketing publication wanted to reprint a chapter I wrote on online marketing years ago, it wanted to cut out this "signature" point as too "small time." It didn't understand the personal touch.

In one survey, the most effective method of getting people to your Web site was responses to your e-mail and signature. Even where self-promotion is sometimes frowned on, your signature line is acceptable.

2. Give Away Advice

Giving away free advice to various forums, chat groups, and mailing lists allows you to build relationships. Many "big" names in online business got that way because they facilitate online discussion groups.

When contributing advice to an online discussion, learn the rules of the group first. Observe for a while, or read past issues.

Build Relationships Think of e-mail as a chance to build relationships, just as you would have done by letter in the old days. Customized e-mail is the ultimate in one-to-one marketing.

Friendly E-mail Pays Off

One online marketing consultant makes a point of sending people e-mail notes when she sees something they've written online that she likes. She compliments them and adds information from her own experience. She doesn't promote herself at all, but about half of the recipients go to her Web site on their own *and* e-mail her about publishing something from it on their sites. She's had two job offers, many business leads, and developed "pen pal" relationships, about both business and nonbusiness topics.

Trade Links

If you search for "Link Exchange" on a search engine such as Google.com, you'll find exchange sources for many countries and interest groups. Banner exchanges and Web rings do something similar.

E-mail combines features of the phone and writing. People often dash off quick responses. Thus, e-mail often has a less-polished feel than might a letter you edited and thought about.

Of course, I recommend that you edit carefully. Everything that you produce should represent you exactly the way you wish.

3. Links

One of the major features of the Web is hyperlinks. There are two ways to use these links to market yourself.

Links to You The first way to use links is to get other sites to provide links to yours. This is the second-best source of site visitors. And, of course, a link from another site is an endorsement that your site is worth visiting. Some search engines use it as a measure of your site's value.

Links Away from You The other way is to link your site to other sites where your customers will want to go. This makes your site more valuable. Your Web site becomes the central resource. By constantly adding interesting links, people will have an incentive to come back and see what's new.

Of course, there's a danger in providing links *away* from your page. Even if they'd been intending to come back, something in another page takes them to another page, and so on. Pretty soon they've forgotten where they are. This leads us to method number 4.

4. Encourage Bookmarks

Bookmarking is a way of recording or indexing the Web pages you've visited. Tell people on your first page to bookmark it so that they can get back easily. You might want to mention this several places on your site, especially near material that is updated regularly, or near your best material.

You can also use technical devices such as frames to keep people on your page. Some systems even go too far by making it hard to escape a site when you're done with it!

5. Web Page Design

Proper design is aesthetically pleasing as well as effective.

Practical Graphics Tips In addition to the general value of "good design," there are some specific things to consider.

One design issue is *where* you link to other Web sites. You don't want to put links on your first page. You want visitors to leave your page only after they have read something valuable.

Another simple point is to remember to put your name, address, phone, fax, or e-mail address on every page—as the computer presents them to readers. If browsers print any page, they will be able to contact you.

Remember that not everyone uses the same browser. View your page using different browsers to see how the presentation looks. For instance, your type is read and shown different ways by the various browsers. And people with slow modems can't wait to download complex graphics.

Title Your Graphics

Many people turn on the "ignore graphics" option in their browsers. This means all the viewer sees is "[graphic]" in the place the graphic would be.

HINT: Construct your Web page using the "ALT=" feature. This allows you to include a one- to four-word description. Instead of seeing "[graphic]", viewers will see "[CEO photo]." That way viewers can decide if it's worth clicking on a particular photo. Some search engines will also pick these up as key words and improve your ranking.

6. Fresh Content
I call old pages "cobweb sites." If you aren't constantly adding new links, new articles, new research, and other items, your page becomes old news. Give people a reason to come back by telling them what is coming, as well.

7. Custom Pages
By linking your Web page to a database, some programs let you create custom material for each person who visits you.

8. Search Engines, Directories, and More
One of the best ways (first to third in various surveys) to be found on the Web is to get yourself listed in the top search engines and indexes. This is a topic that has its own specialists (SEOs: search engine optimizers) and courses. For the average firm, building relationships online (such as with links) will be more important than search engine listings, but I'll touch on the topic here.

Of course, if you're not in the top twenty or so listings, they're not of much value. Some directories try to cover most Web pages. They combine directories and search engines to help users find resources that they need.

Reasons to Visit a Site

One direct mail consultant has a "critique of the week" on his page. He takes a mailing he receives, scans it in, and tears it apart. He also has databases of marketing statistics and an index of articles people can order. By constantly updating all these, people have lots of reasons to visit his page regularly.

The Name Is the Thing

The title of your page is your first set of key words for some search engine listings. Leave your ego behind. Maynard, Garcia, Beck may be a fine name for a law firm, but is difficult to remember. Patentlawyers.com would be a better name for a Web page.

When a poster and framing store changed its Web page name from artuframe.com (not a bad name since it states the product), to the simpler art.com, the owners experienced an immediate 30 percent jump in site traffic.

There are also services that will list you in multiple directories. The rules for getting listed on each search engine are different, and they change. For instance, paying for listings is now common. (For an ongoing discussion on how to get listed, check out www. searchengine watch.com.)

Key Words This brings us to the idea of key words. Most directories and search engines look for key words (including meta tags). Make your key words plural. Searches for the singular will find it, and searches for the plural don't find the singular.

What you name your Web page and what key words you use to describe it are important marketing decisions. You have to think in terms of the users. What are they going to be looking for?

Because my URL for one Web page is "rickcrandall.com," people have to know my name to find it easily. To reach the "masses," I should call a page the "online marketing, consulting, advertising, publicity, merchandising, retail, customer service page from Rick Crandall"! Of course, that's too long for a URL, but I can put words like these in the text or meta tags.

Invisible Text or Pixels This is an example of the technical approach to rankings that change as search engines and Web site designers play games with each other to improve rankings. If you want to add extra key words to your page that some search engines will find, but users won't see, you can make text the same color as the background. This makes the text or pixel image invisible to your users, but recordable by search engines.

Some search engines hold this trick against you. One way around this is to use a white background and black text, then a black background image. The engines then see your page as black text on white, but users don't. (If this seems complicated, or more trouble than it's worth, it may be, but these games can help your rankings.)

The invisible pixel is a 1" × 1" pixel image the same color as your background. The search engines and users won't see the image. But some search engines will read the "alt" tag labeling the image, so you get more key words on your page.

Buying Rankings More and more search engines are allowing you to bid on clicks from their listings. For instance, the person who bids thirty cents per click would be ranked ahead of ten cents per click. If users click through to you, you pay the search engine.

The way to handle this cost-effectively is not to bid on the popular terms. It is to bid on *many* lesser terms. For instance, at Overture.com, you can find a list of what terms were searched how many times. Start at the bottom and bid on all the ones that relate to your site. For the same budget you would spend to get, say, one hundred clicks from one top searched word, you can often get five hundred clicks from hundreds of less-often searched words.

The Open Directory Project (http://dmoz.org) There are some places to be listed that are disproportionately important because they are used by other search engines. The ODP is one of those. Here human volunteers review every listing. One hundred other search engines make some use of these listings. Make sure you submit to the correct category. Some volunteers get grumpy when you waste their time.

9. Advertising on Other Sites
Entrepreneurs are constantly inventing new types of advertising to buy on popular Web sites and new technologies to present it.

As you know from the chapter on advertising, I don't like having to pay your money before you know how effective an ad will be. Fortunately, there are per inquiry, per order, and barter methods of advertising where you know what you're paying for. For instance, ad exchange services put your ad on smaller sites in return for you placing ads on your site.

Most common are "per click" arrangements where you pay for each visitor delivered to your site. Unfortunately, even with targeted clicks, it usually takes several hundred visitors to your site to make one sale, or produce a strong lead for your services.

10. Give Away Something
People like free things. When you can give away valuable information (e-books, postcards, graphics, and so on), people will come to your site, tell others, and remember it.

If you give away information you've developed, it is a work sample demonstrating your expertise. For instance, several people have given away the first chapter of a book and sold the rest. Or they've given away one version of their software and sold upgrades.

11. Viral Marketing

A variation on giving something away is called *viral marketing*. If you were a big fan of some popular music star such as Britney Spears, and you saw her having lunch at your local restaurant, you might go online and tell your list of chat buddies about it. They would share it with theirs, and so on.

Viral marketing spreads like a virus because it is something considered valuable by the recipients. It might be a new joke, a free resource only available for a short time, or a choice bit of gossip.

The difficulty is to motivate prospects to *want* to spread the word. Many "hip" movies and parties are promoted successfully this way. For those of us who are less hip, we can try to come up with the right material to start a "virus" creating word-of-mouth for us.

The King and Queen of Spam

Spamming was made notorious by attorneys Laurence Canter and Martha Siegel. In 1994 they posted ads for their immigration services in every usenet group they could find. People hated it and the lawyers' computer service was closed down from the "flames" and "mail bombs" they received. But they claim that they also got $100,000 of business from it, and they wrote a book.

12. Spam

Spamming is the Net's junk mail. As of 2003, only a few states had laws regulating spam. And under these laws, you are allowed to solicit people once as long as you tell them it is advertising and let them tell you not to contact them again. While few people recommend spam, it is legal.

Netiquette The online world was originally used by academics. Most material was given away. It was considered poor taste to actively promote yourself or to impose yourself on users.

In addition, much like junk faxes, users pay for their accounts and their time online. If you spam them, they are paying for your marketing. This is an area where there will continue to be lots of conflict and evolution.

13. Your Online Newsletter or E-zine

While this is a form of e-mail, it is so important that it deserves its own section. Creating a brief newsletter online is a great way to keep in touch and build relationships. It gives people a sample of your expertise and philosophy, lets them become familiar with you, and encourages responses. Having a good e-zine and list can be more important than your Web site.

The trick is to develop an opt-in list where people *ask* for your newsletter. Start by inviting your existing customers and contacts to subscribe. Add notices of your e-zine to your signature, Web site, and other ads. Then, ask for referrals. You can also register with e-zine directories.

14. Encourage Referrals

You can create ways on your site for visitors to easily refer you to others. For instance, you can have a "postcard" on your site that people can send to friends just by filling in the e-mail address. Or think of eBay, where you can forward the description of an item to a friend.

By making it easy for people to forward a free tip sheet, an article, or something else from your site, you create referrals and build traffic.

15. Affiliate Programs

Amazon.com popularized affiliate programs. In its case, you recommend books on your site, and people can click and go directly to Amazon to order. Amazon then pays you a commission (usually under 10 percent) on all sales from your site. With the success of the Amazon program, thousands of other online affiliate programs have been created. For instance, you can earn commissions for recommending search engines, graphics sources, consultants, and almost anything else.

If you can pay commissions to encourage other people to sell or recommend your products or services, you may be able to set up a successful affiliate program. The best programs are really just referral sources. People put a link to you on their Web sites and recommend what you offer because they use it themselves. (Web rings linking related sites are somewhat similar.)

Unfortunately, most affiliate programs sell things that people don't need—at extremely high prices—and often the programs don't pay their commissions reliably. There is also a sense of people "taking in each other's laundry" because many of the programs involve selling courses on how to market online. If everyone makes their money from selling instructions on how to market online, that means that everyone is just selling to newcomers who hope to sell to more newcomers! To succeed online, ultimately you'll have to sell something that isn't available everywhere else.

16. "Cold" Individual E-mail

The definition of spam is not really fixed. It tends to mean mass, impersonal, commercial mail to people you don't know, but some people resent any contact they didn't ask for. However, I have had success sending individual notes to people I don't know.

For each note, I type in the person's name and customize the message when I can. However, I may send a similar note to many people.

For example, I may search online for Web sites of marketing consultants. I then send all of them an e-mail inviting them to sell my marketing books to their clients, to write a chapter in a book, or to subscribe to my free newsletter. The connection is commercial and "cold," but it potentially fits them.

I might also be researching a topic and ask for information in their area.

I've done a great deal of business online with this approach. While very few people ask me not to contact them again (less than 1 percent), sometimes up to 20 percent respond positively.

Another firm, net-market.com, located e-mail addresses for a client in a directory maintained by the client's competitor! Thirteen percent responded to a custom e-mail. Speaker Steve Waterhouse received a 50 percent response from e-mailing associations about his speaking to their groups.

Web Malls

You may notice that Web "malls"are not in my list of techniques. While they work with good promotion, they are usually a marketing dead end. They tend to be overpriced deals promoted by seminars around the country or low-level junk sites run by exploitive marketers.

NEW MARKETING MODELS

You need to develop acceptable new ways to invite people to receive more information from you without offending them.

We don't have to reinvent the wheel here. In direct marketing, advertising, and telemarketing, two-step marketing has been developed. This is probably the best model from traditional marketing to apply to online marketing. In fact, online will probably end up popularizing three- and four-step marketing programs.

Marketing Is About Relationships

Let's say you have a list of e-mail addresses of people you think might be interested in your product or service. Or, even worse, you have a large list of e-mail addresses about which you know nothing. You're tempted by the fact that it may cost you only a little time to send them all e-mail messages.

So you give in to this temptation. If you send a commercial message, you'll be guilty of spamming. You'll get flame-mail and your service provider may even disconnect you!

Step 1: Try an Invitation

Is there another way to open the relationship? What if you sent people an invitation that said, "I wasn't sure if this was appropriate for you, but if you're interested in information on XYZ, just respond and I'll get you more information free. If you don't respond, I'll take you off the list and not bother you again. Thank you for your time." This would be legal spam. You are asking for permission to contact prospects further (see Seth Godin's *Permission Marketing*).

Try to offer people something of real value that "fits" them. In direct mail, you might get a .5 percent response from a list that fits your product. My research suggests that if you spam people you don't know anything about, you might get only a .05 percent response. (That's 400 per 800,000 messages.) With my personalized "cold e-mail" (method number 16), I might get a 5 percent response or better—that's a hundred times better than bulk spam.

Meta Search Engines

Searching online is still inefficient. For instance, in a study we did, no single search engine was best for more than one test search. For completeness, save time by using meta search engines—they simultaneously search about twenty different search engines. (I use dogpile.com at present.)

Step 2: Start a Relationship

For the people who actually identify themselves as interested, the second step is to send them the material you promised them.

You'd start off by saying, "Here's the information you asked for on XYZ." Then, in a low-key way, you would explain any offer to them. Because these are selected prospects, you might get a 10 percent response, or better. And some of the others would buy later.

Multistep Marketing

Where it would become three- or four-step marketing is when you might not even ask for the order the second time. You might say, "We're very interested in getting input from new people and seeing what they like in this area. We'll keep you informed with free reports and other material that become available in this area, unless you send us an e-mail message that says you don't want to hear anything more from us."

First they had to "opt in" to get on your list (they had to make a positive response). Now they have to "opt out" to get off your list. It's like the continuity book clubs. Subscribers will get more information unless they explicitly ask to be removed from your list.

The Relationship Builds

You can now send these new people your newsletters, press releases, or other nonpushy communications that build the relationship and express your personality. This allows them to get used to you and builds potential trust. You might also start creating a community because you'll want to build relationships with many people at the same time. You'd do this with a discussion group or other tool that allows your audience members to interact with each other under your sponsorship.

At some point, it will become appropriate to make recipients an offer. Your newsletter may have interesting articles and information. It may also have a note attached to it that says, "Special this month. If you'd like me to critique your internal policies manuals for the newest HR law at half price, send them to me." Or you may say, "We've just written a book on this topic and we have a free report or we have a paid report." Gradually it becomes more and more natural to offer recipients things that they could pay for.

SUMMARY

The good news is that you are still on the ground floor of a major new business medium. There's still time to be a pioneer, despite the fact that others have been experimenting with the commercial Internet since 1994.

The bad news is that there is lots of worthless material online. Big companies waste money on beautifully designed pages, but don't connect emotionally with their customers. And most "fancy" pages aren't designed to load fast or be user friendly. Small companies get involved in scams and "garbage," and search engines still waste lots of time and find much unrelated material.

Online Mortgages

Eastern Mortgage Services got fifty to one hundred home equity loan applications a week from its Web site within months of creating it. Plus, the applications were for higher average amounts but cost Eastern only $10 to handle online versus more than $100 the traditional way.

The company approaches its offer as it would any other direct mail solicitation by making it to the point and easy to read, offering free twenty-four-hour approval, and calling for action. To attract people, Eastern employs the "traditional" online marketing techniques of registering with search engines and linking with more than two hundred other sites.

Test Before You Spend

Success in any marketing comes from testing, and online is a great place to test. You can test different ads or offers to be used "offline." You can test different places to market online. You can track from which directories your inquiries come by using Web analysis tools or a variety of e-mail addresses (equivalent to post office boxes in direct mail). You can post notices to different groups using codes. You can begin to understand from where actual business or viable inquiries come.

In other words, just because online is a new and exciting medium doesn't mean old rules don't apply. Find people who need what you have to offer. Track your responses. And build relationships to do lots of business over time.

Those are the basics of good marketing—both online and offline. They will apply to any new medium.

AGENDA

We must either find a way or make one.
HANNIBAL

Your Web Site

▶ If you don't have a Web page, look for a free place to practice with one (for example, aol.com, tripod.com, or geocities.com).

▶ Consider creating multiple Web pages, each focused to reach one group of customers. Then link them together.

▶ Improve your Web site with forms and small Java programs (applets).

▶ Ask people you know for links.

Your E-mail

▶ Improve your signature line.

▶ Work to build your own list for an opt-in e-mail newsletter.

▶ Send lots of e-mail correspondence and answer your e-mail promptly.

▶ Write articles that go on e-zines and their Web sites.

▶ Contribute to discussion groups, or run one.

Your Search Efforts

▶ Get on mailing lists relevant to your interests. The I-advertising Digest (internetadvertising. org) and I-sales Digest (audettemedia.com) are good marketing ones.

▶ Do searches for people who could link to your Web site.

▶ Search for directories of e-zines and discussion forums.

CHAPTER THIRTEEN

CUSTOMER SERVICE

Where the Real Gold Is Buried

*The Platinum Rule™ goes beyond the golden rule.
Don't treat people the way you want to be treated,
treat them the way they want to be treated.*
TONY ALESSANDRA
The Platinum Rule

GOOD MARKETING CAN MAKE YOU *FAIL* FASTER!

Good marketing gets people to try you sooner. If you're not any good at what you do, customers won't come back, they'll tell others you're no good, and you'll fail sooner. If you're good at what you do—and at relating to clients—marketing will bring you increased success.

Providing great customer service is the *most effective, least expensive* way of marketing. If you are established in business, this is the most important chapter in this book! Building relationships with existing clients should receive the majority of your marketing budget and attention.

Building Repeat Business

If you are new in business, you can't get repeat business yet. But you should be thinking of the lifetime value of potential customers, not just the profit to you from one transaction. This can change the way you conduct your marketing, handle problems, and invest in clients for the long term.

If you're established in business, at least 70 percent of your business should be from past clients and their referrals. Across many services, from legal to construction, most profitable firms meet the 70 percent figure, and very profitable firms often reach 90 percent. This doesn't mean that

Repeat-Customer Value

Taco Bell has determined that a repeat customer is worth about $11,000 in lifetime total sales. At Sewell Cadillac, that figure is $332,000. A recent study found that reducing customer defections by just 5 percent resulted in an 85 percent profit increase in a bank's branch system, a 50 percent profit increase in an insurance brokerage, and a 30 percent increase in an auto service chain.

Harvard Business School
Achieving Breakthrough Service

70 percent or more of your clients do business with you every year. It means that more than 70 percent of your revenue comes from past clients. In some fields, clients don't need you every year. To make up for this, you must provide new services to existing clients.

For instance, Brian Farley estimates that 60 percent of his yearly loan broker business is repeat and 30 percent is referral. He prefers to put his marketing dollars into building relationships with customers and referral sources; and, of course, it pays off.

Brian has been one of the top two hundred mortgage brokers in the United States since starting his business. He tries to provide super service to clients, such as prefilling out all mortgage applications. And he cultivates real estate agents and other referral sources. For example, he faxes updates to agents so they can keep their clients informed. And he makes donations to the favorite nonprofits of key referral sources, as well as throwing an annual client party.

THE LOYALTY EFFECT

Principles of Loyalty

- Play to win/win: Profiting at the expense of partners is a shortcut to a dead end.
- Keep it simple: Complexity is the enemy of speed and responsiveness.
- Reward the right results: Worthy partners deserve worthy goals.
- Listen hard, talk straight: Long-term relationships require honest, two-way communication and learning.
- Preach what you practice: Actions often speak louder than words, but together they are unbeatable.

Frederick Reichheld
Loyalty Rules!

Perhaps the most practically important findings in marketing over the last few decades have been the studies that documented the true value of repeat business. In *The Loyalty Effect*, Frederick Reichheld summarized studies that showed that a 5 percent increase in customer retention can lead to 25 to 95 percent increases in long-term profits.

The reasons that small increases in retention lead to much larger increases in profits are complex.

1. It is at least five times more expensive to get a new client than to keep an old one. I believe that ratio is much higher. Marketing costs are reduced and reductions in expenses go straight to your bottom line.

2. Just as reductions in expenses have direct effects on profits, additional services to clients can

often be added at no cost. If you are not booked 100 percent, new income from your previously unused capacity becomes straight profit.

3. There are also considerable efficiencies in time when dealing with familiar client situations.

4. To produce service that leads to high loyalty, firms also must have a happy staff. This leads to less turnover and internal expense. Lower turnover in staff, in turn, supports better client relationships.

When we talk about repeat business, I mean from *good* clients. We all know that there are some clients you should fire! And as your marketing gets better, you will be able to pick and choose clients based on profitability and your own preferences.

Most of this chapter will focus on how to create thrilling service. You need to start with the premise that average service is a negative for your business.

Most customers don't leave you because of your technical incompetence, or to go to your greatest competitors. As the figure shows, they leave because of small disatisfactions with your service.

How Clients Are Lost

- 16% Product/ Service Dissatisfaction
- 11% Competitive Inroads
- 68% Staff Discourtesy
- 4% Move
- 1% Die

IT'S NOT ENOUGH TO BE GOOD AT WHAT YOU DO

It was Ralph Waldo Emerson who said, "If you build a better mousetrap, write a better sonnet, . . . the world will beat a path to your door." Well, Ralph Waldo Emerson may have been well known as a philosopher, but I don't think he knew too much about business!

Too many professionals want to agree with Emerson that it's enough to do a good job at what you do, and the business will follow.

Unfortunately, it is generally not enough in today's day and age, unless you have no competition.

Top customer service should mean three things:

1. How well you do your job delivering the service customers purchase
2. How well you and your staff treat customers in your little interactions and the extras you give them
3. What kind of *overall* relationship you build with customers

CREATING YOUR OWN LEGENDS

It's much easier to find stories of bad customer service than great service. It isn't easy to generate such stories, but you can do it if you look for opportunities to thrill customers.

Take the case of Sheldon Bowles, who has now written books about service. In the 1970s when self-service was taking over in gas stations, he created a chain of *full-service* stations in Canada.

Sheldon wanted his service to be great *and* fun for users. So he designed his stations like Indianapolis 500 pit stops. Attendants dressed in red jumpsuits and raced to your car. One pumped gas, one looked under the hood, and a third offered you coffee and a paper while vacuuming your car.

Sheldon's retro stations were better than the past. They were impressive and enjoyable for customers. So, naturally, they prospered and created raving fans who sung their praises.

CUSTOMER SATISFACTION VERSUS DELIGHT

Use a Guarantee

Products often have guarantees of satisfaction or your money back. Services are less likely to have guarantees. But according to Christopher Hart of the Harvard Business School, "A service guarantee can be a turbocharger to force change and quality improvement, making a good company much better."

The book title *Raving Fans* makes a point: *Satisfied* customers are not enough. Satisfied customers are just people who don't have a better alternative and will leave as soon as they find one. What you need is *delighted* customers, *ecstatic* customers, *raving fans*! You need clients who love you and want to do anything to help you succeed.

The difference between satisfied customers and delighted customers is night and day in terms of customer loyalty and repeat business. For instance, Xerox found that customers who rated them a 5 instead of a 4 on a five-point satisfaction scale were *six times* more likely to buy more! This means that measuring client satisfaction is very important and that distinguishing between degrees of satisfaction is crucial.

Plan for Great Service

My guess is that most of you *want* to give great service, but you don't actually have a plan to create it. Without that plan, it's not likely to happen, but it can change your business from struggling to successful. Remember that making only 5 percent more customers into repeat customers can improve your profits by 25 to 95 percent. So if you shoot for perfection, perhaps you'll retain 10 percent more customers and double your profits!

In addition to staying with you, customers who really like you will buy new services from you. For instance, some banks are now targeting existing customers with new offers, based on detailed demographic and psychographic profiles. By changing a mailing based on customer qualifications, response to one offer went from about 1 percent to 10 percent. That's what raving fans (and more targeted marketing) can do for you.

Once you have a strong relationship with clients, it's easier to create new services for them than to find new customers. For example, a health club added singles events, wine tastings, and travel packages to become a one-stop social center. A law firm manages all client legal services, even the ones they don't provide. A landscape firm hires other contractors and manages the job for homeowners who want a swimming pool.

Treat People as Special

Every customer wants something "just for them." That's what one-to-one marketing is designed to provide. Look for custom services to offer existing buyers. Develop customization by:

- making customers your partners and involving them
- designing services for each customer
- using customer relationship management (CRM) software— if you are large—to track what customers actually do or request as you build many customer relationships

HOW GOOD IS YOUR SERVICE, REALLY?

You have to find ways to thrill customers so they will love you, help you suceed, and tell stories about you to others.

> **How to Create Raving Fans**
>
> 1. Decide what you want to do.
> 2. Discover what the customer wants.
> 3. Deliver your vision plus 1 percent (exceed customer expectations).
>
> Ken Blanchard

Above and Beyond the Call of Duty

A city awarded a first-ever commendation to the contracting firm hired for a $1 million paving job. What prompted the city to take notice? It wasn't because the job was finished on time or to specification—that's expected from a professional.

It was the firm's effort to protect the well-loved trees along the street, and more important, the special effort it took to minimize inconvenience to the residents affected by the work. As an example, the city manager cited the instance where a woman and her two small children weren't able to park near their house and the construction company employees carried groceries to the house. Such treatment is apparently so rare that the residents called city officials with their praise.

The construction company ended up with an enhanced public image that would have cost it thousands of dollars spent on public relations to achieve.

How Is Your Phone Handled?

- When you or your staff answer the phone, do you sound glad that people called? Exactly what do you say? If you don't know, your customer service can't be too good.
- If you answer, "Sally Smith," it's not that pleasant. If you answer, "Can I help you?" that's not actually logical. Of course, they called because they want something.
- Is the tone of voice "professionally friendly" or actually warm? Most phones are answered with a neutral-friendly tone. It is quite impersonal. Try answering like you know it's a friend, or you just laughed at a joke.

Develop a greeting that works for you; for instance, "Sally Smith, how can I help you?" or "Hello, this is Sally Smith, how can I help you?"

You may think I'm making too much of little things, but when people call your office, all they hear is the tone of voice of the person on the phone and what is said.

Now let's take a bigger case of customer service by phone. The Canadian Imperial Bank of Commerce has more than a thousand phone service reps. Three million of its customers are registered for telephone banking. By improving training and reducing turnover, this department has achieved the highest customer service ratings in the bank (84 percent), and reduced costs besides. If you have a smaller operation, you should be able to do even better, but it means you have to measure and train.

Your Call-Return Policies

Next question: Do you return all client calls within two hours? A division of Snell & Wilmer, the largest law firm in Arizona, does. If you don't, your customer service may be just average.

If customers or prospects call you, do you call back once, playing telephone tag, waiting for them to call you again? If so, you're not making much of an effort. You should call back multiple times and leave specific hours when you can be reached. You should ask callers to leave more details in their messages, so you can get back to them with information about what they need. Also, ask when they're available.

Do you *not* receive or return calls after 5:00 P.M.? Not such great service.

Speed

One way to improve customer service across almost any industry is to establish standards for speed. The example above of returning calls in two hours is a simple one that is greatly appreciated by clients.

Several insurance companies have been successful largely because of their speed. In one case, when what actually happened to a policy application was analyzed, it was found that the process took about a month. However, about twenty-eight days of that time the policy was sitting on various desks waiting to be worked on! CGU Life USA makes speed its centerpiece. It responds to agent questions within forty-eight minutes, makes commission payments to agents within twenty-four hours, and issues customer policies within forty-eight hours.

When Northwestern National Insurance provided immediate bids with a portable computer, it increased sales 50 percent, while cutting costs.

Response times to customers' e-mails were pitiful in one study. If you responded within six hours, you were among the top companies in a study by Jupiter Media Metrix. (A third of responses took three days or more!) You should be able to thrill customers by responding within a couple of hours, even if it is to tell them when you'll get back to them with details.

Improvements in speed can give you a service (and sales) advantage in almost any service business. And a goal such as speed tends to push internal changes, which can further improve your service efficiency.

WHAT EXTRAS DO YOU GIVE?

- When you bill clients, does your itemization include things for which you list "No charge?" If not, what's special?
- Do you call or send clients things when it's *not* business, so that they know you're thinking of them when you're not charging them?
- Do you always meet deadlines?
- If you're going to be late on work, do you call clients well ahead of time and discuss it? Or do you wait until it's too late for them to do anything?
- Do you send out a newsletter to customers and prospects? Or do you send customers personal notes or clippings about them or their industries, or things designed directly for them, at least once a quarter?
- Have you socialized with your customers when you weren't working with them? Have you invited them out for a drink or coffee, or to a client party, or to your house?

Remember, service is more than the work you do. It's the little things and the relationship too. If you don't do all of the above, what makes you think your service is special?

HOW WOULD A
"MYSTERY CUSTOMER" RATE YOU?

Candid Camera

The shadow agency helps clients hire mystery shoppers equipped with video cameras in their buttons! This gives you complete sound and picture of how customers are treated.

In retailing, there are services with names such as "mystery shoppers." You pay for anonymous people to shop in your store and provide a report on how they were treated.

Your picky customers can be a great asset. By listening hard to unhappy customers, you could even use them as a service-training tool. Unfortunately, they usually don't take the time to complain to you. They just downgrade you in their minds, stop giving you referrals (or start making negative comments), and leave you when a better opportunity comes along. And you don't know how many of your clients are just putting up with you until another provider makes it easy to leave!

CUSTOMER DISSATISFACTION

Think about the times you've been a customer in the last month—at the grocery store, drugstore, or gas station.

The odds are you didn't receive any kind of extraordinary service. For instance, at your regular bank, do tellers greet you by name? Probably not. We've become accustomed to mediocre service. Many customers also build up a generalized grudge or hostility.

As customers and clients, we're often:

- on edge, expecting to be abused and ready to defend ourselves
- resigned to mediocre service or even to being mistreated

As a customer, if you catch a mistake, you go in ready for workers to make excuses and not take responsibility. So, it's easy to become angry. Some of this creates unprovoked unpleasant customers.

CLIENT SURVEYS

Few firms do client surveys. If you are a one-person shop with only a few customers, you *may* already know how they feel. But if you don't talk with customers in depth, I'd wonder. If you are a larger business with lots of clients, how could you possibly know which customers are ready to defect and what new services they want unless you ask them? Areas with high impact on customers and low ratings are where you should work harder at improving.

Chapter One included a three-item customer survey and explained why it could be very useful. Here, let's talk a bit more about ways to get input from your customers and others.

First, remember that few of your clients will be interested in "filling out a questionnaire." The one-minute survey in Chapter One is about as much as people will do happily without some incentive.

By casting any survey as an attempt to find out "how we can serve you better" your clients will feel less put upon. And, if you are sincere about making great service a centerpoint of your firm, your staff will also feel good about collecting information.

Try a new technique called *fogging*. Don't challenge the complainer. Cool his intensity by saying things like "That's really interesting," or "Yes, that might be true." It's like pouring water on a fire rather than adding fuel.

Ken Blanchard

What's for Lunch?

When you give a luncheon or open house for clients or prospective clients, call their secretaries to find out the clients' favorite food items, soft drinks, and so on. If clients don't know that you did this research, they will be especially comfortable at your function. If they find out, they will be flattered and impressed by your effort. Either way, you make a favorable impression.

Personal Contact

You should be in regular touch with your biggest clients. It sounds obvious, yet one company maintained a list of three big clients in each region of the country to give out as references. Surprisingly, when I called them, it turned out that 25 percent of the phone numbers were out of date, about 15 percent of the key contacts had changed, and about 20 percent were unhappy with the company and did not provide good references!

Are you in regular touch with your twelve biggest clients so that you'll always have their correct phone numbers? When your contact is on vacation, are there other people who know you? Are you giving out as references people to whom you haven't spoken for some time?

For any survey, you should contact your most important clients personally. You might do that before contacting others. Ask for their suggestions. This way, their input can help you determine what type of questions to ask others. And your big accounts might be flattered to be helping set the agenda. Have a conversation, not an interrogation. Don't make them feel like they're filling out a survey.

The Phone

Up to about ten minutes' worth of questions can be asked on the phone. By speaking directly with people, you have the flexibility to talk *with* them. Again, this is more desirable than a questionnaire.

Written Surveys

Here are some of the potential dimensions you could measure:

- quality of service
- speed of service
- pricing
- complaints or problems

A little less traditional, and more important, are:

- trust in your staff members
- closeness of relationship with contacts in your firm
- types of other services needed
- percent of business you receive that you could do
- your positioning in clients' minds

If you're just starting a business, you may want to gather information about your expected competitors. This can help you both position yourself and make initial contact with prospective clients.

You should involve staff and clients in designing a questionnaire. Don't get carried away. The odds are that once you start discussing questions with staff and clients, you will come up with more than you should ask. You can also share some of the results back with clients, which allows you to discuss important issues further.

"Big" Surveys

If you have a big client list and lots of questions to ask, split your survey. Ask half the questions to half your clients and half to the other. To get more sophisticated, randomly assign clients to versions of the questionnaire and have a few questions that overlap both groups, which will give you an estimate of similarity between the halves (reliability).

E-mail/Your Web Site

If you have a simple, brief survey, e-mail can be the way to go. Clients can either respond directly on a form you provide, or link to your Web site to fill out the survey.

EMPLOYEES COME FIRST

In a groundbreaking book, *The Customer Comes Second*, Hal Rosenbluth emphasized the point that how you treat your staff will determine how they treat customers. When your staff are not happy, they will not be motivated to thrill customers.

Employees Want to Be Part of Something Great

On the positive side, if your firm is sincere about making customer service great, staff will support you if they are well treated. Good employees want to

Benefits of Employee Satisfaction

Firms that are great at hiring and reinforcing employees have lots of advantages. Companies that have distinguished themselves in the way they hire, train, and treat employees have experienced the following positive benefits:

- increases in service, quality, and customer satisfaction of over 50 percent
- growth rates 60 percent to 300 percent greater than their competition
- return on sales 200 percent to 300 percent greater than their competitors
- return on assets 150 percent to 300 percent greater than their competitors

William Fromm
The Ten Commandments of Business and How to Break Them

The key to great customer service is a satisfied employee.

Roger Dow
Marriott Hotels

be part of a superior organization. They want to be proud of what they do. And focusing on customer service is a lot more motivating to staff than a "program of the week" or higher profits for partners!

In a survey by Watson Wyatt, only 55 percent of employees said they had the power to make decisions to satisfy customers. I like the rule at L.L. Bean that you must get permission to say *no* to a customer, not yes! One accounting firm gives each accountant $100 a month to take clients to lunch and expects them to spend it. The Ritz Hotel gives every employee $2,000 a year to spend on extras for customers, and pressures them to use it. Think what these things say to employees about your belief in serving customers. And think of the empowerment for the employee to take care of problems, rather than wait for permission.

What Employees Want from You

Abraham Maslow's hierarchy of needs is well known. But Frederick Hertzberg provided evidence for a crucial distinction between needs that can make employees happy and things that can make them unhappy.

Lower-level needs such as pay and job security are taken for granted by employees. Their *lack* can make them unhappy, but their presence doesn't make people happy. Higher-level needs such as social acceptance and intellectual stimulation can make employees happy.

Now use this distinction to look at a sample research finding in the sidebar on the facing page of the difference between what bosses think employees want and what employees actually want.

I've focused on employees' top six wants. Note that supervisors have the order almost completely backward! They think people want pay and job security, but they really want to be involved with interesting work where they receive appreciation.

Employees want to be treated as part of the team, given responsibility, and appreciated. When they are treated the way they *want* to be treated (the Platinum Rule), they will be motivated to deliver great customer service. When people just do their jobs, customers receive average, mediocre service—like most of what we see around us. To provide great service—the type that produces loyal customers—you need *motivated* employees.

Employees Are Your First Customers

If you're building a firm, you must first sell or inspire your employees to help you. If you can't enlist employees' full cooperation in serving clients, you can't deliver great customer service.

Your employees are crucial. Oftentimes, prospects and clients spend more time talking with your receptionist on the phone than they do with you. Having their names used, being remembered, and being treated as if they are special may go further to building relationships than the quality of your work. Yet how many receptionists are called "Director of Client Relations" as in one law firm? How many are even asked to build relationships and told how valuable they are?

If employees are your first customers, other employees are *their* first customers. This is obvious when the work of one employee is necessary for other employees to do their jobs. It is less obvious when one corrosive employee is allowed to undermine morale in your whole firm. When you reward employees for great service, include internal service.

If you are a one-person shop, you get the rewards from your performance directly. Employees will be motivated differently than owners. It's up to you to reinforce people the way they prefer.

What Employees Want in Their Jobs: Rankings by Employees and Supervisors

	Employees	Supervisors
Interesting work	1	5
Appreciation	2	8
Feeling "in" on things	3	10
Job security	4	2
Good pay	5	1
Promotions	6	3

From a George Mason University Survey

PROACTIVE SERVICE BUILDS RELATIONSHIPS

The value of *personal* service to build relationships is obvious. What may be less obvious is the value of *proactive* versus *reactive* service. Reactive service gives you less opportunities to thrill clients. You have to wait until they ask for something. When you reach out, you not only have more control, you get more credit for taking the initiative.

For instance, at the new Park Hyatt Hotel in Japan, many of the staff have two-way radios. The doorman peeks at the name on the new arrivals' luggage tags. Then he radios the front desk clerk, who can rush to the door to greet people by their names and take them straight to their rooms. Surprised customers get excellent personal service, feel like VIPs, and avoid the boredom and time wasted in a check-in line.

Here are some ways being proactive lets you provide great service and build long-term relationships. You can:

- notify customers when you learn something new in their area
- send them a regular newsletter or e-zine
- acknowledge them on their anniversary of doing business with you
- send clippings of personal interest to them, such as on their children's interests or achievements
- make random calls to say hello
- invite them to a seminar you give *or* attend
- survey their satisfaction
- invite them to a customer focus group
- have an open house
- give them tickets to an event
- go to their trade group or convention with them
- give them a referral

I'm sure you can think of specific ideas for *your* clients. When you take the initiative, clients are flattered and you have more opportunities to make a good impression. And by including many nonsales contacts, you create a more sincere relationship.

SEEK COMPLAINTS TO BE SUPERIOR

If someone brings you a complaint, is the first thing you say, "Thank you for taking the time to bring this problem to my attention"?

Or do you give explanations or excuses, or ask the person questions that imply he or she may not understand the situation? You've heard statistics about happy customers telling six people, and unhappy customers telling fifteen. Handling complaints is where "the rubber meets the road" for customer service. Even more, you have to *encourage* complaints. Most clients with a problem won't tell you, yet complaints allow you to excel.

Customers who have complaints that are listened to are *more* supportive of you than the average happy customer. But 90 percent of customers who have a complaint never bring it to you.

If you have staff, they may pick up a few complaints, but 90 percent of these aren't passed on to you. If there is any feeling of "blaming the messenger" in your organization, or in your response to complaints, then you have a problem.

Don't defend your mistake. Never argue with customers. Start by assuming they're right.

Ken Blanchard

Internal Customer Complaints

One way to change the handling of complaints in your firm is to start with an *employee* complaint session. The first half can be devoted to complaints that employees have about their jobs. The emphasis should be on policies that make it harder for them to deliver great service, and you must guarantee no punishment. Internal service complaints will give you a good start to restructuring your bureaucracy.

The second half of the session should cover customer complaints of which employees are aware. You will be surprised by the number you hadn't heard. Then gather employee suggestions on how to improve your customer service. You may find you need more than one session.

Customers Do Hold Grudges

Here are some personal examples of how long customers can remember slights.

My father worked for Chevron Oil. Once its local gas station upset him, and he quit going there for twenty years. I don't even know what the problem was. (Perhaps he felt the station cheated him on a repair.) He probably took away thousands of dollars in business over that time span. He had a similar experience with Bank of America. He had been a good customer for years, and when he actually wanted something from them, they treated him like a statistic, rather than as an "important" customer. In that case, he didn't do business with that bank for forty years. I still remember it, since thirty years later, they did the same thing to me.

Why Don't Customers Complain More?

In order to complain, customers know that they will have to confront someone. Combine this with the fact that many complaints aren't resolved satisfactorily and you have a losing combination. Most take the lower-stress path and just stop doing business with you, or give you bad word of mouth. When they do complain, they are negatively "psyched up" for a fight, so they're harder to handle or make happy.

!

Customer Complaint Scarcity

It's hard to get customer complaints in most service businesses. People know that their criticisms are more personal for you because services are more personal in their delivery.

For one of the newsletters I owned, we used a postage-paid card in *every* issue to offer free issues if readers would send us a complaint. Yet we were lucky to get one complaint per six hundred subscribers.

Don't think of handling customer complaints as an *expense*. Think of it as a *marketing tool* that can create loyal customers. And if you do something really dramatic to make a good client happy, think of it as advertising. If you do something great, you will receive a lot of word of mouth from it. And as you know, good word-of-mouth advertising is "worth its weight in gold." (For more on this, see Chapter Fourteen.)

SEVEN STEPS TO HANDLING COMPLAINTS

Here are a few specific steps to help you turn complaints into stronger customer relationships.

1. Be on Their Side

Don't ask questions first. State your intention to help them first. Only then will your questions not seem hostile.

2. Validate Their Feelings

Statements such as "I understand that you're upset" help build trust and reassure people that you may understand them. Don't say, "I know how you feel." That will usually make them angry.

3. Accept Responsibility

Don't pass the buck or refer them elsewhere. Stay with them as their advocate. If you have to get back to them, tell them what you are doing and when you'll respond. Then do it.

4. Keep a Positive Attitude

A complaint gives you an opportunity to create a very loyal customer. Remember that attitude, even if the customer is still unhappy. Be sincere and enthusiastic about helping him or her.

5. Ask for Help

Ask for customers' input. They may suggest solutions or "make-goods" that are far less costly than you would be willing to do.

6. Don't Make Promises You Can't Keep

Since you have lost the complainer's trust, you need to be extra careful. Do what you say you will and keep customers informed.

7. Follow Up

After a problem is resolved, customers may feel guilty that they made such a fuss. As a result, they may avoid you. If you want it, ask for their continuing business. Let them know that they are still welcome.

Making It Easier for Customers to Complain

Canadian Tire retail outlets had a video booth in the center of the stores to record customer complaints. Merely having their complaints recorded probably calms down some customers and also gives the company valuable information.

THE CUSTOMER IS *NOT* ALWAYS RIGHT

I'm not saying that the customer is always right, or that there aren't "terrorist" customers out there—there are. Sometimes you need to support your employees in a conflict with a client.

Customer Focus Groups

As discussed under research in Chapter Three, a focus group is an attempt to get ideas and input. You bring in five to ten customers or prospects and ask them questions or have them react to material. You can pay a professional facilitator and videotape the whole session, or just lead an informal discussion yourself. In either case, you have a chance to gather ideas about customer needs, reactions to your company, suggestions for new services, and other topics.

If a customer is totally unreasonable, and you cannot meet his or her needs, that's probably a customer you can do without. As you develop your complaint-handling skills, you will better recognize ahead of time those prospects who won't be satisfied customers. Don't take on cases where you think you can't meet clients' needs.

A CUSTOMER ADVISORY BOARD

One way to get regular input from customers—good and bad—is to put together an advisory group. This can act like a focus group, but is set up to provide input over time. You may pay members, or simply buy them dinner. If you create a good group, members may also enjoy meeting each other.

Sheraton Hotels found that if it only put loyal customers on its advisory board, it received little useful feedback. By adding people from firms that did little business with it, it got better discussion and input.

There are many benefits to such groups. They give you a source of input from the customer viewpoint. They provide a sounding board to ask specific questions. They enhance your relationship with good customers, who become more committed to your success. And they can move relationships with prospects ahead.

Advisory boards are a much underused way to improve customer service, develop new services, and encourage repeat business. Even the smallest firms can use them effectively.

REPEAT BUSINESS

Repeat business should be the most profitable you have. You are familiar with the client, and you can save time in estimating jobs. Clients trust you, and everything falls right into place. For instance, in the case of my newsletters, we almost never make money the first time someone subscribes because our marketing costs are so high. But when a subscriber renews, we make a lot of money.

Your marketing costs are probably not that high, but looking at the lifetime value of the customer is both a sophisticated view of marketing and makes good common sense.

That's why going out of your way to satisfy customer complaints is often both the right thing to do and of practical value. Take a tip from Nordstrom's department stores and create legends about yourself by meeting *unreasonable* customer demands. Even if you take a small loss because of a customer mistake, it can mean thousands or hundreds of thousands of dollars' worth of future business or publicity.

SUMMARY

Loyal customers can be worth a tremendous amount of business to you over their lifetimes.

At Mackay Envelope Corporation, you wouldn't believe how much we know about our customers. . . . We want to know, based on observation and routine conversation, what our customer is like as a human being, what he feels strongly about, what he's most proud of having achieved, and what the status symbols are in his office.

When you know your customers, . . . you always have a basis for contacting and talking to them. I have a customer who's a devoted Chicago Cubs baseball fan. That's usually good for at least half a dozen condolence messages a year. I don't sit there scribbling notes about the latest fashions in envelopes. *I* write about the Cubs; *he* writes about the envelopes.

I have another customer who's a stamp collector. No matter where I go, all over the world, I send him unusual and exotic stamps. I think he must like that. He's been a customer for twenty years, and in all that time, I've met him only once.

Knowing your customer means knowing what your customer really wants. Maybe it is your product, but maybe there's something else, too: recognition, respect, reliability, concern, service, a feeling of self-importance, friendship, help—things all of us care more about as human beings than we care about . . . envelopes.

Harvey Mackay

Keep in Touch

There's nothing sadder than hearing a satisfied customer say, "Oh, darn. Someone just asked me last month for a referral to your field, and I forgot all about you." That means you haven't been doing your job of cultivating the relationship. Keep in touch with prospects *and* customers.

!

The other nice thing about satisfying customers is that often you work with numerous people at larger firms. If you build relationships well, they will refer you to other divisions within the company, and some of them will move on to other companies where they then can also use your services. If you do good work for a large company, you eventually could have other jobs with several companies, as well as with the original one.

Once again, your success will come from relationships. That's one reason that your marketing should become more fun as you go along. As you make progress, you make new friends and strengthen ties with the friends you already have.

AGENDA

We cannot do everything at once,
but we can do something at once.
CALVIN COOLIDGE

Look at the Client View

- ▶ Call clients and ask how they've been. Say that you've been meaning to call. If you have a tip for them, that's even better.
- ▶ Create a client advisory group if you don't have one.
- ▶ Organize a client survey.
- ▶ Create a list of reasons to proactively be in touch with people.
- ▶ Figure out ways to encourage customer complaints.
- ▶ Hire a "mystery shopper" or call your own office anonymously.

Involve Staff

- ▶ Have a staff meeting about complaints and reward staff for collecting them.

▶ Talk to staff about things you could implement to improve service.
▶ Give each staff member a small budget to spend on customers at his or her discretion.

Thrill Clients

▶ Decide what free extras you can include in client bills.
▶ Plan and budget for ways to thrill customers when you really need to make up for a mistake.
▶ Have all partners or executives spend one day a month at client sites.
▶ Collect information on good clients in an ongoing fashion so you'll know what they care about in business *and* personally. Often you can get it from their employees.

CHAPTER FOURTEEN

REFERRALS AND WORD-OF-MOUTH MARKETING

Satisfied customers are an organization's most successful salespeople.
EBERHARD E. SCHEUING
Creating Customers for Life

I f the best way to get more business is from existing customers, then the best way to get new customers is word-of-mouth referrals from people who know and trust you.

That's not just my opinion, it's the opinion of nine hundred sales and marketing professionals surveyed by New York University. The value of referrals was rated 4.8 on a five-point scale compared to personal selling, 4.5, and cold calling, 1.5!

This chapter will show you how to increase referrals ten times if you're willing to ask for them aggressively. To get the best referrals, you need more than naturally occurring word of mouth. You need to have a program to actively encourage referrals in multiple ways.

Remember, referrals can be for more than direct business. It may be much more valuable for you to be referred to a potential referral source, a friendly competitor who can show you the ropes, or a good networking group.

You can obtain referrals whether you have clients or not. But if you're new in business, you need to start with referrals from nonclients who know you in other ways. If you're starting a business, you need to talk to everyone you know and meet. As discussed in Chapter Eight on networking, you can even ask for referrals from people you've just met.

WHY DO PEOPLE GIVE REFERRALS?

The most common reason people give referrals is because they like you or your service. However, as is the case with customer service and repeat business, *liking* you is not always enough.

As discussed in Chapter Twelve on online marketing, referrals can be stimulated by an extraordinary offer that others want to share. When something of real value is available free online, word-of-mouth "viral marketing" kicks in. E-mail makes it easy. When one person tells several, and they do the same, awareness of the offer grows like a virus.

Less obvious reasons for referrals include that you have given those people referrals or they expect referrals or your own business in return.

Some people are just more likely to give referrals than are others. When you identify someone who is liberal with her referrals, cultivate her. She will be worth several people who like you just as much but aren't in the habit of giving referrals.

FOUR WAYS TO GET REFERRALS

Now let's look at getting referrals. There are actually four general methods of obtaining referrals.

Remember—Referrals Can Come from More Than One Source

Referrals can come from people with whom you've done business, from people you know in business but haven't worked with, and from people who know you but not in a business context. These could include relatives, bankers, neighbors, and people with whom you commute, play ball, socialize at the club, and others.

1. The Prayer Method!

Most people use what I call the *prayer method*. They do nothing and pray that others will give them referrals! You can look at your own experience to judge how this works for you.

You will get occasional referrals without working at it. If this is your approach, you can do better, but it takes initiative. You have to *ask* for referrals. You have to put your ego on the line a little bit. It may be painful until you get into the habit. But isn't success in your business worth it? As discussed in Chapter One, if you provide a valuable service and are not personally sleazy, you shouldn't be ashamed to ask for referrals.

If you think the suggestions I'm going to make here are radical, wait until you hear the last description of the most aggressive referral-gathering program that I've ever heard of.

2. Ask for Them

The second way to get referrals is to *explicitly ask for them* but not do any follow-up.

You might give contacts business cards and say that you hope they'll keep you in mind. One of my past students gives people four to six cards instead of one. He says it increased his referrals. (With multiple cards, people may be less likely to file them away and also feel more pressure to give them out.) Have plenty of business cards wherever you go, and don't be shy about telling people you're looking for leads.

A good time to ask for referrals is when people compliment you. A financial planner said that her clients sometimes thank her effusively for helping them with their money situations. She tells them, "The best way to thank me is to send me your friends who might need the same help."

Attraction Versus Intimidation

Years ago, Peter Blau, a sociologist, pointed out that to build relationships you must be attractive enough to draw people to you but not so attractive that they are intimidated.

In other words, you have to be both attractive *and* approachable. When you're trying to impress people, you need to come across well, but not create the impression that you don't want new clients.

If You Don't Ask, Why Should They Assume?

If you don't ask for referrals, why should people assume that you want them? If you're established in business, you need to be clear that you want more business.

In addition to calling current clients and asking them for referrals, you can call past clients and ask them for the names of people who might need your service. Often they also turn out to be interested in trying you again.

In some businesses, such as hair salons, you can reward people for bringing you business. It's illegal in other cases, such as for therapists, and it doesn't fit the ethics of many professions. But for some services it is appropriate and acceptable. Even my accountant gives a restaurant gift certificate for successful referrals.

Newsletters Create Referrals

One professional worked with a good client for eleven years, but he said he just didn't give referrals. Finally, she offered to send her newsletter to his associates. He asked if this was another way to ask for referrals, but was impressed and gave her three referrals.

!

3. You Ask, You Follow Up

Referral approach number three is the second-best one. Ask people for referrals and then follow up.

Try to get specific names from people, then ask if they mind if you call people to say that you were chatting and it was suggested that you call them. Of course, this is hard to do. But all that networking you'll be doing from what you learned in the chapter on networking will give you a lot more people you can ask for referrals. If you can have "normal" conversations with people you call, good things will often result.

Help People Think of Referrals

When you ask for people's names, your contact might think of a few. A classic way to get more names is to "prime the pump." Develop a list of *types* of people who do business with you and and remind people of them. For instance, ask who they know in real estate, who has young children, who works for a large company, who knows a lot of people, and so on.

Asking for referral suggestions makes good sense. As I mentioned in Chapter Eight on networking, you can continually increase your pool of referrals by getting several leads from each person, a couple more from each of them, and so forth and so on.

4. You Ask, They Follow Up

The fourth approach to referrals, and the best one, is to ask and have *them* follow up. This approach is used in the strictest tips and leads groups, in which others are required to bring in appointments for you. (See Chapter Eight.)

Let's say you're talking to someone at a business function. Tell him or her you're looking for ideas for new business. Some people will say they know someone who might have an interest. Say that you'd like to talk with the person but don't want to bother him. Then ask the person who knows him to see if the prospect would like you to call.

You have other people acting as your "sales agents" and doing all the work. Yet, in many ways, it's easier for them to do this than for you.

Maybe they'd like to talk with the person anyway. And the person being approached realizes that someone is trying to do her a favor (both in thinking of her need and in not having a stranger call uninvited). Your helpers won't feel rejected if people turn them down. They're doing it as objective observers because they think the person may have a need.

It's actually easier for others to sell you than it is for you to sell yourself.

COMPETITOR REFERRALS

One big source of referrals is people in lines of business related to yours. Competitors need not always be competitive.

Here's a simple example: Bill is a landscaper. He gets a large percentage of his business from two or three referral sources—in his case, it's a tree service, a deck contractor, and a patio contractor. If his customers are having work done in their yards, they often need cement or deck work, or trees trimmed. Since Bill doesn't provide these services, and vice versa, these businesspeople are in a great position to mutually refer each other.

Even direct competitors will refer to each other under some circumstances. Thus, people who look like your competitors may actually be good resources for you. Perhaps you'll cover for each other when you're on vacation, or you'll consistently refer certain types of clients to each other. And there are many generalist-to-specialist referrals (and vice versa), such as between a small-business attorney and a litigation specialist.

A Wedding Mafia

One wedding planner I know is a member of a self-defined "Wedding Mafia" that cross-refers. The group includes a cake maker, a bridal shop, a florist, a rental hall, and almost everything else someone needs to hold a wedding. Once you contact one of them, they all have access to you, and vice versa.

CLIENT-CENTERED REFERRALS

Whenever you have a client in common with another service provider, it's logical to get acquainted so you can coordinate in serving the client. And when you know each other better, more cross-referrals should follow if you do your part. Build the relationship and send referrals his or her way.

One large consulting firm uses this approach almost exclusively to add new clients. For every client it has, there are often four to five other professionals it can contact. And often it has multiple clients in common with other firms, creating a stronger tie.

MAJOR REFERRAL SOURCES

Some sources are in a position to make many referrals. For instance, a banker deals with many businesses who may need professional services. Accountants also have broad contacts. It may take a long time to become a preferred referral source for these key people, but building a relationship with one such person a year can make your entire business.

Many such referrals are also available on a simpler level:

- a personal injury lawyer and a medical doctor
- a medical doctor and a chiropractor or fitness trainer
- a psychologist and a psychiatric facility
- a business lawyer and an accountant
- a banker and a financial planner

The list could go on and on. You should be making your own list of possible referral sources.

One of the most interesting ways to build high-level professional referrals is discussed by consultant and author Troy Waugh. He works largely with accountants and attorneys who are good referral sources for each other. In addition to building individual relationships, he uses a hosted mixer format. One firm will invite the other over to get acquainted.

Rather than letting haphazard mingling occur, he starts events with a structure. For instance, the hosts prepare "stations" representing all of their areas of expertise. As the guests arrive, they are escorted through the "stations" where someone discusses each expertise briefly. Everyone is introduced. This helps professionals with similar interests to immediately identify possible referrals or clients in common. At the end of the circuit, guests are taken to the food and drink and tentatively paired up with a host to create a potential relationship.

Such a structured mixer is ten times more efficient than the traditional kind at making connec-

Encouraging Referrals

For many services, direct payment for referrals is not professional. However, there are many ways to encourage referrers:

- do business with your own clients
- encourage your staff to do the same; ask clients for coupons or business cards to distribute to staff
- encourage clients to trade with clients; introduce a few prospects each year to your best clients
- refer prospects to your referral sources
- send out notes to your client list for key referral sources

Troy A. Waugh
Power Up Your Profits

tions. The visiting firm's professionals start out knowing something about their hosts and introductions are accomplished all around. In a normal mixer, you never meet 90 percent of the attendees and often spend most of your time talking with the people you came with!

Referrals Help Your Customers—and Prospects

Cross-referral arrangements with other service providers, you also help your clients. Together you create a "group" that is a more complete organization to serve each customer better (like the Wedding Mafia on Page 287).

Your prospects would prefer to hear about you from someone they trust who has their interests at heart. By setting up referral arrangements, you help yourself and your prospects.

EMPLOYEE REFERRALS

Your own employees can be a big source of referrals, yet they are often ignored. Or worse, if they aren't treated well, they may be giving you negative word of mouth!

Bring a Friend

Andrew Wood's karate schools always invited a new child signing up to bring a friend or two free to her first lesson. The child felt more secure with a friend there and was more likely to continue. Parents appreciated the thoughtfulness, and some of the visitors became students.

Informed Employees Build Referrals

Your employees not only provide customer service that can create good or bad word of mouth; they are talking about your company to their families, friends, others in the community, and your suppliers.

These positive (or negative) messages are going out to potential customers. Do some public relations with your own employees. Don't assume they already know the positive things that have happened. Use personal notes or stuffers in their pay envelopes to spread good news (anniversaries, a public pat on the back to an individual for a job well done, positive comments from a client, public service undertaken, and other activities). Then watch the good news drift out into the community.

One of the smartest accountants I know, Christian Frederiksen, has built and sold several practices. He works to encourage employee referrals. First, he gives employees their own cards and encourages them to pass them out at meetings they attend. For many clerical staff this is the first card they've ever had. Second, when people ask them what they do, he encourages them to say, "I work for the best accountant in town." (If your employees don't want to say this, you may have a problem.) Last, he rewards employees for referrals with a dinner out. This also reminds their spouses about his practice, opening up another referral source, and perhaps making up for some of the times the employee may have worked overtime in tax season.

A study by the Gallup Organization found that employees who said their company's mission statement made their jobs important were more than *three times* more likely to recommend their company's products and services. Similarly, they would recommend their companies as places to work and planned to stay in their jobs. The Conference Board found that about 60 percent of companies did not have strategies to "sell" their companies to their own employees. Your employees should be the first audience to which you sell your value. If they don't believe, why should your customers?

REFERRALS TO DIE FOR

Why don't people give more referrals? Three reasons: 1) because they're afraid you'll foul up, and they'll be blamed; 2) because they don't care enough about you to go out of their way; and 3) because they don't remember you when referrals are possible.

This means that getting more referrals is logically easy. You just have to:

1. build people's confidence in you so that they are sure they'll get credit for a referral to you, not blame;
2. build strong relationships with people who will care about your success; and
3. project clearly who you are (positioning) so that you are memorable. Then keep in touch so you are in "top of mind" awareness for more people.

Other reasons people don't give referrals vary from being afraid you'll get too busy to thinking you are too expensive.

1. Building Confidence

To build people's confidence in you, small consistent actions are more powerful than any other service tool. It's *always* being on time; it's *always* communicating the truth, no matter what. Time and consistency are the two best tools for building people's confidence in you.

You need to not only be there for the customer with a problem, you need to solve it with him or her as a partner, and do a little more than expected. These actions build confidence.

Only when you are considered a high-value resource will customers be confident enough that they'll win points by referring you, and not worry that they'll *lose* points.

Many people will need ten-to-one odds of getting "brownie points" instead of complaints before they give you referrals. Let's take a simple example. Pretend that you knew a car mechanic. The mechanic worked for $30 an hour, made house calls at your home or office, and was extremely courteous—the kind of person you liked having around. He always took the time to chat with you after the job was done, cleaned up, and never made a mistake.

If you referred this person to your friends, you'd be doing them a favor! You might even say to your friends, "Don't tell anyone else; I don't want him to get too busy and not be able to be at my beck and call."

To get great referrals, that's the way *your* customers and friends should think of your service. They have to believe you really care about them and any referral they give you.

Surprisingly, one thing many people forget is to thank referrers. Be sure to thank the referrer whether you get the job or not. And when you do the job, be sure to thank the referrer again. Then enc further feedback from the "referree" to the referrer so he knows he's appreciated. An easy way to do this is to make a policy of collecting a testimonial letter from each client. Then show the letter to the person who referred you, while thanking him and treating him to lunch.

2. Building Relationships

There are many pointers about how to build relationships throughout this book. Here, I'll summarize a few things from common sense and social psychological research. Many of the points fall under the heading of reinforcement. We respond positively to people who provide rewards for us.

You can reinforce others in many ways. The most basic involve giving something to others. That can be as simple as money (such as paying for referrals), or more subtle attentions. If you are of high status, or wealthy, or beautiful, it may be reinforcing for others to simply be around you. If you are more like me—not blessed with status, wealth, or beauty—being a good listener or a source of ideas or referrals can be reinforcing to others. The key is to understand what others find reinforcing.

Another common basis for friendships is similarity. As noted elsewhere, when talking to a stranger, you can look for points of similarity. When we have something in common with others, it feels safer. We assume that we have more overlap in values, and we have something comfortable to talk about. I know many people, such as my friend Andrew, who've turned their love of golf, for instance, into an ongoing source of social and business contacts.

Fortunately, time alone works in your favor. If you can stay in touch, you become more familiar, safer, and more likely to provide reinforcements. As Woody Allen said, "Showing up is 90 percent of success."

Last, I'll simply remind you to keep a database. Doing something with those cards you obtain makes the information available for you. In order to keep in touch, you must have a system. Once you develop a regular system, it can be managed by staff and becomes easy to do. Like all successful marketing, once you know it's effective, setting up a system makes referrals automatic, productive, and easy!

Media Referrals

Note that one reason publicity is so good is that it's an implicit referral. When the newspaper does a story about you, people often take it as if the newspaper is endorsing you. It's a kind of mass-media testimonial.

3. Building Memorability

It's called "word of mouth" because people are talking. To generate talk, you need to be memorable. What are you doing that would give people a reason to talk favorably about you? People have other things to think about unless you do something extraordinarily well or very interesting.

The best way to be in your clients' (or referral sources') minds when opportunities for referrals come up is to have done something dramatic. For instance, when I talked with the biggest customers of a major computer company, only one had a story of great service that the firm was still telling seven years after the fact. The office had been robbed on a weekend. The dealer for the company threw everything into helping the client get back up and running, including lending it computers and software and working round the clock.

The other way to be dramatic is to use flair or panache in delivering your services; for instance, wearing an unusual costume. If this fits your image, it works.

It's hard to find occasions to be really dramatic or "knock someone's socks off." Nordstrom's is often cited for great customer service. What people don't realize is that Nordstrom's looked for opportunities to give unusual service in order to build word-of-mouth marketing.

A more normal way to be memorable is to have a niche or specialty that is easy to understand. In Chapter Eight on networking I mentioned your "elevator speech." If you can't explain what you do in an interesting way in twenty words or less, you won't be memorable. This should come from your USP or positioning—clarifying your uniqueness or what you offer compared to alternatives.

Of course, keeping in regular contact helps you be in people's minds when referral opportunities come up. That's where your newsletter, e-mails, or regular "lunch with clients" programs come in.

THE MOST AGGRESSIVE REFERRAL SYSTEM

What's the most aggressive referral system I ever heard of—the one I threatened you with at the beginning of this chapter?

A consultant in one of my "Marketing Your Services" seminars explained his system years ago. I immediately realized how effective it was, and was surprised that I hadn't heard about it before. The reason probably is because most people would think it's too aggressive, if it occurred to them at all.

Some people feel that being aggressive about marketing is unprofessional. As mentioned in Chapter One, this doesn't have to be the case.

There are ways to be aggressive without offending people. If you believe that you help people, and spend time and money reaching out to let them know about your service, you could be doing them a favor. Your marketing efforts can save them time and money in finding someone (you) to meet their needs.

Get a Written Referral

Try this for an aggressive referral program. When my student had a satisfied client, he talked to him or her and said, "As you know, I get most of
my business from referrals. For instance, you heard about me through So-
and-So. Would you be willing to write a letter commenting on how I've
helped you in your business?"

If clients are satisfied, normally they'll agree to write a letter, and often
will say, "Oh, sure. *You* write it on my letterhead, and I'll sign it. No problem." To help them, you could interview them and draft the letter based
on their comments.

Think about different things you want your referral letters to cover. One
might speak about speed of service, and another might mention how
much money the client saved. One might discuss how much money you
made for the person, and another might say what a pleasure it was to work
with you. Try to decide what your different strengths are and make sure
you have a variety of letters that cover the different benefits you provide.

But Wait, There's More!

It isn't terribly unusual to ask for a letter. It's the next step that takes the
method into the stratosphere!

After satisfied clients agree to write a letter, my ex-student says to them,
"Would you mind if I sent this letter to some people you know, rather
than just keeping it as a general letter for the files?" Then he asks them
who comes to mind. Maybe they'll think of one or two people. *Then* he
says, "Could we go through your Rolodex (or database) to get ideas about
to whom to send it?"

Now he has the client's contact list of a hundred people from which to
draw. There may be ten or twenty customers, competitors, suppliers, or
colleagues who are appropriate.

By going through the possibilities, one at a time, you can make a couple
of notes on who these people are in order to customize your letter. That
means from every engagement with a satisfied customer (and he has a lot),
he might send out five to fifteen letters! With this kind of aggressive program, he can't help but have a waiting list of clients.

For the Shy

I know this idea takes a lot of getting used to for most people. But if you have even *one* person in your life who is completely on your side and wants you to succeed, you can use this database approach. I hope with time, you'll have many more people who would be happy to open their Rolodexes to you. And if you join a tips-type group, you may have lots of such people (see Chapter Eight).

Group Referral Help

It's clear that you could use this approach with people other than satisfied clients.

When you're asking for referrals from friends, family, and social acquaintances, you could also go through their Rolodexes. In talking to your suppliers or other partners who are interested in the success of your business, you could go through their lists, where appropriate.

He's Not Unique!

A related approach is a "Rolodex Party." As described in the book *Marketing Without Advertising*, by Michael Phillips and Salli Rasberry, someone invited close friends to a party. Everyone brought their Rolodexes. The hostess provided envelopes and brochures for her business. She asked her friends to address envelopes and write a short note to their contacts about her! It was very effective.

Why not have a Rolodex party where everyone helps everyone else by sending out notes to their networks? Then everyone at the party would both benefit and help others.

AFFINITY MARKETING

Now, let's generalize this idea one step further. Consider something that big companies do called *affinity marketing*. (Even smaller companies do it online now too.)

One type of affinity program is where a group such as your college alumni club makes a deal with a credit-card company, so that if you sign up for the MasterCard or Visa, some percentage goes toward supporting your group. You benefit the school, the company benefits, and the charge card offers your group a number of specials.

Affinity marketing can be when big companies send letters on their stationery, recommending someone else, and get a percentage on the business generated. Or two businesses do it for each other. Just find yourself a complementary business and do it.

Your Affinity Programs

Who would do an affinity marketing program with you? Could you get a local college to send out a letter to its business school alums, and offer them a percentage of the business generated?

Many local business newspapers will sponsor seminars and give you free ads in the newspaper, just to offer their readers more and to have their names associated as sponsors. Local banks will do the same thing for their business customers. They'll send out letters to all their customers to offer a seminar, often for a small charge. This is an endorsement of you by this institution. The Small Business Administration also used to cosponsor seminars and pay for the mailings for them.

Look at the MCI "Friends and Family" program as an example of referral marketing. Some people find it obnoxious that their friends turned over their names to MCI salespeople, who then called and suggested they join the program (everyone who joined got a big discount when they called each other).

No matter what you think of the program, it was massively successful for MCI. It allowed the company to add millions of new customers who had a personal reason for joining.

CROSS-REFERRALS

Many people give each other regular cross-referrals. This means that they are endorsing each other.

My old friend Bill gets more than half his business from referrals from the two or three people who offer complementary services to his, and he does the same for them. Their mutual support didn't develop from anything as planned as I've suggested above. It took years of getting to know each other. But you shouldn't have to wait years for things to happen "naturally." Don't you think a little "artificial" effort could speed things along?

RELATIONSHIPS AND REFERRALS

Even if it's only an annual photocopied or e-mailed Christmas card, you should be in touch with people regularly.

That's why there is a chapter on newsletters in this book. But there are a lot of other ways to keep in touch with people. Insurance agents are trained to send you—or your cat—a birthday card. But most other service providers don't systematically keep in touch. You should call people once in a while just to say "hi," drop them a note every quarter, or send them a reprint by you (which you'll be generating now, because you've read Chapter Seven on publicity). Or send them clippings that are helpful to their industries. Even if they've seen the articles, they'll appreciate the fact that you thought of them.

You'll Stand Out

Interestingly, even when you send them things, very few people reciprocate. That will make you stand out all the more. Don't overdo it and send them junk that is not applicable. Always personalize everything with a little Post-it or handwritten note, and try to make what you send specifically relevant to them.

Perhaps the best thing about the best-selling book *Swim with the Sharks Without Being Eaten Alive* was the checklist in it that salespeople use to gather information about prospects and clients. (See the Appendix for a somewhat similar list.)

You may not need to collect so much information, but most of you probably collect way too little. You can't build relationships if you don't know—and remember—things about people.

REFERRALS CAN BE ANYWHERE

Perhaps the most unusual referral for its time was from someone my friend Steve had never met, to someone he'd never met.

This was in the early days of computer networks and bulletin boards in the 1980s. He lived in San Francisco and developed a "pen pal" on a bulletin board, a woman in Wisconsin. He told her he was a marketing consultant. She told him what she did, and they had lively exchanges. She eventually referred him to a friend of hers in her geographic area who needed some marketing material written. Steve sent a proposal and got the job.

> Once you discover an individual's interests—or even better, his passions—you tap information that will help you build a much stronger relationship.
>
> R. Misner and R. Davis
> *Business by Referral*

The Internet

Because it's so easy to contact a lot of people online, your referral sources are greatly extended. You can be in multiple industry and other discussion groups, receive e-zines, and so on. Most encourage input, so you have a chance to demonstrate your expertise.

If your business is largely in your local area, you'll want to get on regional discussions, or perhaps even run a forum. You can impress people with your knowledgeable commentaries on issues they care about. For instance, from one list, I was solicited to help a magazine in Holland develop an American edition.

Even worldwide discussion groups can be useful. People in other countries have valuable ideas. For instance, I've received two e-mails from Russia with suggestions and offers of ideas for my books and Web sites. And people in other countries may know people closer to you.

"Referring" Yourself

Long-Lasting Signs

One home-siding company offers a discount on some work in return for keeping a sign on the house for sixty days.

Bottomline Business

!

If you have a service such as landscaping or painting that people can see, one way to get "referrals" is to introduce yourself to people in the neighborhood in which you're doing work. (Job signs and your name and number on your truck are designed to do this too.) Or leave flyers in the immediate neighborhood, pointing out that you're working across the street at number 7, and inviting people to talk to you or call you. Thus, your work becomes a referral for you. It's a good idea to mention this to your customer. But the fact that the person hired you usually becomes referral enough.

Many consultants make a living by being referred from one division of a large company to another. For instance, attorneys should make an effort to introduce themselves to other divisions in client companies.

SUMMARY

There are many individual marketing techniques covered in this book that could be the basis for all your marketing—from speaking to sales letters to writing articles. However, you should clearly understand that referrals are the most effective, least expensive marketing method for obtaining new clients.

You should also be aware that referrals don't "just happen" because you do good work. You need to decide what you're comfortable doing to encourage them, and get started.

AGENDA

To move the world, we must first move ourselves.
SOCRATES

Be Memorable

▶ Make sure you can describe what you do in a brief, interesting way.
▶ Is there any way you can become more exciting or dramatic, such as by wearing a costume or becoming a crusader for a cause? (See Chapter Seven on publicity.)

Steps to Take Now

▶ Take your best friend out for a drink and ask him to write you a letter of recommendation to his list of contacts. Next week, try it with your second-best friend!
▶ Call current clients who like you best and ask for advice on referrals. Ask them for a nice letter as a start. (Or ask about using their Rolodex.)
▶ Offer your employees an incentive for referring you.
▶ Look for online discussion groups to join.

Long-Term Referral Building

▶ Call people you share clients with and start to get better acquainted.

▶ Call competitors who might become referral sources for you.

▶ Call someone with whom you might set up a cross-referral program or a "Wedding Mafia."

▶ Develop a contact list of potential major referral sources—people such as bankers for an accountant—who can be referral sources for years.

CHAPTER FIFTEEN

YOUR MARKETING ACTION PLAN

Implementing Your Success

> *Somebody said that it couldn't be done,*
> *But he with a chuckle replied*
> *That "maybe it couldn't" but he would be one*
> *Who wouldn't say so till he tried.*
> EDGAR A. GUEST
> *It Couldn't Be Done*

Throughout this book, I've tried to show you how you could strengthen your marketing *and* your customer relationships at the same time. Now it's time for you to act, and I have a challenge and a promise for you.

GUARANTEED MARKETING RESULTS

The time to apply what you've read is as soon as possible—like now. I challenge you to use this chapter to create three mini–marketing plans for yourself. They will take about five minutes each. If you've read at least half this book and you'll commit to working on your three mini-plans in the next month, I promise that you'll see results. If you don't get results, write me in care of the publisher or through my Web site (rickcrandall.com) and I'll either give you free consulting, or I'll personally refund the money you paid for this book.

Your mini-plans should be created within the context of a more general marketing plan. You want your smaller marketing efforts to be directed at the right target audiences, to represent you correctly, and to position you to meet your long-term goals. Such a general plan is also covered in this chapter.

If you don't know where you are going, any path will take you there.
The Cheshire Cat
Alice in Wonderland

A SPECIFIC COMMITMENT

Nothing gets done until you commit to doing it. Once you have a goal to improve your marketing, you need to make it specific.

For instance, in some chapters, I suggest that you write three letters, and so forth. List your goals like these in specific numerical terms and then give them time lines. If you have decided to produce a newsletter, give yourself a one-month deadline to get the first issue out, and so on.

IF YOU DON'T LIKE PLANNING

Planning can be guesswork. However, *if you have no plan*:

- You tend to set no specific goals and time lines.
- Others may doubt that you are serious.
- You tend not to budget your time and attention.
- You can let things slide.

If you don't like the idea of planning, please use the "mini-planning" approach throughout this book to overcome your reluctance. Agree to give it a try, even if you aren't sure yet that it will work.

If you have a plan and get started, you gain more valuable information than if you don't have a plan. Even if the plan changes totally, its existence tends to get you going.

- A plan helps you find information that can help you.
- It helps you inspire others and enlist their aid.
- It helps you direct your efforts to get where you want to go.
- It motivates you to accomplish your specific goals.

IT'S EASY TO GET STARTED

A small marketing plan for a big company such as Procter & Gamble might be fifty pages. A marketing section of a business plan, with which you raised millions of dollars for a new product, might be twenty-five pages. But *your* first marketing plan can be as small as one page. Once you begin marketing, you'll gain more information to make better plans.

To me, marketing means *doing*, and that's what it takes to sell your services. Hopefully, you've already taken a few steps suggested in other chapters.

Here, I'm going to focus on things you can do in the next day, week, and month. This gives you deadlines that are close enough so you can begin to see progress. Your progress should, in turn, encourage you to tackle bigger jobs.

Partial Mini-Plan

Goal number 1: To get publicity with X target audiences.

- find likely publications
- analyze what they like
- call editors
- offer three types of stories
- other

GOALS WORK

I remember a study done over thirty years ago. The main variable that predicted success in the Peace Corps was that people had five-year goals. Peace Corps applicants with five-year goals handled their assignments better and were less likely to come home early than the applicants who had no five-year goals.

This doesn't mean that people stayed with their five-year goals. They simply had them. Whether they wanted to go to law school or start their own businesses, they aimed for a goal.

It's all right to change goals. Having goals tends to get you moving, and when you are acting, *you gain more information* to either refine or change your goals.

Five Years Can Zip By

If you've been around a few years, you know that five years can go by rather quickly, and leave you no better off than you were before.

But if you have a plan to educate yourself or to invest a little money, in five years it can add up to big results. I'm focusing here on marketing

2004						
			1	2	3	4
5	6	7	8	9	10	11
12	13	14	15	16	17	18
19	20	21	22	23	24	25
26	27	28	29	30	31	

goals from which you can see results in the short term. But I want to encourage you to give yourself one- and five-year goals as well, so that you'll know *why* you're working. Presumably, you're trying to develop your business so that it supports you, rather than you supporting it.

For instance, a five-year goal in monetary terms could be that you want to be earning $200,000 a year from your business. Or, in lifestyle terms, it might be to have your business at a level at which you have to work only three days a week. Or it could be to develop one product a year, such as an audio, video, or newsletter, which will "work" while you're sleeping. Then you wouldn't just be selling your hours.

These are long-term goals that can put you in a better position than you are now. Without such long-term goals, your short-term work can keep you in the same rut forever.

To help put your marketing planning in the full context of your life, let's take a look at the broad picture before we work down to your marketing planning. To jot down a few preliminary long-term goals now, answer the questions listed below.

If you prefer to work from the general to the specific, you can skip now to page 312 and do your general marketing planning. Then come back to the previous section to fill in your specific "mini-plans."

Your Long-Term Personal Goals

- What do I want to have accomplished personally in five years?
- What do I need for my family?
- How many hours a week do I want to work in five years?
- What can I do to develop myself personally?

Your Long-Term Marketing Goals

- What type of clients do I want in five years?
- What type of work will I be doing for them?
- Will I have any products that work while I sleep?
- If yes, what?
- What will I do in the next year to find the clients I want?
- What will I do in the next year to strengthen my relationships with current clients?
- What will I do in the next year to improve or extend my expertise?

YOUR OVERALL ACTION PLAN

Your marketing planning must fit within the context of your life to be usable. What you need to do in marketing may not get done if you have a conflict with your other life priorities.

To look at the broadest context possible, it can be helpful to create a brief "Action Plan" for your life. Under that umbrella are *Personal Goals, Business Planning,* and *Marketing Planning*. All of these should funnel into your goals for the next week, the next month, the next year, and the next five years.

Under *Personal Goals*, you need to deal with your personal priorities. Think about your self-development. Set life goals for balancing work and leisure. Determine the work habits or discipline that are best for you. Commit to spending more family time.

Under *Business Planning*, you may need to research different possible services to offer. You may need to train your staff or add a marketing coordinator. (But don't use this to dump the responsibility.) You may need to make client development a formal part of each partner's or employee's job with appropriate compensation. Or you could seek alliances to strengthen your competitive position.

If you're a new business, you may need to seek financial support for your efforts to build your business. You may need to set up the legal form of your business, get a fictitious business name, hire people, and similar activities.

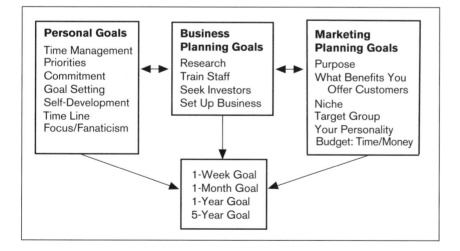

There may be a number of general budgeting, accounting, and business planning issues that you need to deal with to be in business. (Of course, there is much business planning software available.)

For *Marketing Planning*, if you've been answering the questions and making notes on ideas that appealed to you in each chapter, you have almost all the material you need to write both mini–marketing plans and a more general overall plan.

HOW DO YOU CHOOSE MARKETING METHODS?

Now you know a lot more about marketing than you did when you started this book. You know about many different methods. You have inside information about low cost and guaranteed methods. And you know that you should track and test your results before you spend big money.

The major question people ask at this point is "How do I choose specific marketing methods from among so many?"

No one can tell you what will be best for your particular service and style. Four of your many jobs in determining your marketing approach are to:

1. Look at a broader range of possibilities than you're doing now.
2. Apply choice criteria to decide what new methods to try.
3. Test, test, test—inexpensively—to see which approaches work best for you.
4. Implement a system to repeat the methods that work so they become easy and routine.

Choice Criteria

Criteria you might want to consider for choosing your marketing approaches include:

- cost
- convenience
- whether an approach fits your image and style
- how fast you expect it to be

- how easily you can do it
- its effectiveness for similar service providers

You can weigh your criteria any way you want. Cost, fit for your style, and time should be important. One of the criteria might be a "veto" if it is very important to you.

Don't get hung up deciding how to decide. If you're unsure—guess. You'll be better off making a decision and getting test results than doing nothing.

MINI–MARKETING PLANS

Now let's talk about your mini–marketing plans. Many marketing consultants will spend a long time with you, asking questions about your positioning, target audience, and the other technical factors we talked about in Chapter Three. You'll remember that these types of questions were used in a number of chapters, but here we'll focus on some specific tactics.

Several people have suggested ways to create marketing plans by answering just a few questions. For instance, Ray "Rocket" Judkins, a direct-mail expert, uses an eight-point plan: objectives, timetable, budget, audience, offer, creative, production/media, and analysis/measurement. Jay Levinson, the author of the best-selling *Guerrilla Marketing* series, has used the answers to seven questions for mini–marketing plans (purpose, target audience, methods, niche, your identity, budget, and schedule).

Here is my version of how you can do a mini–marketing plan in only three steps:

1. *What is the purpose of your marketing?*
   Purpose #1: _____.
   How you answer this question is the key to getting moving. We are looking for a simple, specific marketing goal. Something general, such as making more money or getting more clients, is not useful.
   Here are some possible purposes:

   - to get publicity for your business in local newspapers
   - to get publicity for your service in trade and technical publications
   - to get more *new* customers of a certain type or industry

> **A** journey of a thousand miles begins with the first step.
>
> Ancient Chinese adage

- to get more repeat customers
- to get more business from each customer

The purpose might be even more narrow, such as to get on radio talk shows, or to write a regular column in your local paper. Perhaps the simplest purpose of all was given in Chapter Two and Chapter Eight. One goal discussed there was to get a letter to the editor published.

Choose a purpose that's limited, doable, and focused on one small aspect of your marketing. That's why it is called a mini–marketing plan. When you put a series of these together, you will soon have a comprehensive marketing action plan.

2. What is your budget?

- I have this much time per week: _____.
- I have this much money to spend: $_____ .
- I can "budget" the amount of emotional energy and attention.
  I need to accomplish this purpose and keep my focus on marketing enough to make it work.

If you are a big company, advertising and marketing budgets are often determined as a percentage of your gross sales dollars. This can work when you have historical data relating your spending to results. However, by using the techniques recommended in this book, you'll be able to get much better results with a lower budget.

If you're a small business or just getting started, you have to budget enough of your time, money, and attention to get results. At the extreme, if you have no clients, like a beginning insurance agent, you should be marketing most of the time.

If you are big and established, you may have a lot of money and little time. Then you can hire other people to do most things for you. If you have lots of time and no money, you can do it all yourself. You can educate yourself. You can use techniques from this book and other sources. But, no matter how you balance time and money, there must be some focus and attention from you. You are ultimately responsible.

3. Can you make a real commitment to a schedule?

This last point is often left out of discussions of these "mini-plans." If you're busy like most of us, it's easy to put things off. You're already using all the hours in your day, and no new ones will miraculously appear to be spent on marketing!

Item 2, your budget, called for a general commitment about how many hours you will spend on marketing. Now you need to be more specific.

Marketing does take some time. First, you have to work on it; then it can work for you. While we all need relaxing downtime, you must commit time to your marketing to make it work for you. If you watch TV, you can make time for your marketing. Do it!

The nice thing about committing to a specific schedule is that it makes it easier to motivate yourself to reach goals. A schedule represents a direct commitment to finish a task at a particular time. It helps you focus to finish your mini-plan.

Decide now what you might do soon on this first mini-plan.

Tomorrow I will _____ .

_____ .

_____ .

The hours I'll work tomorrow are _____ .

Within a week, I will _____ .

I'll work these days and hours _____ .

Within a month, I will finish _____

You May Want to Review Other Factors

I've put the mini-plans before your general marketing planning. As discussed in Chapter Three, you should know your target audiences, identity, positioning, the niche you want to dominate, and similar information.

You Need Deadlines

"A goal is a dream with a deadline" is an old saying, but a good one.

I'm guessing that after reading this book, you have a good sense of these factors. Or, at least you wouldn't pick a mini-plan that didn't make sense for you. As I've said before, I believe that taking action and building positive momentum is very important. That's why the emphasis is on immediate mini-plans.

Strategy Versus Tactics

Another reason I like to start with mini–marketing plans and their specific focus is that tactics can be more important than strategy. Traditionally, "experts" think your broad marketing strategy should determine which specific tactics you use. Then they want you to shape your personal style to fit the strategy. However, it's worth noting here—as did Al Ries and Jack Trout in *Bottom-Up Marketing*—that tactics often dictate strategy, rather than the other way around.

For instance, if you have a great referral source who wants to help you succeed, it can be worthwhile to shape your business to serve the kinds of clients the source can deliver. Similarly, if you are better at using a particular marketing tool, you should develop your strategy around that tactic.

Multiple Mini-Plans

You should be able to create a mini–marketing plan in five minutes, by simply making choices from those I've listed. Hopefully, you've already filled in answers as you read this chapter. If not, go back and fill in your tentative answers.

It's actually most effective if you develop two or three mini–marketing plans now. Decide which activities look most interesting and fill in the blanks from copies of the next page.

For instance, let's say that of the things you've read, you could see trying to get some *publicity*, doing some *networking* in groups, and making a few *phone calls* to clients, referral sources, and past clients. After narrowing these down, each could be pursued in a small amount of time.

Your progress on each plan will help you learn which activities are most effective for you. As you take action in any area, new possibilities will suggest themselves. As you work on your goals, you'll gain information to improve both your planning and action.

Here's a summary of the three questions that you can use for your plans:

GUIDE FOR MULTIPLE "MINI–MARKETING" PLANS

1. Plan number and purpose of your marketing

   Number_____:

   Purpose: _____

2. What is your budget?

   I have this much time per week: _____ .

   I have this much money to spend: $ _____ .

   I have the emotional energy for this purpose: ☐ Yes   ☐ No

3. What is your committed schedule?

   Exactly when will you work? _____

   When will you be finished with this mini-plan? _____

   _____ .

   _____ .

   _____ .

Mini-Plan #3

Mini-Plan #2

Mini-Plan #1
Publicity

Steps
1. _____
2. _____
3. _____

Note: I prefer to have several mini-plans on the table at the same time. However, you'll probably find it most effective to work on one area at a time. When you have to wait on one project, however, it's handy to have other plans available.

It's useful but not necessary to write an overall marketing plan to implement and organize your mini-plans. You should probably take at least a moment to put the big and small planning perspectives together.

YOUR OVERALL MARKETING PLAN

We've now covered a range of plans, from your five-year life and marketing goals to mini-plans that might take you a few hours.

Here I'll briefly cover what a general marketing plan might look like, with some questions for you to answer. The main purpose of this plan is to make sure that all your specific marketing efforts fit within the overall context of your broad goals; in other words, that you perform short-term marketing activities—or tactics—that contribute to your major goals and are the most effective use of your time and efforts.

For instance, one mini-plan suggested above was to get some publicity. To do that, you have to decide who you want to reach and what image you want to convey. These determine what specific media you try and what you say to them.

OUTLINE OF YOUR OVERALL PLAN

I. Executive Summary

This is a brief overview of your entire marketing approach. It could be from a paragraph to a couple of pages long. Outside readers of your plan may only read this and then glance at one or two sections of the specific plan.

II. Your Markets

Who are the major end users of your services? Be as specific as possible in listing all groups or types of customers who account for at least 5 percent of your business.

Major Customer Groups:

1. _____

2. _____

3. _____

4. _____

5. _____

6. _____

7. _____

8. _____

9. _____

10. _____

Here are some questions to answer:

Your Market:

- Which of these market segments has potential for expansion?
- How profitable for you is each group?
- In which segments do you have the least competition?
- Which of these groups does your expertise best fit you to serve?
- How long is the purchasing cycle in each of these groups?
- Which of these groups have the most urgency to hire someone?

Your Positioning:

- How well known are you in each of your customer groups?
- How would you like to be seen compared to your competition?
- How do you think you are seen now?
- Do you need to build your expertise and contacts in any of the areas in which you want to work?
- How do your price, quality, and value compare to each major competitor or type of competitor?
- How well do you really know major competitors or types of competitors?

Your Customer/Prospect Needs:

- What are the major benefits you offer customers? (See Chapter Three for a discussion of features and benefits.)
- What are the major needs that customers say they have?
- What benefits can you offer that your competitors can't?

III. Market Research

What kinds of information do you need to gather to know your markets, your prospects, your customers, and your competitors better (for instance, to answer the questions in section II)? How will you track the results of each of your marketing efforts and the effectiveness of each method for different target markets?

IV. Marketing Objectives

In this section, you should set clear goals for the types of customers you want to reach and how many new customers you want to gain each month. Set goals for each person in your company, with time lines.

V. Your Marketing Outreach Program

Briefly describe the key methods you are relying on to reach your prospects. Use the lists in Chapter One of where your clients come from now. Then add new methods from this book as you experiment with them.

- What are you doing to assure that you (and everyone in the company) meet new potential prospects on a regular basis in natural settings?
- What business group meetings do you regularly attend?
- What social groups (leisure, church, PTA) do you regularly go to where you can meet new people?

- Is advertising effective for you?
- Do you have a publicity campaign?
- Does your Web site bring you clients?
- Do you regularly create useful checklists and handouts to give away to prospects?
- Do you regularly ask customers for referrals?
- Do you regularly write letters to possible prospects?
- Do you regularly phone possible prospects?
- Do you regularly give talks to groups of possible prospects?
- Do you participate in online discussion groups?
- Do you have a source of names of possible new prospects?
- Do you have a newsletter for prospects and customers?

VI. Customer Service and Relationship Building

- Do you regularly develop repeat business?
- Do you spend at least 80 percent of your time with existing customers?
- Do you have a system to build relationships with new people you meet?
- Do you regularly send customers personalized notes? (A newsletter can also help here.)
- Do you empower employees to deal with customer complaints?
- Do you have customer service policies that make it easy for customers to reach you any time? (See also Chapter Two and Chapter Thirteen for discussions of returning calls, answering the phone, and other customer service behaviors.)

VII. Your Budget

Describe here the time, money, and emotional attention budget for your total marketing program. This may also include a budget for any necessary outside help.

SAMPLE MARKETING PLANS

When you're sure that you know what market segments you're targeting, and how you're positioning yourself, you can pull together a set of mini-plans to serve as your general marketing guides.

Here are two examples of marketing plan overviews that might be used by service providers.

A Traditional Implementation Plan

The mini-plans in a traditional marketing plan might look like this:

1. Create a brochure. (See Chapter Five.)
2. Advertise in places your prospects read. (See Chapter Four.)

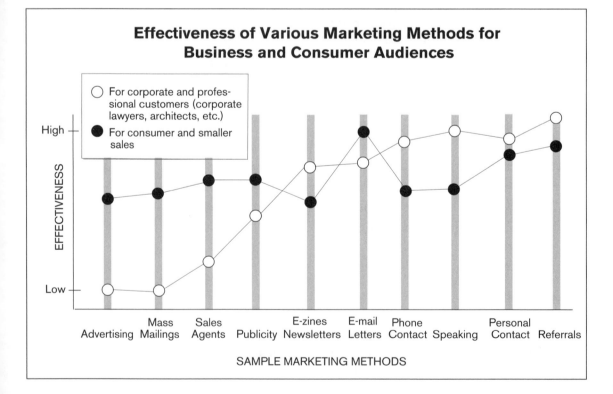

Effectiveness of Various Marketing Methods for Business and Consumer Audiences

3. Write letters to big companies (Chapter Five) and follow through with phone calls (Chapter Nine).
4. Give a talk at an industry conference. (See Chapter Eleven.)

This approach is traditional in two different ways.

First, it focuses on activities that are easy to do and cost money. Even worse, it is the type of plan that any nonservice, product-oriented company might follow when it has a marketing budget and directs a general marketing assistant to "do something."

Second, it is the same approach that any of your competitors might take. It doesn't set you apart in any way or take advantage of your unique personality and strengths.

Other reasons I don't particularly like this plan include:

1. You can spend a good bit of money on brochures and advertising without getting much response.
2. If you don't have an effective marketing program now, you won't know how to do effective brochures and advertising.
3. Approaching big companies is a long-term process. It can take you a year to find out whether it will work or not.
4. Getting to speak at an industry conference will usually take at least a year. Instead, start to speak at local groups of your customers. This will also give you more direct contact with people who could use your services.
5. There is little direct relationship building with prospects or customers in this plan.

A Less Traditional Plan

A less traditional, relationship-oriented, less expensive plan might look like this:

1. Create a one-page quarterly newsletter or e-zine to send out to prospects, past clients, and current clients. Borrow some material from this book to get started. (See Chapter Ten and the Appendix.)

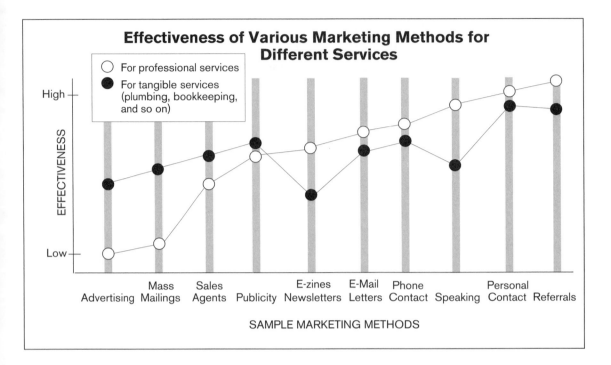

Effectiveness of Various Marketing Methods for Different Services

○ For professional services
● For tangible services (plumbing, bookkeeping, and so on)

EFFECTIVENESS: High — Low

Advertising, Mass Mailings, Sales Agents, Publicity, E-zines Newsletters, E-Mail Letters, Phone Contact, Speaking, Personal Contact, Referrals

SAMPLE MARKETING METHODS

2. Send five personal letters a week to new prospects. (See Chapter Five.)
3. Talk to your best clients or prospects about their needs.
4. Ask your best clients or friends for referrals.
5. Increase your "specialization." Become the expert in a certain problem or for a specific group.
6. Make ten follow-up phone calls a week to people whom you've written, or met networking, or for whom you have worked in the past. (See Chapter Eight.)
7. Start working now on getting publicity in your local paper or trade publications. (See Chapter Seven.)
8. Begin doing research on a possible new service to offer, or type of client to approach. (You can also obtain publicity from this. See Chapter Seven.)
9. Call other service providers who serve your clients and could be referral sources for you. (See Chapter Fourteen.)
10. Arrange links to your Web site from referral source sites. (See Chapter Twelve.)

HOW TO GET STARTED

How Do You Decide What to Do?

Getting started on a new marketing program is a bit like raising children. It's a big job, but you only have to handle one day at a time. The trick is to get started—with marketing at least. (With children, you may already be started and are now just trying to survive!) The more practice you have, the better you get at marketing (and children).

Earlier in this chapter, I mentioned a few criteria you could use to choose a marketing method. To review, those criteria are: *cost, convenience, fitting your style, speed, ease of implementation,* and *effectiveness.* These criteria are all relevant. But there is often no way to know how effective a marketing method will be until you try it.

At some level, deciding what you will do is not a rational, deductive process. It is simply your best guess and something you like. The act of committing to a decision can make your choice more effective than if an outside consultant like myself told you to do it.

> **Focus, Focus, Focus**
>
> Research by Charles Garfield on peak performers shows that they focus on only a few things at a time.
>
> **!**

He Who Hesitates Is Lost

If you're not sure what to do, you are left with five possibilities:

1. Do nothing, stall, avoid.
2. Pick something arbitrarily.
3. Do what is easiest.
4. Get someone else's advice and follow it.
5. Go with what you like, what feels right.

Of course, I have a very strong bias for number 5, some bias for numbers 2 and 4, and a strong bias against number 1. You want the time (not to mention the "big money") you've invested in reading this book to pay off.

If some methods haven't already appealed to you, I urge you to pick something *now* and get started. You'll be better off taking action.

Starting your marketing will help you learn more, and be more effective with each subsequent action. Like all good things in life, you get better with practice. And you usually will like a method more as you become more comfortable and familiar with it.

Create Your Own Support Group

If you have a few close friends or colleagues, you may be able to create an informal marketing support group. All you need is an agenda, regular meetings, and a commitment.

Such a "support group" could be as simple as a phone appointment once a week with one friend. You each report in and encourage each other. I've done it—it works.

This book could be your agenda outline or "textbook" for a group that gets together. In my experience, meetings every week or two are necessary to keep your momentum going. Try committing to 100 percent attendance for at least a month to try out the group. Keep meetings brief at first—one or two hours.

Here are some things you can do at meetings:

- Have everyone say what marketing they've done to date that has been effective.
- Have everyone pick something specific that they will do in the next month. At each meeting, they report in on their progress and get input from the group.

These two steps alone will keep marketing on your agenda. Just having to report in to someone makes a huge difference.

Other things you can do:

- Each person can be assigned to research something that will benefit the group.
- People can bring in marketing material that they admire.
- Guest speakers can be invited.
- People can bring in leads or ideas for each other.

In Larger Companies, Assign Responsibility

If you're a marketing manager with a staff, make sure that the responsibilities for all marketing activities are clearly assigned. Each mini–marketing plan should have a project manager. With whom does the manager need to coordinate to handle subparts (such as obtaining mailing lists, doing physical production, and so on)? What results do you expect to see that you would consider a success? Who do they need to contact outside your company to make things work?

If you're a marketing manager in a large professional firm, you have my sympathy. While you can produce a newsletter, Web site, and leads, you still need to "teach" the professionals that *they* have to build the personal relationships and sales. Hopefully, your senior partner will reinforce professionals for "rainmaking."

Be a Fanatic

Like Peter Drucker, I believe that, ultimately, you have to create a little fanaticism to focus and energize any serious activity, including marketing. This means that you have to believe in the value of what you do.

Being a fanatic keeps you working when you don't feel like it. It helps you call people who could reject you. It makes you persist even when you're not sure that what you're doing will work.

The good news is that you don't have to be a fanatic forever—except about the quality of your customer service. Remember, the purpose of a marketing program is not to always be trying new things. It's to create a system to use the things that work, and systems become easier to carry out with use.

Once you've found what works for you, you can rebalance your life. When your overall life is in shape, your marketing and business will go better. And when they go better, this will feed back and enhance your overall life too.

> Anyone who ever accomplished anything has been something of a monomaniac—they focus intensely on one thing at a time.
>
> Peter Drucker

SUMMARY

When your plans are in place, you'll be in a position to move forward. Start your journey to success by taking that first step now!

Remember that good marketing should not be a hardship for you. It should make your life *easier* and you more successful. You do some front-end work to find the methods that you like and that attract the types of clients you want (your niche). Then you set up a system to make marketing routine while you have fun building relationships with your clients and prospects.

Good luck (and don't forget that there's more material for you to use in the Appendix).

AGENDA

Success usually depends on two methods only—
energy and perseverance.
JOHANN VON GOETHE

If you've done the exercises in this chapter, you have several mini–marketing plans. Commit now to taking the steps necessary to begin your marketing. I promise that you will see results. In fact, I've already given you a money-back guarantee. The ideas here work if you do! (In the first 20,000 copies of this book sold, not one person took me up on the guarantee.)

I'd love to hear about your successes (www.rickcrandall.com). Please write and let me know what you've done that has worked—or failed. Please send marketing forms or checklists you use (like those in the Appendix material in this book), and tell me what you could use.

In return, I'll send you some extra material to give you new ideas for your marketing, and perhaps I can feature your "case" in a future book.

CHAPTER SIXTEEN

THINGS YOU CAN DO NOW

An Expanded Action Agenda

AGENDA

Unused talents give you no advantage
over somone who has no talent at all.
MARK TWAIN

You'll have noticed that at the end of each chapter there were quotes about the benefits of taking action. Hopefully they inspired you to take some marketing steps. There are many ideas about effective marketing actions you can take in each chapter. These Action Agendas cover only some of the things you can do.

Sometimes you may have a few minutes to spend on marketing and not know what to do. This chapter has some examples you could do in these "found" moments.

Below is a group of further little ideas that can help get you started on your marketing. Some of them are not mentioned in the book, some are. Most are small things, but they may help to get you going. They won't all be appropriate for you, but I'll bet a lot of them would fit your situation.

This list is formatted differently than the chapter Action Agendas. For this one, put a check mark in front of each marketing step that fits your situation. Put two checks by the marketing activities you can do soon. Then, refer to the list often.

You now know a lot about marketing, but, as Mark Twain said, if you don't put what you know into action, you'll be no better off than if you knew nothing.

150 Small Marketing Ideas

_____ 1. Create your own name tag for events. Keep one in each purse or coat pocket.

_____ 2. Pick one small goal to achieve today.

_____ 3. Create one new business card that you can print on your computer—perhaps with a particular group of prospects in mind.

_____ 4. Choose a cause for which to be an advocate.

_____ 5. Have a good suit or dress cleaned and always ready.

_____ 6. Change your invoice to include mention of new services.

_____ 7. Put new signs up in your office.

_____ 8. Create a flyer on your business that kids can pass out.

_____ 9. Change your available hours to include unusual times.

_____ 10. Answer the phone in a more cheerful way.

_____ 11. Develop "free samples" of your services.

_____ 12. Volunteer for a group that gets you involved and meeting others who are involved.

_____ 13. Clean your desk or office.

_____ 14. Put a display in a local library or bank window.

_____ 15. Join a new group.

_____ 16. Create a specialized one-page résumé on your computer for one service or target audience.

_____ 17. Up to 60 percent or more of the impact of an ad depends on the headline. Write six new ones and test them with friends.

_____ 18. Train your staff thoroughly on how to greet people on the phone or in person.

_____ 19. Sponsor an employee or Little League team.

_____ 20. Create an insert of tips on a topic for your bills.

_____ 21. Smile at everyone today.

_____ 22. Reprint your best ad or PR material.

_____ 23. Put a "take-a-card" holder in a neighboring business.

_____ 24. Create a contest for the best or worst "something" related to your area.

_____ 25. Offer free coffee and tea to clients in your office.

_____ 26. Create a one-page capabilities sheet for a new service.

_____ 27. Approach a competitor about mutual referrals.

_____ 28. Analyze your pricing policy to see if you can improve it.

_____ 29. Provide a new specialized service no one else does.

_____ 30. Figure out what your current phone numbers could spell.

_____ 31. Add an 800 phone number—perhaps one that spells out something related to your business.

_____ 32. Call ex-clients and try to bring them back.

_____ 33. Get a specialty ad catalogue and look for novel items.

_____ 34. Consider a searchlight for an open house.

_____ 35. Write a guest column on your expertise.

_____ 36. Give evening seminars in your office.

_____ 37. Create a one-page newsletter for one type of client.

_____ 38. Throw an open house at the office with wine, cheese, and crackers.

_____ 39. Change your phone greeting to "*How* can I help you?"

_____ 40. Send out a news release.

_____ 41. Research your industry's award competition and submit your work. You may be a winner!

_____ 42. Go on a local talk show.

_____ 43. Call ten people you've been meaning to talk to.

_____ 44. Find a new online discussion group.

_____ 45. Buy an unusual postcard on which to send notes.

_____ 46. Give a referral to a colleague who gives you referrals.

_____ 47. Give a guest lecture at a local school.

_____ 48. Go to the library and research local companies.

_____ 49. Create a gift-certificate form.

_____ 50. Add a touch of color to your letterhead.

_____ 51. Offer faster service on one service with faster payment.

_____ 52. Request testimonials from good clients.

_____ 53. Create a joint ad with another service provider.

_____ 54. Ask a supplier for a referral.

_____ 55. Refer business to a client.

_____ 56. Invite several similar clients to a meeting at your office to share business tips.

_____ 57. Sponsor a talk by a visiting expert on a topic for your clients.

_____ 58. Create a client update sheet with information on changes of interest to them (for example, tax laws, investment opportunities, or management techniques).

_____ 59. Create a description of your ideal client.

_____ 60. Gather a list of questions clients ask most often.

_____ 61. Create a reference list of recommended books, tapes, and courses.

_____ 62. Create a policy of returning client calls within one hour.

_____ 63. Develop a free handout of tips to give to inquirers.

_____ 64. Offer a money-back guarantee for some service.

_____ 65. Produce a video of your next talk.

_____ 66. Develop a "survey of your needs."

_____ 67. Go to free SBA/SCORE sessions for consulting on marketing.

_____ 68. Give subscriptions to clients for Christmas.

_____ 69. Attend a chamber of commerce mixer.

_____ 70. Send a lottery ticket with a note that says, "If you want better odds, talk to us."

_____ 71. Go to free talks on marketing by authors at bookstores.

_____ 72. Try third-class mail with a postage meter or stamp. People don't notice actual postage. Your mail will be treated as business mail by most businesses/mail rooms.

_____ 73. Household service businesses can advertise with doorknob hangers distributed by kids.

_____ 74. Create an unusual name for a particular service package.

_____ 75. Find a marketing mentor and meet with that person regularly.

_____ 76. Set up a fax-on-demand service to send out literature twenty-four hours a day.

_____ 77. Create a 900 number which sells information (perhaps tied in with your fax-on-demand service).

_____ 78. Test offers with small classified ads.

_____ 79. Create a public service announcement.

_____ 80. Set up an Internet call box.

_____ 81. Broadcast your press release by fax.

_____ 82. Put your face, your service message, and a phone number on a billboard.

_____ 83. Send greeting cards to clients or prospects on birthdays and more unusual holidays such as May Day, VE day, and others.

_____ 84. Barter your services for other services you need (such as printing) and ordinarily pay for.

_____ 85. Donate a certain amount of company time to a charity; for example, for answering the phones on a telethon. (PBS fundraisers give great exposure.)

_____ 86. Host a party during a nontraditional time of year.

_____ 87. Do a client survey to uncover possible weaknesses and find additional opportunities.

_____ 88. Create a dramatic stunt. One landscaper has a "precision lawn-mower team" marching in local parades.

_____ 89. Create an employee marketing-suggestion contest. Everybody who submits an idea wins something.

_____ 90. Put a company logo or sign on your car.

_____ 91. Buy a license plate frame with your name or slogan on it.

_____ 92. Use a second color in your Yellow Pages ad.

_____ 93. Write a booklet.

_____ 94. Buy T-shirts, hats, or other wearables with your company logo displayed.

_____ 95. Create a new twenty-word description explaining your business.

_____ 96. Develop a special offer.

_____ 97. Offer free reprints of previously published material.

_____ 98. Sponsor a community event.

_____ 99. Do a remote radio broadcast from your office.

_____ 100. Encourage your employees to spread the good word about your service.

_____ 101. Take a former client to lunch.

_____ 102. Create a board of advisors.

_____ 103. Have a professional picture taken.

_____ 104. Send a fortune cookie to clients and prospects with the message wishing them good fortune in the new year.

_____ 105. Take a current client to a ball game.

_____ 106. Tape audio testimonials from some clients.

_____ 107. Write an article explaining something about your philosophy for your Web site.

_____ 108. Write an article with ten tips in your area and submit it to e-zines in your area or your clients' areas.

_____ 109. Plan to develop a new specialty. What would you need to establish yourself?

_____ 110. Set up a program to take clients and referral sources out to breakfast three days a week.

_____ 111. Put together a folder of information about you, your firm, and your approach.

_____ 112. In the next two minutes, write down twenty ways you could thrill clients. They don't have to be practical; write anything. Then go through and sort out the ones you can do now.

_____ 113. Study individual differences. Classify the people you come into contact with and see if your knowledge helps you relate to them better.

_____ 114. Do an online search in your area looking for consultants. Then start going to their Web sites and getting on their e-zine lists. Ask for links.

_____ 115. Do an online search looking for competitors. Catalogue their sites and see how you compare. Now improve your site to compare better.

_____ 116. Ask your best customers how you could help them with their customers.

_____ 117. Set up a clear reward system for employees bringing in referrals, leads, or business.

_____ 118. Write down what you don't like about marketing or sales and then write how you can overcome or change each point.

_____ 119. Pick a regular time every day to contact customers or do marketing.

_____ 120. Create a checklist or flowchart showing the process you go through as you build a relationship with a prospect and a customer.

_____ 121. Create a set of visuals that cover the key points about working with you and your firm. (Different prospects like to see information different ways.)

_____ 122. Develop ways to tie what you do to the highest priorities of your clients.

_____ 123. Practice your nonverbal listening skills, such as nodding, leaning forward, making eye contact, and saying "uh huh."

_____ 124. Practice your active listening skills, such as restating what you hear.

_____ 125. List two personal activities you'd like to increase. Schedule them in the next month to meet more people in leisure settings.

_____ 126. If you don't like small talk, decide on five topics about which you'll be willing to talk to strangers.

_____ 127. Decide how you're going to follow up with people you meet: postcard, faxed cartoon, e-mail, phone call?

_____ 128. Make a list of the reasons your services are worth a premium. Write down the differences between cost and value of your services.

_____ 129. Implement a self-training program to increase your skill in one area every week.

_____ 130. Contribute to an online discussion group today.

_____ 131. Start writing material for your own online e-zine. Create a mailing list to send it to some of your current contacts.

_____ 132. Build your e-zine list by asking your current contacts to forward it to friends and including it in your signature line.

_____ 133. Decide what trade show in your industry or your clients' industries to visit.

_____ 134. Make a list of the people in your community who you would most like to have as referral sources. Then make a list of what you can do for them.

_____ 135. Make a list of the people who can refer others to you online. Then figure out the benefits for each one linking to you.

_____ 136. Add a resource center to your Web site. Summarize valuable material with links to more details.

_____ 137. Visit the nearest college. Go to the department most relevant to your services and chat with whomever is available. Ask about possible interns, what research is being done, guest lecturing, cosponsoring a seminar, and other activities. Check out the library resources.

_____ 138. Put something attention-getting in your office. Have a competition for staff to bring in the most unusual item that will give visitors a chuckle.

_____ 139. Create a wallet-sized card with twenty tips on it for clients and prospects.

_____ 140. Go to Google.com. Search on "marketing" and your field and check out some of the sites that come up.

_____ 141. Go to my Web site (rickcrandall.com) and see if there is an
article about something relevant to you. If not, ask me for
an idea.

_____ 142. Think of something unusual to get attention outside your
office. For instance, for about $75, you can buy a pole and
official-looking street sign with your name on it for in front
of your office.

_____ 143. Visit the offices near you, introduce yourself, and ask employees what they do. Invite interesting people out for lunch or a
drink after work.

_____ 144. Use a Web analysis tool to find out where your site visitors are
coming from. Then use it on your competitors' sites.

_____ 145. Ask your favorite clients who their other favorite service
providers are. Then call them and arrange a meeting.

_____ 146. Offer your house or office to a nonprofit group for a fund-
raiser or board meeting.

_____ 147. Find a movie or book you could give out to clients (for example, for contractors, *The Money Pit*; for medical groups,
The Doctor.

_____ 148. Put some of your marketing material on a CD that people
can view on their computers. Include your Web site.

_____ 149. Create a separate Web site for one subgroup of your clients (a
niche). Register a good URL for about $10 a year and site it
with your main site for nothing.

_____ 150. Look at your Web site using at least two different browsers.
Note the differences in how it looks and optimize it for
all browsers.

MARKETING YOUR SERVICES

CHAPTER ONE

MARKETING FOR REAL PEOPLE

Hiring Help

There are many sources in the world where you can get help with your marketing if you have more money than time. They are advertising agencies, freelance copywriters, publicity agencies, graphics design firms, and others.

There are Yellow Pages listings for advertising, marketing, business consulting, and so on. You'll also see ads in business publications.

In searching for people to help you, you will want to use many of the marketing techniques we've discussed. Word of mouth, direct referrals, and testimonials will be important.

The best way to use word of mouth is to ask everyone you know if they know someone who's good at marketing services. Ask competitors of yours, or you might see brochures, ads, or publicity from similar services that you admire. You might call them and ask who did their marketing. Ask people in your networking groups and general business groups.

Having read this book, you'll be better able to deal with consultants, weed out the B.S., and get better work from service providers. Most consultants respond to people who appreciate their work, give them clear direction, and are intelligent critics. If they don't respond to your questions and criticisms with better work, you probably shouldn't be working with them.

Good marketing consultants, whether they're focusing on one aspect of marketing such as telemarketing or broader issues, should do some of the same things. They should have a sense of strategy and tactics. They should have a conceptual view. They should be able to use words, and understand both your services and the market to which you're appealing. They should be well organized and frank, but supportive.

If you ask people to judge whether they can help you, good consultants should ask a lot of questions about your service. They should essentially ask you for your positioning statement, your USP, your prime benefit, and many of the things we discussed in Chapter Three and elsewhere. In other words, they shouldn't just crank out a brochure, sales letter, or telemarketing script; they should want to understand your unique positioning, the best things you offer, and exactly to whom you are trying to appeal. You should see them as strategists or tacticians.

Questions that the consultant might ask you are (like in the mini–marketing plan in Chapter Fifteen): What's the purpose of this marketing? Do you want to create a particular document, such as a brochure, or are you just trying to attract more new clients? What is your budget? Who are the prospects you're targeting here? What sort of competition do you have? What specific benefits can you offer? Can you offer a strong guarantee?

If consultants don't know your marketplace, they may want to do some research, paid or unpaid. For instance, they should ask to call some of your satisfied clients. They might ask you to gather testimonials if you don't have a set of them. But they should want to understand your marketplace.

Costs
Rates vary considerably, yet consultants with different titles may do much the same thing. Graphics consultants tend to be the least expensive. Graphics consultants can be hired for as little as $35 an hour, and often not more than $50 an hour. Many editors are available for $35 to $50 an hour, but they would normally be editing something you've written. If you go to an advertising agency, you'll be billed at a higher rate. The average marketing consultant probably earns in the neighborhood of $100 an hour.

Many consultants offer a special $50 or $100 flat fee to evaluate your brochure, sales letter, publicity release, or other material. This is a good way to test them out. If they just give you general feedback—that it's too long—without any details, they are probably not someone with whom you want to work. If you're paying them $50 or $100, they should at least give you a number of specific criticisms and suggestions for improvement, so you can see the types of things that they would improve.

Ad Agencies
Ad agencies are probably the most expensive and traditional place to go for marketing help. They are sometimes paid on a percentage of media

placements. For instance, some get 15 percent of all your advertising expenses on newspaper, radio, and other media. And, historically, many ad agencies worked for just this 15 percent, which they got from the media. Therefore, they were apparently free to you. Nowadays, most advertising agencies charge for their time by the hour, and many would not take on a campaign unless it was for many thousands of dollars and you were going to do substantial advertising.

Public Relations

Most good public relations people will want to work on a retainer basis of, give or take, several thousand dollars a month. They also will not guarantee results and will want a contract of several months. It takes time for their efforts on your behalf to begin to come to fruition. It could be three months before you see items in the press.

Many people say that you're paying people for their time, but I much prefer results! There are occasional PR agencies (such as ours) that will work on a performance basis, getting paid for each placement. PR people and others like to say that you're hiring them for their knowledge, not their contacts. But if they don't have a database of the type of media that you're trying to reach, they'll have to get a general directory and make phone calls. They'll spend a lot of time building up their database at your expense before any results occur.

Results?

The funny thing about marketing consultants is that almost none will work on a results basis. Logically, if marketing consultants aren't confident that their services will make you far more than enough money to pay them, why should you have any faith in their abilities? But, unfortunately they get paid for their time, not their results, in many cases.

Contracts

You don't need a contract with a consultant, but it makes sense to have a one-page memo of agreement on services to be rendered, and a payment-due agreement. Most marketing people will want 50 percent up front and 50 percent when the job is completed; or one-third of the payment up front, one-third when the job is 50 percent completed, and one-third when the job is finished.

Build Relationships

Once you've actually produced a letter, script, or whatever, and tested it, tell the marketer the results. Compliment him or her if things go well.

Build a relationship for the future just as you would with a customer. Once the preliminary groundwork has been done, the marketer may well be willing to write a single press release or a single ad, quite inexpensively, as part of an ongoing relationship. If results are really good, write an unsolicited testimonial to the marketer for use as a reference. If you are easy to work with, he or she will do better work, and you'll get more for your money.

CHAPTER TWO
WHAT YOU CAN DO TODAY

Customer Feedback Letters

**A Letter Asking Customers
How They Feel About Your Service**

Dear _____ :

We've been working with you on _____ over the last _____ . One of the things we try to achieve is to do more than satisfy customers. We want to delight you. In order to constantly improve our service, we're always eager to receive any input.

Could you help us improve our services by taking a few minutes of your time to respond to the following questions? We'd appreciate your answers, whether or not you wish to identify yourself.

You can have questions rated on a one-to-ten scale, such as:

How satisfied are you with our services?
How satisfied are you with _____ ?

You can also ask if there are future jobs for which customers would consider you. You'd normally include a self-addressed, stamped envelope. Also add a note:

If you wish to put your name and phone number here, we'd love to talk to you further if you have the time.

Cover Letter for a More Extensive Questionnaire

Dear _____ :

I have a favor to ask that you may find interesting. As one of our important customers, I hope you're aware that we really value your input. In order for us to keep in touch and improve ourselves, we occasionally ask a few people to respond to some questions about our services and to tell us what things they think are important.

I know you're busy, and filling out a questionnaire might not be at the top of your list for today. But if you could take a few minutes and return the questionnaire in the postage-paid envelope, I'd really appreciate it.

Last year's suggestions resulted in some important changes that enabled us to do a better job for you. Even a hint of an idea would be greatly appreciated.

A Thank-You Note for Returning a Questionnaire
(If People Are Identified)

Dear _____ :

Thank you for returning your completed questionnaire. I just want to let you know that I especially appreciate it. For your information, a very brief summary of the results is attached.

You may give clients the option of receiving results of the questionnaire.

If you'd like more information or would like to share more ideas with me, I'd love to get together any time and take you to lunch.

As a bonus, you might also include a gift certificate or something for their response.

CHAPTER THREE
YOUR "MINI–MBA" IN MARKETING

Ways to Price Your Service

There are three general ways to price your service from the theoretical perspective. The first is *based on your costs*. This approach is more appropriate for manufacturing than service. Your direct costs may not be significant compared to the fees you want or need to charge.

The second is *based on the competition*. In practice this is the way most people price their services. They aim to be in the neighborhood of other people like them. For instance, people in the graphics or editorial industry tend to be on the lower end of the price spectrum, maybe $30 to $50 per hour. Attorneys tend to be on the high end, ranging from $100 to more than $300 per hour. Most other services fall in between. In most cases it's relatively easy to find out what your competitors are charging.

The third way to price your service is *what the market will bear*. If you have a unique resource and great demand for your service you can theoretically raise your price until demand and supply are equalized. Very few of us are in a position to be in such great demand that we can charge almost anything. Speakers such as Tom Peters and some celebrities fall into this category. They can only do so many talks a year.

From an analytical point of view, here are the kinds of steps you'd go through in setting prices.

1. Decide what your objective is in setting a price. Are you trying to make a certain amount per hour or per year? Are you trying to attract more or less business?

2. Identify constraints on pricing. What does the competition charge? Are customers willing to pay within a certain range but no more?

3. Estimate demand and revenue based on each price.

4. Determine your cost, expected volume, and profit you'd make.

5. Select an approximate price level.

6. What "price list" or set of prices will you quote? For instance, you may have a flat hourly rate, you may have a retainer rate that's less, you may have cost-plus that's billed in a different fashion, and you may have flat bid rates or procedures.

7. Make adjustments to your list prices and quoted prices depending on market feedback.

8. Other factors that may influence your pricing are characteristics of your buyers. Different industries may be willing to pay different amounts, and certain geographic regions may be willing to pay more. For instance, urban area prices are generally a bit higher than rural areas, even from the same service provider. General economic conditions can also have an influence.

In pricing, you may be trying to buy market share. You may be trying to maximize volume. You may be trying to balance your workload. There may be social or ethical considerations, image considerations, and so forth.

For instance, if you're a professional service you don't want to set your rates too low. It raises questions about your competence and value. It's better to offer fixed pricing or special arrangements but keep your quoted and hourly rates at the normal level.

CHAPTER FOUR
ADVERTISING

Letter Ad Using Personal Style
Here are some ideas for doing a column type of advertisement such as the one for the chiropractor in Chapter Four.

I've been in our community for __ years. I've seen many changes, some good and some bad. As a ___ I like to feel that I can contribute to the community both in working with individuals and companies, and as a citizen serving on the boards of _____ and _____ and contributing my time to the school and _____ . In this column I'd like to share a few ideas from my field that you might find useful.

Then would follow a brief set of tips or a short article on your expertise that might help readers to take care of their trees better, handle their legal affairs, buy or sell a house, buy insurance more intelligently, and so on. Anything you might put in your newsletter could go in the paper, designed like a column. This could include humor, trivia, how-to's, and personal opinion. See Chapter Ten for more ideas that you can use for an advertisement of this sort.

CHAPTER FIVE
WRITING YOUR WAY TO CLIENTS

Fog Index

One fog index, by Robert Gunning, is constructed by taking a sample of writing (about a hundred words in length). Perform the following steps to get a measure of readability.

1. Count the number of sentences in that sample. (Pick a word length that allows you to end on a complete sentence.)
2. Divide the number of words in the sample by the number of sentences. That gives you the average sentence length.
3. Count the number of words with three syllables or more. Do not include capitalized words or combination words that come from simple roots (like "bookkeeper" or "created").
4.. Add the average sentence length to the number of words with three syllables or more and multiply this by .4.

The number you arrive at is an approximation of grade-level readability. A 10 would be high school sophomore—a level accessible to most people in the country who read. Anything over 12 is into the college level and is considered too difficult for most people to easily and enjoyably comprehend.

Other measures of fog estimate how formal or personal your language is. There are many ways to calculate formulas like this, but the one above will give you a rough idea of how readable your material is.

CHAPTER SIX
HOW TO LIKE PERSONAL SELLING

How to Write a Sales Proposal

Some service businesses are required to submit formal proposals. Proposals outline the scope of the work and specify what will be done, when it will be done, and how it will be done. In the most structured case, a company will issue a request for proposal, or RFP which will specify exactly what it wants to see. Many times these are government agencies or companies that are trying to satisfy affirmative action or other requirements. In the case of government agencies, they are often required to accept the lowest qualified bid on such a proposal.

While there are good sides to doing proposals, there are also expenses and dangers. A complete proposal can specify exactly how the work will be done. It can take you dozens of hours in a new area, and it can provide great value for clients. Yet very seldom can you get paid for doing this proposal. It's very dangerous to invest time in a proposal when you haven't talked to the people who will be making the decision.

In less formal cases, a company will request a few pages outlining your approach and proposition to it. Normally, this will confirm what you have already agreed on verbally.

Ideally, a proposal should only be done when you've already agreed on a contract. When proposals are competitive, such as law firms trying to win major accounts, they can become work samples and can cost thousands of dollars for a major account.

Since you don't expect to get all the jobs you make proposals on, you have to be very careful of your investment of time and resources in creating them. For instance, recently a large automobile company changed advertising agencies and requested proposals. The advertising firms estimated that each proposal with video, sample ads, and so on would cost them well over $100,000. The advertising firm that had been doing the work declined to compete with a new proposal. It had already analyzed the situation and decided the client was looking for a change.

In the worst case of wasted time, a prospective client may ask you to develop a proposal and then turn around and give that proposal to competitors as a job specification. By saving your competitors the time of outlining the work to be done, this can allow them to give a much lower bid by stealing your approach. That's one reason I don't like doing proposals unless I know the situation well and believe I have a good chance of winning the contract.

You should work to build up a "book" of proposal material in your word processing program. This means that after you've done it a few times you can create new proposals very quickly by putting together relatively standard pieces. Of course, you'll want to customize material for each proposal based on your detailed conversations with the company. In particular, you'll want to customize your cover letter, which is all that most people involved in the decision will read closely.

Proposal Styles and Politics

One reason it's a bad idea to do a proposal when you don't know the people involved is that you may not understand both their needs and their approach or style. Some people are engineering or technically oriented, and they want many technical details. If you're dealing with an engineering audience, this is often the case. Other people are very practically oriented; they just want to believe that you can solve their problem and don't want to be bothered with all the details. You need to make them comfortable working with you and build your general credibility.

You also must make a distinction between the people who solicit the proposal and the people who actually make the decision. Is the decision going to be made on staff review of technical criteria or is it going to be based on the comfort level of the CEO in working with your company? Some decision makers are interested in not rocking the boat, bringing in suppliers who fit the general pattern of the industry. Others have the vision of new ways to do things and are looking for cutting-edge approaches.

These factors make a big difference in how you position yourself. By carefully constructing the index of any larger proposal you can make it easier for people to find the types of information they want. For instance, some will look largely at financials, others will look at technical detail, others will look at the statement of your philosophy and style of approach.

Protecting Proprietary Ideas

If your proposal discloses proprietary information that is a special advantage for your company, you may want to try to get the recipient to sign a "nondisclosure" agreement before submitting your proposal. Such an agreement briefly states that you are disclosing the information only for proposal purposes. It is not to be shared with other people, and it represents trademarked or copyrighted material or trade secrets that are not publicly disclosed.

Many companies will not sign such a nondisclosure agreement because they feel it limits their ability to share the proposal with people within their firms, but this may be necessary for you in some situations. You can also copyright part or all of your proposal, or put a notice on the front page that the proposal contains proprietary information and is submitted only for purposes of evaluating your bid for the contract and should not be shared with others without obtaining written permission. In some cases you may be able to avoid disclosing full technical details so that your proposal talks about your capabilities but not exactly how you'll solve the problems. In other cases companies will want to see that you know how to solve their problems before they'll give you a contract.

Sample Cover Letter with a Proposal

To: _____

From: _____

Re: Increasing your productivity in _____ area.

As I understand your current problem, you are not able to be as effective as you'd like in _____ area. I believe that we have an approach that can markedly increase your productivity there.

Next, provide no more than one paragraph of technical details about why your approach is the best.

The next paragraph should talk about benefits to the user.

I estimate that this approach will save you _____ hours and _____ dollars over the next year. Since our cost will be only _____ you should see an immediate return on your investment.

Another Sample Letter

Date _____
Mr./Ms. _____
Director _____ Systems
Company _____
Address _____

Dear Mr./Ms. _____

I very much enjoyed our meeting last Monday. As I understand what you said, you are looking for ways to greatly
increase the speed and cost-effectiveness of your legal
services at no increase in budget.

Today legal costs are escalating out of sight. We agree
with your perspective that steps need to be taken to control
them. We have a custom program which guarantees legal
costs within defined parameters.

If you'd like to get started inexpensively we can do a low-
cost analysis of your legal needs for the next year. It will
take us about a week of interviews with your top executives
and then we will come up with an exact budget guarantee
for the upcoming year. The cost for our analysis is only
_____ dollars and you receive a fifty-three-point, twenty-
page report that you'll find valuable even if you decide not
to use our full services.

Attached are more details about our successful experience with other companies like yours, and brief descriptions of how we structure the service to control your legal
costs to protect you in today's litigious marketplace.

Formal Proposal Outline
A formal proposal will normally include:

1. A brief cover letter of one page.
2. A title page with possible statement of your proprietary interest.
3. A one-page table of contents.

4. An executive summary of no more than two pages which provides a complete overview for those who don't want to read the entire proposal.
5. The body of the proposal. This will often include technical capabilities or issues, detailed costs, time lines and PERT charts, specific descriptions of what you'll accomplish, when payment will be made, training provided, and backup documentation.
6. Appendixes, including capability statements, résumés, and so on.

Build Relationships

The approach to marketing advocated in this book of building relationships with people will generally eliminate the need to do proposals.

When proposals are needed you should have an advocate at the company who helps guide you through the process and simply needs the proposal as a formal tool to meet internal contracting requirements while he or she sells your services for you.

Many references are available for more details. Because very few people actually read your proposal closely, how it looks and how it's "packaged" can be very important. That's why your executive summary has to be the best part of your proposal, and that's why your outline should be very clear to the reader at a glance. In today's busy world, people are more likely to skim than to read word for word, so use subheads, short sentences, and other approaches discussed in the writing chapter (Chapter Five) to make your proposals appealing to both the eye and the mind, which doesn't have a long attention span.

Points to Cover in a Written Proposal

1. Decide each major function in the contract.
2. Specify unique, unusual, interesting, or technical approaches for each function.
3. Describe how the client's management will be utilized and kept informed.
4. Explain what inputs are necessary from the client.
5. Describe interim objectives and outcomes resulting from each major function.
6. Describe final objectives and when they occur.

Typical Sections of a Proposal

Front Section
Title page
Table of contents
Executive summary
Client problem
Goals
Objectives

Main Section
Proposal narrative
Functional flow diagram
Project time line
Personnel loading analysis

Budget Section
Project budget or budget summary
Statement of your capabilities

Appendix
Supporting articles and technical documents
Testimonials and client list
Résumés and other evidence of abilities

Personal Attributes of a Good Salesperson
A survey of a manufacturer's customers listed ten attributes of salespeople, and asked which were the most important. In order of importance, the top five were: 1. Knowledge of the product; 2. Ability to make a concise sales talk; 3. A pleasing personal appearance; 4. Knowledge of my needs; 5. Warmth of personality.

Here are five qualities people don't like in salespeople: 1. Sloppy appearance; 2. Overaggressiveness; 3. Inability to see the other side; 4. Overly lengthy sales talk; 5. Slow, halting speech. I want to reorder these slightly and point out that what people like in salespeople is being likable and nice and being knowledgeable about their service area, and what people dislike is the "pushy," "hard-sell," myopic salesperson.

CHAPTER SEVEN

FREE PUBLICITY

More Ideas for Holiday PR

HOLIDAY	SERVICE	PR IDEA
Administrative Assistants' Day (4/26)	Anyone	Article on why administrative assistants should receive more respect.
Thanksgiving	Banker	Article on how early crop failures of the Pilgrims were due to their socialist economic system.
St. Patrick's Day	Insurance	Article about the potato famine and how insurance covers crop failures, job layoffs, and other disasters.
Valentine's Day	Realtor	Discuss how houses can reflect the relationships of the couples who live in them.
Release of new wine (Nouveau Beaujolais 11/17)	Anyone	Use French stamps as extras on letters to media.
Trade show for your clients' industry	Anyone	Advice for that industry about your field.
Presidents' Day	Marketing Consultant	How the creation of the holiday was a marketing effort.
Veterans' Day	Business Consultant	Article on SBA veterans' preference programs.
Pearl Harbor Day	Beauticians	Be prepared for surprises with your makeup.
Longest Day of Year	Architects	How to protect your house from sun damage.
Shortest Day	Heating Services	How to inspect your furnace for cold days ahead.

HOLIDAY	SERVICE	PR IDEA
9/11/01 Anniversary	Therapist	How to deal with old stress.
	Builder	How new buildings are stronger.
Lincoln's Birthday	Mortgage Broker	How you can free yourself from the "slavery" of high interest rates.
Washington's Birthday	Anyone	Why honesty is important in business.
Halloween	Anyone	How not to be scared of a particular problem in your area.
Martin Luther King Day	Business Consultant	Why having a "vision" is important to success.
New Year's Day	Anyone	How to start the year off right in your area.
April Fool's Day	Marketing Consultant	How not to be fooled by advertising salespeople.
Groundhog Day	Housecleaner	How to conduct a more efficient spring cleaning.
First Day of Spring	Car Detailer	How to protect your car finish from rains.
Daylight Savings Starts	Therapist	How light affects our moods.

Ideas for Press Releases for Different Services
(Note that many of the ideas can be used by other services too.)

SERVICE	PRESS RELEASE IDEA
Accountant	Offer a discount package with a bookkeeper for books and tax work.
Acupressure	Write an article for a local magazine or newspaper on pain reduction.
Architect	Write articles on low-cost additions or alterations that add value to homes.
Astrologer	Predict the winners in a local election.
Beauty Salon	Create a combination deal: customers receive a hair styling and tickets to an event (which you can buy in bulk at a discount).

SERVICE	PRESS RELEASE IDEA
Bookkeeper	Offer family seminars on budgeting or bill paying.
Business Consultant	Create a business roundtable—give a free consultation once a month for four hours at a popular restaurant.
Career Consultant	Appear on radio about the job market. Organize a career day.
Carpet Service	Carpet the sidewalk on your block and have your neighbors call the newspaper.
Caterer	Write about different ethnic cuisines.
Clothing Designer	Give items to auctions given by highly regarded charities. Usually the women working for these charities will want to buy your designs.
Computer Consultant	Present free mini-seminars at computer stores. Then offer follow-up services that meet the needs of the people who come.
Consultant	Write a column for your target audience. Donate your services to a charity auction.
Contractor	Offer an open-house session where you use CAD to show people the house of their dreams on a computer.
Dating Service	Offer a free seminar for those reentering the dating market who are aged fifty and older.
Employment Service	Offer a free résumé workshop or write an article about doing a résumé.
Event Planner	Donate your services to a charity that caters to your prospects.
Executive Recruiter	Write an article on why executives fail, how to assimilate newcomers into jobs, and so on.
Financial Planner	Write articles for your local newspaper on how money affects relationships or the role of money in divorces.
Graphic Designer	Offer a course on business graphics. Create a striking mural in your office or on an outside wall.
Hairdresser	Do a makeover on a reporter, perhaps on computer if you have that system.
Hospital	Broadcast a radio show on health issues from the hospital.
Housecleaning Service	Write about housecleaning tips that save time.

SERVICE	PRESS RELEASE IDEA
Interior Designer	Offer clients a one-hour consultation where you visit homes and rearrange the environment. Create the world's biggest pillow. Cosponsor seminars with a store and show how the items can be used in different decors.
Investigator	Adopt a colorful "persona" to intrigue the media, such as wearing a Sherlock Holmes hat and using a magnifying glass.
Judo Instructor	Write a pamphlet on self-defense specifically aimed at your target audience.
Laundromat	Have "singles sessions," "housewife hours," or other events.
Limousine Service	Write about the history of the auto in America.
Massage Therapist	Publicize a backrub-at-work service.
Mover	Specialize in moving computers. Write articles on how to lift properly, how to protect household goods, and similar tips.
Optician	Write about how to exercise your eyes to improve vision.
Packing Store	Give a seminar in the store on how to do special gift wraps.
Painter	Create a pamphlet on how colors affect your mood.
Pet Groomer	Create a summary sheet on what qualities different dogs have.
Photographer	Use a dramatic photo on your business card. Take pictures free at political events. (You can still sell prints to individuals.)
Plastic Surgeon	Discuss why self-esteem, not vanity, is a deciding factor.
Podiatrist	Send out releases on healthful footwear.
Psychologist	Develop a new term for an old problem, such as "Sunday Blues."
Real Estate	Do a booklet on creative financing.
Rental Service	Offer seminars on tenant or landlord rights.
Secretarial Service	Publicize a remote dictating service to your voice mail that is available twenty-four hours a day. Create a writers' support group where people encourage each other and set goals.
Travel Agent	Do press releases on travel to areas in the news.
Upholsterer	Have a contest for the city's oldest chair. Give seminars on how to preserve furniture.

Sample Press Release

NEW BOOK NEWS

For Immediate Release
Contact: Randolph Hugo,
ABC Publishing Co.
(555) 932-1612

AUTHOR GUARANTEES READERS MORE MONEY
Corte Madera, CA (March 29)—ABC Publishing Co.
announces the publication and release of <u>Marketing Your
Services: For People Who Hate to Sell</u> by Rick Crandall. In
an unusual twist in bookselling, the author guarantees the
book will help readers market their professional or contract services or he will personally buy the book back. "If
this book doesn't boost your income this year," says the
author, "I'll give you your money back in full!"

"One of the key points I make in the book is that good
marketing is built on relationships with your customers
and clients," states author Crandall. "An exceptional guarantee is just one feature of a successful marketing plan.
But also, it's a good way to start or keep a strong client
relationship. It earns immediate trust."

In keeping with a relationship approach to marketing,
Crandall is also asking for reader input for future books
and editions. In return, he promises to send readers more
marketing material for their use.

Crandall belongs to a new school of marketing (with
Michael Phillips, <u>Marketing Without Advertising</u>; and Don
Peppers, <u>The One to One Future</u>) that challenges traditional
approaches such as advertising. Once called "grassroots
marketing" and practiced by Apple Computer and others,
many experts now call this "relationship marketing."
Crandall says, "I can't overstate the value and cost-
effectiveness of knowing your customer and I mean knowing more than his zip code. In marketing services, the
client should be king."

Crandall advocates spreading the word about your services from inside your current customer base. "Let your clients do the selling for you," says Crandall. "This is a one-to-one, person-to-person process that gets you better results and more referrals." Crandall claims this <u>inside-out</u> approach is the reverse of how most people try to market their services. "Most of the time, they want advertising to achieve instant rapport with the outside world. But advertising does little to build relationships."

Before you advertise, you should read this book. Why? "Because advertising is the first thing that can kill you," says Crandall. Nevertheless, if you insist on advertising, the author shows you how you get the most bang for your buck. The book is packed with "fill-in-the-blank" exercises for writing headlines and ad copy, worksheets, checklists, sample letters, and press releases. Crandall gives you the materials you need to get started right now. The appendix alone ensures that Crandall won't have many takers on the guarantee.

Crandall has a Ph.D. (University of Michigan) and has taught marketing at colleges and universities for twenty years. He has lectured for various professional groups.

<u>Marketing Your Services</u> is a book that means business—new business for you or your money back!

Title: <u>Marketing Your Services: For People Who Hate to Sell</u>
Author: Rick Crandall, Price: $18.95 (Paper, 380 pages)
Publication Date: April 2, 2003
To Order: 1-555-555-5555
Reviewer copies and interview slots are available.

Sample Letters to the Editor

Perhaps your best letters to the editor are to the trade publications that your customers read. Those are too specific to cover here.

Here I'll cover general letters to the editor that you might send to your daily newspaper to gain overall visibility and to build up a reputation as a concerned citizen.

These samples are necessarily generic. Remember that the more individuality you can express in your letters, the more you'll create and build the image that you want.

On Education

I was moved to write about the status of education in this country from some of the recent news. It appears that our country is willing to spend more on prisons to hold people who the system has failed to educate, than it is on education to avoid such lifelong consequences.

It's an accepted fact that all taxpayer dollars spent on education are well repaid by those with more education paying more taxes over their lifetime. So, even the arguments by people without children that they shouldn't pay for education are false. Education helps everyone in society directly and indirectly.

What disturbs me about the educational system today is that it doesn't seem much different than twenty years ago. We have more computers in the classrooms but teachers still stand in front of classes and give lectures geared to the pace of the average student.

It's time that we applied what we know about technology, and not only the technology of using computers, to teach rote material. Surely educational research has developed better ways to educate and inspire children today than we had twenty or thirty years ago. That's the most important thing.

Our education system serves a function as simply a "holding pen" for children. Its higher function should be to inspire them to a <u>lifelong</u> love of learning. The information they learn may be out of date as soon as they graduate. But we could teach basic skills like how to learn, how to read more efficiently, and how to memorize necessary facts. What about how to judge the arguments of politicians? These are lifelong skills that could benefit us all.

On Crime

I'd like to weigh in with one more voice about the ridiculous crime problem in this country. We are spending a fortune building prisons and creating a clogged court system that legal experts say is almost impossible to utilize efficiently.

What about crime prevention? What about exercising better judgment and throwing out ridiculous cases that never should have come to court, or about assessing court costs to the losers to discourage frivolous suits?

The most pessimistic people I've heard talk about the crime problem are those in law enforcement and judges. The legal system appears to be breaking down all around us. We need to do something <u>now</u>, at least on a local level.

Statistics Can't Measure a Problem's Importance

The old saying that statistics can be twisted to support anything is not necessarily true, but as a _____ I believe that I have a basic understanding of the scientific method. So many of our problems in society such as _____ and ___ are really a matter of value judgments and priorities, not statistics. It doesn't matter what the exact number of homeless people is or the exact number with a certain disease, what matters is our willingness to commit to improving the situation. If we can't afford to attack it full bore we have to at least be clear what we're willing to do, and use our resources in an efficient way. Too many times advocates and opponents, even within advocacy groups, argue about details when what we need is more consensus on the importance of the problem and the value of getting started now.

On Politics

Like many people I'm a bit disillusioned about the political process as it's practiced. The Democrats and Republicans seem to spend time jockeying for position. Lobbyists seem to be able to buy influence in legislatures. It's easy to get discouraged.

We need to focus on things we can do within the political system to improve matters. And the media needs to focus on bringing out clear and detailed information about the politicians and issues at stake in each election. As individuals, we can be overwhelmed by the task of being informed citizens. But we all have that duty. Let's encourage our media to do a better job of bringing us the facts so we can do a better job of voting our consciences.

On Volunteerism

As a _____ I've decided to make an effort to volunteer for community agencies that can use my skills. I'd like to urge all people to pick one agency this year. If you don't have technical skills to improve its functioning, volunteer to make phone calls. Volunteer to help out at the office. America is often considered a land of volunteerism. But most of us don't give blood, and don't regularly give volunteer time to help others. A few hours a week or even a few hours a month can make all the difference. And surprisingly, in my experience, I've gotten as much out of volunteering as the people I volunteered to help. I've learned things, I've met people, and I've had good feelings about contributing. I urge everyone to reach out to the agency of their choice.

CHAPTER EIGHT
NETWORKING

Twelve Tips for Running a Business Mingler
Many tips for how to run a good business mingler or mixer are implied by the tips in Chapter Eight in the text on how to benefit from going to a group. To summarize some of the obvious ones here:

1. *Have name tags.* Provide as much information on the name tags as possible such as name, company or type of service, and geographic region if relevant. The more you put on the tag, the more points people have to strike up conversations.

2. *Have multiple food and drink centers.* If you have food or drink, set it up in more than one place to encourage circulation and make it easier for people to move through the room.

3. *Seek out cosponsors if your group is not large.* The easiest way to meet a lot of new people at one mixer is to cosponsor it with other groups in

town. They'll appreciate your overtures, and many times you'll have double the mixer than either one of you could have by yourself.

4. *If your object is to help people make connections, think of ways to do it.* Set up some sort of game that encourages people to talk to each other, rather than just talk to their friends.

For instance, if you put two colored dots on each tag, people can be told that if they collect dots from five different people in five different colors, they can win a small door prize, or they get to introduce themselves to the group. Or colored dots can have numbers or letters added to them and people can play "bingo" by spelling out words with the letters they find, and making a note on whose tag had each letter.

Or you can sit participants down at tables where all people with the same color tags have a chance to introduce themselves before going back to general mingling or before rotating to another table. There are many different ways to facilitate contact.

5. *Have official greeters at the front door.* As people come in, ask if they've been there before or if there's anyone in particular they'd like to meet. Then have someone take them over to an appropriate person and get a conversation started. The old-fashioned host and hostess help make parties successful.

6. *Make sure you have friendly people at the front door.* Some of us are better than others at greeting strangers over and over. Make sure you have a smiling face there.

7. *Collect people's business cards as they come in the door.* You'll know who's there, and you can put them on your mailing list. Have literature about your group on a table.

8. *Have a place for people to put their own literature during the mixer.*

9. *Encourage people to not stay with the people with whom they arrived.* Post a list of official "networking rules" by the front door with suggestions on mingling or the rules of the games you're playing.

10. *Have roving hosts.* They should move from group to group and make sure that everyone has someone to talk to, and otherwise help the social flow. It's actually easier for individuals in the group to act as hosts than to act on their own behalf, so both parties benefit from this.

11. *Have half a dozen people come early.* Then when the first people come there's a small group, and they don't feel that they're the only ones there. These people can be officers who work the door during the evening

and they can act as the initial seeds to create clusters of interesting conversation early.

12. *Remember that it's easier for people to stay late than to come early.* Expect your mixer to get off to a slow start. Arrange for some early birds to create a crowd. And allow the mixer to extend beyond the formal ending time if people are still enjoying themselves.

CHAPTER NINE
USING THE TELEPHONE AND FAX

A Telemarketing Script to
Set Appointments for a Service Provider

Hello, I'm _____ calling for _____ . Do you have a minute to talk? _____ helps companies like yours. Would you be interested in a free meeting at your facility for him to give you a little feedback on any problems you may have?

Or

She's offering a free assessment session. She comes to your facility and covers a twenty-five-point checklist that you may find helpful for gaining perspective on your company. Who do I talk to in your company to see if this would be useful to you?

Or

We're offering a free assessment session to analyze your _____ . Who in your company should I talk to about this?

If you get a yes that someone is interested, then you should have a few questions that qualify him or her, such as: How many employees in the company? What are its major markets? Or, if it's for an individual, questions that allow you to know what category of customer he or she falls into. For instance, if you're a financial planner, you'd want to know clients' occupations, how long they've been on the job, income level if they'll tell you, tax bracket if they'll tell you, and amount of savings or financial goals.

CHAPTER TEN
KEEP IN TOUCH

Newsletter and Electronic Publishers Association
National office: 1501 Wilson Boulevard, Suite 509, Arlington VA 22209; (703)527-2333, (800) 356-9302; (newsletters.org). You can visit local chapters for the cost of a lunch, rather than joining immediately.

Editorial Material You Can Use or Modify in Your Newsletter

Travel Plans: A Private Matter

High on the list of travel safety tips is this caution: Discuss travel plans on a need-to-know basis. Don't tell everyone that you will be out of town for a period of time. Those answering an office phone should not disclose that you are on a trip or how long you will be away. William Ethridge, manager of corporate security, says a traveler should confirm arrivals and destinations with his or her office and family. Stick to an itinerary.

Ask the Right Questions to Improve Quality

The traditional approach to quality improvement is to teach improvement of skills. But some contend that skill is not the issue, that people already have the skills they need. Dramatic improvement comes not by teaching skills, but by asking people questions that help to create ownership of the improvements you want.

Many questions have negative effects. For instance, if a supervisor asks, "Why are you behind schedule?" or "What's the problem on this project?" or "Why did you do that?" the response is likely to be defensive. The questions focus on what's wrong and who is to blame so people get caught up in protecting themselves instead of finding answers. Better questions to ask are:

"How do you feel about this project so far?"

"What have you accomplished that you're pleased with?"

"What kind of support do you need to assure your success?"

For better questions, make them open ended so they can't be answered with "yes" or "no." Be forward focused, directing energies to what needs to improve.

Use questions to help people. Behind all questions should be the guiding principle: How can I help this person gain more clarity by answering this question?

Negotiating Hotel Discounts on the Spot

There are a number of things you can do to get better hotel rates ahead of time, such as calling the hotel directly and inquiring about its commercial rates. When you arrive in person and want to negotiate, one manager's advice is to be discreet. Always avoid a crowd. Allow the hotel staff to give you a special rate without interfering with their business with other customers.

How to Jump-Start TQM (Total Quality Management)

Should quality efforts be tied to early results? Yes, because if you are clear on goals and produce early results, the long-term effort will be energized. Here's a three-step process to jump-start TQM:

1. To begin, ask people to generate specific results in a short time frame. Pick a goal, such as reducing errors, that can be achieved relatively quickly.
2. Once early results are achieved, target the next set of goals. Look for measurable gains that will be part of a total program but provide a short-term payoff.
3. Introduce the quality tools, training, and support material on an as-needed basis. Don't give people a lot of general theory when they don't know how to apply it.

It is management's job to set challenging goals and to help teams succeed quickly with measurable results. Setting goals doesn't mean telling people how to do everything. Selecting the means to achieve the goal is where the creativity of all the team members comes into play.

Late Lunches Boost Productivity

Many workers take lunch breaks at 1 p.m., 2 p.m., or later. People are eating later because they say they can get more work done from noon to one, regardless of what time of the day their work begins. Other reasons for the trend: longer workdays, later breakfasts, and after-work exercise workouts.

Digging Out from Under Your Paperwork

The "Information Age" can drown you in raw data. You need to be in the "Communication Age" where you handle information efficiently. If you get buried under pieces of paper and things to do, here's a saying that may remind you of what you should be doing: "Update and eliminate or you'll accumulate."

Don't Ruin New Workers

When people start a new job with a new company their enthusiasm is often at its highest level. Most companies are so poor at introducing new-comers to their business that they squelch this enthusiasm, rather than tap into it. Talk to people who are new with your company. Let them help design an orientation program that really works.

Old Values Pay Off

Remember the phrase "work ethic"? Sounds a bit old-fashioned, right? Well, it's not. Many CEOs say it's one of the things they look for in job and promotion candidates. They want people who are team players and are committed to their company, who worry more about completing projects than leaving at 5 p.m., and who get along with their colleagues.

The Japanese Recommend Food Variety for Health

When it comes to diet, variety might well be called the essence of life. The Japanese government gives one health recommendation to its citizens: Eat thirty or more different kinds of food per day. This makes sense when you consider the types and kinds of foods available and the spectrum of nutri-ents they contain. Unfortunately, however, North American adults often omit entire categories of foods such as grains, vegetables, or fruit. In the early 1970s, the eating habits of over 10,000 Americans were studied. Researchers found that those whose food choices were the least varied were more likely to have died by the mid- to late 1980s than those who regularly ate foods from five major food groups: meat, dairy, fruits, vegetables, and grains.

Tofu and Prostate Cancer

Tofu may reduce the risk of cancer. The British medical journal *Lancet* describes a study held to discover why Japanese, Hawaiian, and Seventh Day Adventist men had a very low incidence of prostate cancer. The answer appears to be a high intake of foods rich in isoflavonoids—plant versions of the hormone estrogen that inhibit growth of cancer cells. Isoflavonoids are found in lentils, peas, beans, dried fruits, and particularly in tofu. A lifelong high concentration of isoflavonoids could explain why men from these cultures seldom develop clinical prostate cancer.

An Apple a Day Saves Teeth

Dental hygienists at the University of Maryland say you can do your dental enamel a favor by eating an apple after meals. Apples will crush into spaces between teeth, dislodging the cavity creators and stimulating saliva flow to counteract plaque.

Tetanus Immunization Not Just for Kids

About 70 percent of all tetanus cases reported occur in people over age fifty. The infection is rare, but often fatal. Anyone who has not had a booster shot within ten years should get one now to update immunity.

Combating Employee Theft

Workers in retail, most of them poorly paid, often think of theft or sabotage as a way of getting what's owed them. Contrary to what most people think, honesty is not an all-or-nothing trait. Many people readily cheat on their taxes, but would never cheat on their spouses—or vice versa. It's difficult to control theft. Commercial honesty tests aren't reliable. But there are some ways to help deter theft: use surveillance, screen people at hiring, make your expectations crystal clear to employees, set up little traps to see if people take advantage when they think they are safe. The best solution: make your employees feel they are being treated fairly.

Take a Deduction to Clear Out Inventory

You can often support local charities with an "in-kind" donation. Instead of giving money, you give goods or services. The law generally allows you to deduct an amount equal to your average sale price on the item. That means if you normally sell wholesale, you can deduct the wholesale price; if you normally sell retail, you could actually deduct the retail price. In addition to clearing out inventory and reducing costs, your company can get good publicity while helping a nonprofit organization.

Money and Happiness Don't Mix

People say that money can't buy happiness but that it's the next best thing. Now a study published in the academic journal *Social Indicators Research* suggests that the more money people make, the more they want—and the more they want, the harder it is to achieve long-term happiness. The old saying that money can't buy happiness is not just sour grapes from poor people. If your aspirations are focused on material items, money may actually cause unhappiness.

Weekend Car Rental Rates on Thursday

If you have business trips near the end of the week, ask for weekend car rental rates, which are generally lower than the weekday rates. Many companies extend these rates from Thursday through Sunday, but you have to ask for them.

Street Smarts

Always remove badges and name tags when leaving a meeting or a family reunion. The badge identifies you as an out-of-towner, and that information could be useful to a mugger or a dishonest cab driver.

A New Viewpoint

When aluminum foil originally came out, its package was designed to be placed on the shelf endwise so all labels and information had to be on the end of the box. A creative packaging company designed its box so that the end said nothing. Their product had to be put on the shelf widthwise to be read. They dominated the shelf space until others copied them. In today's age of paying for shelf space in supermarkets, you might not be able to get away with this same trick. But there may be other things in your business that you can turn "90 degrees" to gain an advantage.

Five Ways to Stop Being Late

1. Set your watch ahead. 2. Add a time cushion. If the drive should take forty minutes, allow an hour. 3. Buy a beeper watch. Set it to remind you when it's time to make last-minute preparations before leaving. 4. Ask someone to remind you to leave on time. Ask friends to tell you when your lateness has inconvenienced them. 5. Set up a penalty/reward system. If you arrive on time or early for a week, get your reward. If you are late, pay for it in some way.

September Resolutions

Resolutions are traditional at the start of a new year, but September is another good time to take stock of your life. When the children go back to school and summer is officially over, we can focus on achieving goals by the end of the year. September resolutions can help us end the old year on an "up" note. Acknowledge your accomplishments up until now, and use the rest of the time to make adjustments.

First Aid for Cardiac Arrest

When encountering a cardiac arrest victim, call 911 or your local emergency medical service (EMS) *before* starting CPR. Help from EMS is most beneficial in the first seven to eight minutes after a heart attack starts. This is a new recommendation. Previously, one minute of CPR was considered the first action to take before calling EMS. (CPR is still recommended first for resuscitation of children.)

Quality of Sunglass Lenses

Hold glasses at arm's length and tilt them slightly. Look at a distant line and move them up and down. If there's any wavering in the line, especially at the lenses' edges, then the lenses are not shaped precisely.

Cut Purchase Order Costs—Use Credit Cards

On average it costs a company $150 to process a purchase order. It can cost a company $300 to buy a $10 item, says Credit-Card Management. In one analysis of company payments on purchase orders and bills, 60 percent of purchases were items costing less than $500. These items accounted for only 3 percent of total purchasing expenses. By giving managers credit cards, bills were paid faster, and the company saved hundreds of thousands of dollars in processing charges for cutting checks and handling purchase orders. Companies experimenting with this in America and England are reporting a large measure of success, even though banks charge them for the cards.

Break Down a Decision

Break a decision down into importance, risk, and unknowns. Importance is the amount of impact the decision will have. Don't agonize over trivial decisions—just make a decision and forget it. Risk is your analysis of the probabilities for good and bad outcomes. We usually do this intuitively. A clear analysis of what the risks really are can sometimes show that even a worst-case scenario will still be worth the rewards. Unknowns are factors that can add to risk. The more unknowns there are, the greater the margin of error that you need to leave for yourself.

Record Height to Gauge Osteoporosis

Parents often measure their kids and put a mark on the wall to keep track of their growth. Now doctors say adults can benefit from charting their height as well. Research shows that the loss of 1½ inches of adult height in a woman can signal bone-density losses of 6 to 12 percent. Her bones would have the density of someone who is ten years older.

For men, height losses of more than 2 inches were associated with an increased osteoporosis risk. Shrinking may indicate that bone in the spine is condensing, a clue that the hip bone is weakening as well. Other ways to see how bones are doing include X-ray absorptiometry and blood calcium measurements.

Procrastination: A Nice Way to Say No

Perhaps there is such a thing as positive procrastination. When people try to lay tasks on you that really shouldn't be done, one way to avoid confronting them is to put them off. If they're wacky ideas from the boss that would just get you all in trouble, the boss may be grateful later. If they're jobs that others should be doing, procrastinating is a way of forcing the tasks back into their court.

Getting Over Your Vacation

Vacations should make us feel more rested, but the reverse is often true. It's frustrating to come back and see the work that's piled up. Sometimes all it takes to get over the back-to-work blues is a change of perspective. Instead of being mad at your job, appreciate the fact that it gave you the resources to take the vacation. Try to be more patient than usual. And be sure to double-check your work. You may make more mistakes than usual.

How to Save Videotapes

The coating on VHS tapes can loosen over time, destroying your recordings. Before storing a tape, rewind from end to end in a high-quality rewinder. Fast-forward and rewind each tape at least once every three years to keep layers from sticking together. Protect tapes from very high or low temperatures. Store at a relative humidity of 40 to 60 percent.

Cellular Phones Too Expensive? Reconsider Pagers

Cellular phones are a great convenience, but you can get some of the same benefits for far fewer dollars. Pagers are cheaper and can be used to have people call in. If you want still more convenience, you can go with alphanumeric pagers, where brief messages can tell people where to go and what to do. You sacrifice two-way communication, but you save tremendously on cellular phone bills and installation expenses.

Make Your Own Frozen Gel Pack

Mix three parts water with one part rubbing alcohol. Seal in a freezer bag, encase in a second bag; and place in the freezer. The more alcohol you use, the softer the pack will be, making it gentler on injuries than an ice pack.

Handling Interruptions

Men freely interrupt and throw in their own ideas. Women avoid interrupting others and wait for breaks in the conversation. This means that they don't get as many chances to speak. Women expect their input to be solicited. Men expect people who have ideas to put them forward, unasked.

Ask Questions That Encourage Fresh Input

When you talk to the people who work for you, how do you show that you really want their input? If you always ask the same questions, they're probably going to give you the same old answers. You'll be no better off than you were before you tried to get input. Ask questions that make people stop and think—you will be more likely to get new answers.

1. What made the company look bad today?
2. What caused you stress today?
3. What took more time than it should have today?
4. What was misunderstood today?
5. What are we paying too much for?
6. What is being wasted?
7. What wasted your time today?
8. What job was more complicated than it should be?

One answer to any of these questions can be the beginning thread that can allow you to unravel the Gordian knot of the status quo in a company or unit.

Stopwatch Priority Management

How much time do you actually spend on high-priority jobs? Use a stopwatch to document your time. A stopwatch allows you to have a continuous recording mechanism to determine the amount of time spent on your priority items. Pick one item a day and record how much time you actually work on it. You'll often be shocked at how little time your priorities actually get.

Mentally Blocking Yourself

Sometimes we deny ourselves pleasant diversions because we haven't completed an unpleasant task. Rather than providing motivation to take on the unpleasant task, this can have a depressing effect. For instance, let's say you've been looking forward to reading a novel for pleasure. But since you haven't read the technical report for work, you deny yourself the pleasure of the novel. If you don't get down to it and read the technical report, you might as well read the novel and enjoy yourself. This might allow you to go back to the technical report with a fresh mind.

Sample Postcard Newsletter

Your newsletter can be as small as a postcard. Fill it with interesting trivia tips, jokes, or sayings.

Your logo, name, address, and phone number here

Genetics is the study of which parent's family can be blamed for a teenager's behavior.

Want to negotiate a discount at the hotel's front desk? Always avoid a crowd. Allow the hotel staff to give you a special rate without interfering with their other customers.

When all is said and done, a lot more is said than done.
Lou Holtz,
Former Notre Dame
football coach

Take lunch breaks at 1 P.M., 2 P.M., or later. You get more work done from noon to one.

The more money people make, the more they want—and the more they want, the harder it is to achieve long-term happiness.

Buried under paper? Update and eliminate or you'll accumulate.

Tofu may reduce the risk of prostate cancer. A high intake of foods rich in isoflavonoids (lentils, peas, beans, dried fruits, and particularly tofu) inhibits growth of cancer cells.

Quality efforts should be tied to early results. Clear goals produce early results and long-term efforts will be energized.

An apple a day keeps the dentist away. Apples crush into spaces between teeth, dislodging the cavity creators and stimulating saliva flow to fight plaque.

The older I grow, the more I listen to people who don't talk much.
Henry Ward Beecher

You can support local charities with an "in-kind" donation—you give goods or services. The law generally allows you to deduct an amount equal to your average sale price on the item.

Near the end of the week, ask for the lower weekend car rental rates. Many companies extend these rates from Thursday through Sunday, but you have to ask for them.

You may use the items in the postcard newsletter in whole or part. Additional postcard material may be purchased from Select Press (415.209-9838).

Business Quotes for Fax Cover Sheets or Newsletter Filler

A good employee is a valuable resource who can easily be lost forever if placed in a job that is not personally fulfilling and challenging and that does not offer a genuine opportunity for contribution.

> Tom Potts and Arnold Sykes,
> *Executive Talent: How to Identify and*
> *Develop the Best*

Our greatest glory is not in never falling, but in rising every time we fall.

> Confucius

Time passes at a predetermined rate no matter what we do. It is a question not of managing the clock but of managing ourselves in respect to the clock . . . the heart of time management is management of self.

> Alec Mackenzie,
> *The Time Trap: Managing Your Way Out*

There are four steps to accomplishment: Plan purposefully, prepare practically, proceed positively, and pursue persistently.

> Anonymous

Every original idea starts off goofy as hell, then you add to it, take some stuff away, refine it, and it becomes a neat idea.

> Joe McKinney,
> CEO, Tyler Corporation, Dallas, Texas

Anger is never without a reason, but seldom with a good one.

> Benjamin Franklin

Teach once, delegate often. Never teach, and you'll always have to do it yourself.

> George Lumsden,
> *Getting Up to Speed:*
> *115 Quick Tips for the New or Future Manager*

Work is an accumulation of easy things that should have been done last week.

> Kathy Griffith

If you don't expect the unexpected, you will never find it.

> Jurgen Moltmann

The most gifted members of the human race are at their creative best when they cannot have their way.

> Eric Hoffer

The older I grow, the more I listen to people who don't talk much.

> Henry Ward Beecher

Many a standing ovation has been caused by someone jumping to his feet in an effort to beat the rest of the audience to the parking lot.

> Anonymous

Let our advance worrying become our advance thinking and planning.

> Winston Churchill

When all is said and done, a lot more is said than done.

> Lou Holtz
> Former Notre Dame and
> University of Arkansas football coach

Experience is a tough teacher. It gives the test first and the lesson afterward.

> Vernon S. Law
> Former Pittsburgh Pirates pitcher

People are born with an instinctive desire to learn. Rather than encourage learning, schools and social structures frustrate your interest in it.

> Peter Senge,
> *The Fifth Discipline*

Speak when you are angry, and you will make the best speech you'll ever regret.

> Ambrose Bierce

Always do right. This will gratify some people, and astonish the rest.

> Mark Twain

I'm going to live within my income this year, even if I have to borrow money to do it.

> Mark Twain

The more things are forbidden, the more popular they become.

> Mark Twain

The best argument is that which seems merely to be an explanation.

> Dale Carnegie

Daring ideas are like chessmen. Moved forward, they may be beaten, but they may start a winning game.

> Johann von Goethe

True leaders inspire people to do great things and when the work is done, their people proudly say, "We did this ourselves."

> Lao Tzu

The hardest time to succeed with change is when nothing is going wrong. The best time to work on change is when everything is going right.

> Rick Crandall

Show me a thoroughly satisfied man and I will show you a failure.

> Thomas Edison

I don't want any "yes" men around me. I want them to tell the truth even if it costs them their jobs.

> Samuel Goldwyn

Every man desires to live long, but no man wishes to be old.

> Jonathan Swift

The creative mind is like a parachute—it only works when it's open.

> Merrill J. Oster
> *Vision-Driven Leadership*

Work is of two kinds: first, altering the position of matter at or near the earth's surface relative to other matter; second, telling other people to do so.

> Bertrand Russell

Hard work never killed anybody, but why take a chance?

> Charlie McCarthy (Edgar Bergen)

Problems we face today cannot be solved with the same level of thinking we were at when we created them.

> Albert Einstein

Any fact facing us is not as important as our attitude toward it, for that determines our success or failure.

> Norman Vincent Peale

The closest to perfection a person ever comes is when he fills out a job application form.

Stanley J. Randall

File cabinet: A four-drawer, manually activated trash compactor.

Jim Fisk and Robert Barron

Unattributed Quotes
One of the secrets of youth is to lie about your age.

Definition of an opportunist: Someone who sold umbrellas before the Great Flood.

It's still possible to get a high school education. The only trouble is, it now takes four years of college to do it.

It's not so bad sending your kids off to college. The problem is that you have to send most of your money with them, too.

Definitions of meetings: 1. A group of people who keep minutes and waste hours. 2. A group of the unwilling, picked from the unfit, to do the unnecessary.

Last will and testament: Being of sound mind, I spent it all on having fun.

Waste of energy: Often when someone works up a head of steam over something, all that comes out is hot air.

Beware brown-nosers: Be careful of those who kiss the ground you walk on, they may just be reaching for some dirt.

CHAPTER THIRTEEN
CUSTOMER SERVICE

Facts You Could Learn About Customers and Prospects
You don't want to be quizzing customers about a lot of things, some of which might be trivial to them. But you can also gather information about them from their customers and suppliers, banks, newspapers, trade publications, news reports, receptionists, secretaries, and assistants.

One benefit of having this information: If you have salespeople or account managers working with you, when the person dealing with that client leaves, the information about the customer stays in your shop. So, whoever deals with him or her next has a running start in terms of knowing who the person is. There should also be a file with notes on the relationship, purchases, problems, and so on.

Date created: _____

Date: _____   Discussion: _____

Date: _____   Discussion: _____

Date: _____   Discussion: _____

Additional Notes

By knowing a birthday, the customer can be sent a birthday card and be invited out to lunch that day. By knowing the hometown, you can clip items about that person's hometown and send them to him. Knowing their children's interests allows you to discuss things dear to people's hearts. Knowing the person's interests allows you to pass along things that will support her.

Customer or Prospect Information

1. Customer's name
2. Nickname
3. Job title
4. Company name
5. Company address
6. Home address
7. Home phone
8. Business phone, fax, e-mail, URL
9. Birth date
10. Birthplace
11. Hometown
12. Physical condition
13. Physical description
14. Other physical characteristics, such as back problems
15. How does customer like to be contacted: phone, fax, in person, letter, e-mail?
16. Preferred time of day to contact? of week?
17. Secretary's name
18. Assistant's name

Education

19. Name of high school attended and year graduated
20. Name of college attended and year graduated
21. Fraternity or sorority
22. Sports or extracurricular activities
23. Military service
24. Attitude about the service

Family

25. Marital status
26. Spouse's name
27. Spouse's education
28. Does spouse work?
29. Job title
30. Spouse's interests
31. Wedding anniversary
32. Children (names and ages)
33. Does client have custody of children?
34. Children's education
35. Children's interests
36. Jobs held by children

37. Problems with spouse
38. Problems with children,

Business Background

39. Previous employment in reverse chrono-
    logical order
40. Previous positions at present company
    and job titles
41. Approximate salary
42. Professional or trade associations
43. Who are the customer's mentors?
44. What business relationships does the cus-
    tomer have with others in our company?
45. How does the client feel about his or her
    own company?
46. What does our client want to do in the
    long term in business?
47. What are his or her immediate goals?
48. Does this customer put the welfare of his
    company or himself highest now?

Special Interests

49. To what clubs does the client belong?
50. Can you join?
51. Is the customer politically active?
52. Religion?
53. What areas should not be discussed with
    the customer? For instance, is he or she a
    recovering alcoholic?
54. About what personal subjects does the
    customer have strong feelings?
55. Is the customer a fan of a business
    "guru" like Peter Drucker, Tom Peters,
    Ken Blanchard, W. Edwards Deming?

Lifestyle

56. Customer's health and medical history
57. Regular exerciser?
58. Regular sport?
59. Does customer drink?
    At lunch, dinner, or later?
    If yes, what and how much?
60. If no, is customer or prospect offended by
    others drinking?
61. Does client smoke? If no, does he object
    to others doing so?
62. Favorite place for lunch, dinner
63. Does customer buy, like to be treated, or
    split the bill?
64. Favorite foods or items client eats
65. Leisure interests
66. Favorite type of music
67. Favorite TV shows
68. Like to go to sports events?
69. Favorite team
70. Like ballet?
71. Like opera?
72. Like theater?
73. Last business book read
74. Last other book read
75. Last vacation taken
76. Favorite vacation
77. What kind of cars does client drive?
78. Other conversational interests
79. What general business magazines does
    the customer read regularly?
80. What newspapers?
81. What trade magazines?
82. Does the customer like receiving
    clippings on business?
83. Who does the customer want to impress?
84. How would you describe the customer?

85. What is the customer proudest of?
86. What is the customer's long-term personal objective?
87. What is the customer's short-term personal goal?

Customer and You

88. Are there any moral or ethical issues involved in working with this customer?
89. Does the customer feel any obligation to you, the company, or the competition? If so, what?

90. Is customer or prospect very self-centered? Highly ethical?
91. What key problems does the customer see?
92. What are the priorities of the customer's management? Any conflicts between the customer and his or her management?
93. What competitors does the customer work with?
94. How close is their relationship?
95. What customer suppliers do we know?

CHAPTER FIFTEEN

YOUR MARKETING ACTION PLAN

Preparing Effective Marketing Requires Effective Marketing Plan Questions

1. What is the mission of your business?
2. What image do you and your service have?
3. What specific services do you offer?
4. Who are your best customers? What industries are they in? Where are they physically located?
5. What are the main needs and desired benefits of your best customers?
6. What is your unique position that gives you an advantage in the marketplace?
7. Who are your competitors? How are they seen by your prospects?
8. What are the most effective ways to gain the attention of your potential clients?
9. What resources do you require to market?

Thinking

Here are some basic questions. The answers provide the foundation for your marketing. This basic thinking increases the likelihood of accomplishing your objectives.

Use the questions below and others to establish a solid foundation for a new marketing program or to review an existing program.

Past/Present Marketing

- What have you done in the past?
- What are you doing now?
- What works, and why?
- What doesn't work, and why not?
- What are your marketing strengths? Weaknesses?
- Have you developed an overall marketing program or pieced it together with no long-range plan?

Marketplace Orientation

- What is your business?
- What is your current market?
- What is your competition?
- How are you positioning your product or service?
- How are you positioning your company?
- What makes you unique?
- What new markets can be developed profitably?

Company Orientation

- Is your company market, customer, or product oriented? Are all employees included in the marketing effort? Are they told regularly that they are part of the marketing effort? Do they know that the best marketing is building relationships with customers?
- Are employees given information and training that will help them be better marketers and sellers?
- Do they know the marketing goals? Company goals?
- Are they kept informed of marketing plans?
- Are they asked for suggestions?
- Is one person/department responsible for marketing?
- Are there sufficient resources committed to marketing? Time? Money? People?

REFERENCES

ADLER, ELIZABETH W. *Everyone's Guide to Successful Publications.* Berkeley, Calif.: Peachpit Press, 1993. Oriented toward designs for cover brochures, newsletters, and flyers.

BEALS, MELBA. *Expose Yourself: Using Public Relations to Promote Yourself and Your Business.* San Francisco: Chronicle Books, 1990.

CRANDALL, RICK, (ED.) *Celebrate Selling the Consultative-Relationship Way.* Corte Madera, Calif.: Select Press, 1998.

FLOYD, ELAINE. *Marketing with Newsletters.* New Orleans: EF Communications, 1993.

GERSON, RICHARD F. *Writing and Implementing a Marketing Plan.* Los Altos, Calif.: Crisp Publications, 1991. This brief marketing and planning book is somewhat product oriented, but still has lots of useful material.

GODIN, SETH. *Permission Marketing.* New York: Simon & Schuster, 1999.

GUMPERT, D. E. *How to Really Create a Successful Marketing Plan.* Boston: *Inc.* Magazine, 1994.

HANAN, MACK. *Consultative Selling Advanced Sixth Edition: The Hanan Formula for High-Margin Sales at High Levels.* New York: AMACOM. 1999.

HAYES, RICK STEPHAN, and GREGORY BROOKS ELMORE. *Marketing for Your Growing Business.* New York: John Wiley & Sons, Inc., 1985.

KAWASAKI, GUY. *Selling the Dream: How to Promote Your Product, Company, or Idea, and Make a Difference, Using Everyday Evangelism.* New York: HarperCollins, 1991.

LEECH, THOMAS. *How to Prepare, Stage, and Deliver Winning Presentations.* New York: AMACOM, 1993.

McKENNA, REGIS. *Relationship Marketing.* New York: Addison-Wesley, 1991.

MISNER, IVAN, and VIRGINIA DEVINE. *The World's Best-Known Marketing Secret: Building Your Business with Word-of-Mouth Marketing,* Second Edition, Austin, Tex.: Bard & Stephen, 1999.

PEPPERS, DON, and MARTHA ROGERS. *The One to One Future.* New York: Doubleday Currency, 1993.

PHILLIPS, MICHAEL, and SALLI RASBERRY. *Marketing Without Advertising.* Berkeley, Calif.: Nolo Press, 1986.

RIES, AL, and JACK TROUT. *Positioning: The Battle for Your Mind.* New York: McGraw-Hill, 1981.

SANT, TOM. *Persuasive Business Proposals: Writing to Win Customers, Clients, and Contracts.* New York: AMACOM, 1992.

SHENSON, HOWARD L. *The Contract and Fee-Setting Guide for Consultants and Professionals.* New York: John Wiley, University Association, 1990.

STACK, JACK. *The Great Game of Business.* New York: Doubleday Currency, 1992.

STANLEY, THOMAS J. *Networking with the Affluent: Unique and Proven Methods for Influencing the Affluent.* Homewood, Ill: Business One Irwin, 1993.

TROUT, JACK, with STEVE RIVKIN. *The New Positioning: The Latest on the World's #1 Business Strategy.* New York: McGraw-Hill, 1996.

WALTERS, LILLY, ET AL. *Secrets of Successful Speakers.* New York: McGraw-Hill, 1993.

Wilson, Larry. *Stop Selling, Start Partnering.* Essex Junction, Vt, Oliver Wight Publications, 1994.

INDEX